CW01627894

Domestic Violence: Working with Men

Domestic Violence: Working with Men

Research, practice experiences and integrated responses

Andrew Day, Patrick O'Leary,
Donna Chung, Donna Justo

THE FEDERATION PRESS
2009

Published in Sydney by:
The Federation Press
PO Box 45, Annandale, NSW, 2038
71 John St, Leichhardt, NSW, 2040
Ph (02) 9552 2200 Fax (02) 9552 1681
E-mail: info@federationpress.com.au
Website: http://www.federationpress.com.au

National Library of Australia
Cataloguing-in-Publication entry

Domestic violence: working with men:
research, practice experiences and integrated responses
Andrew Day ... [et al]

Includes index.
Bibliography
ISBN 978 1 86287 728 3 (pbk)

Abusive men - Behaviour modification. Family violence- Australia - Prevention.

362.82920994

© The Federation Press

This publication is copyright. Other than for the purposes of and subject to the conditions prescribed under the Copyright Act, no part of it may in any form or by any means (electronic, mechanical, microcopying, photocopying, recording or otherwise) be reproduced, stored in a retrieval system or transmitted without prior written permission. Enquiries should be addressed to the publishers.

Typeset by The Federation Press, Leichhardt, NSW.
Printed by Ligare Pty Ltd, Riverwood, NSW.

PEFC™
PEFC/21-31-17

This book has been printed on Australian offset paper certified by the Programme for the Endorsement of Forest Certification (PEFC). PEFC is committed to sustainable forest management through third party forest certification of responsibly managed forests.

Contents

Acknowledgments

The authors would like to thank the help and support of many people in making this book possible, including all of the women and men who spoke to us about their experiences of the program, the Gold Coast program facilitators, Ann Cunningham and Clare Hallifax at Federation Press, Nadia Boni, Ed Carson and Christine Potito from the University of South Australia, and Catherine Hand and Megan Clarke from the Department of Corrective Services, Queensland. Particular thanks should go to Betty Taylor for her vision and long-term commitment to conceptualising, developing and implementing an integrated response to domestic violence in the Gold Coast region. Thanks are also due to Dr Gary Foster and Sue Moore for their long-term commitment both to this project and to making communities safer places for men, women and children.

The views expressed in this book are those of the authors and do not necessarily represent those of the organisations in which they work. Work on this book was supported by an Australian Research Council Linkage Grant (LP0561991).

Contributors

Laura Bahnisch is a social work and women's studies graduate and researcher at the University of South Australia in the School of Social Work and Social Policy and the School of Psychology. She also works as a counsellor for survivors of sexual assault.

Ed Carson is Professor of Social Policy at the University of South Australia. His research interests include Government/Third Sector relationships, in particular service delivery and workforce development issues in community service agencies contracted to deliver government-specified services.

Donna Chung has a long standing interest in domestic violence having undertaken various research projects and consultancies for Australian national and state governments. She currently works in the UK as an Associate Professor of Social Work and Director of the Centre for Safety Wellbeing at the University of Warwick.

Andrew Day is a clinical and forensic psychologist who is currently Associate Professor at the University of South Australia and an adjunct at the School of Law and Commerce, Flinders University of South Australia. He is interested in the rehabilitation of offenders, particularly violent offenders, and has published extensively in this area.

Tony Fletcher is the Senior Men's Worker at the Northern Violence Intervention Programme in Adelaide, South Australia and a PhD candidate at University of South Australia the School of Social Work and Social Policy. His research interests are men's uses of gendered "violences" and the efforts that workers, agencies, individuals and communities make to both describe and interrupt violence against women, children and men. He also teaches in partnership with the David Unaipon College of Indigenous Education and Research around issues of whiteness and critical social work theory and practice/s.

Gary Foster's work and research interests centre on the problem of violence. He is currently employed as a clinical supervisor at a community agency providing individual and group work that seeks to end domestic and family violence. Gary's doctoral thesis - Male Rape and the Government of Bodies - examined governmental responses to men who have experienced sexual violence. He has lectured and tutored at the University of Queensland, where he co-designed and presented a post graduate advanced counselling practice subject in "Working with Family Violence". Gary continues to be interested in finding creative ways of training and working that limit the influence of violence in people's lives.

Adam Gerace recently completed his PhD in the School of Psychology at the University of South Australia, where he was also a researcher and lecturer. He is currently a Postdoctoral Research Fellow at Flinders University of South Australia. Adam's research interests are in the development of empathy and related social skills, and the evaluation of interventions for offenders.

Annette Hennessy Her Honour Annette Hennessy was appointed a Magistrate of Queensland, Australia in 1999 after 14 years of admission and practice, firstly as a Barrister with Director of Prosecutions and later as a Solicitor of the Supreme Court of Queensland in both urban and regional areas. Her primary areas of practice were in criminal law, juvenile justice, child sexual assault prosecutions, indigenous justice, domestic and family violence, family law and general areas of law. In 2003, in consultation with Indigenous Elders, community organisations and stakeholders, she developed and commenced an Indigenous Justice Program - Murri Court - in Rockhampton, undertaking responsibility for the implementation and development of the Court. The Court was later extended to include Young Offenders. Many of the matters dealt with in Murri Court Rockhampton relate to domestic violence issues. Magistrate Hennessy and other participants in the Domestic Violence and related issues Court processes in Rockhampton are working towards developing practical, appropriate and therapeutic processes to address the underlying reasons for domestic violence incidents and offending and identifying issues related to future directions for the court. Magistrate Hennessy has presented papers at many conferences on the topic of Indigenous Justice and Sentencing Courts including for LawAsia, International Therapeutic Jurisprudence, International Society for the Reform of the Criminal Law and others. She has had articles published in Queensland Lawyer and an AIJA Monograph "Transforming Legal Processes in Court and Beyond". Magistrate Hennessy continues to play a role in the continuing development of the Murri Court and Domestic and Family Violence Court processes in Queensland.

Donna Justo has been the Director of the Gold Coast Domestic Violence Prevention Centre Inc for the past three years and is a member of the Queensland Ministerial Advisory Council on Domestic and Family Violence. She first began working voluntarily in the refuge movement in Queensland in the late 1970s before undertaking paid work in this area. As part of her working career she has managed agencies working alongside women with mental health, alcohol and drug and domestic violence/ sexual violence related issues, and children having children. Donna is a feminist author and activist and has worked extensively in Australia, in Cape York and the Gulf country; the United Kingdom and Middle East, Africa and South America. Donna has attended the past three International Congresses on Women, (Nairobi, Beijing and New York) including representing WWDA - Women with Disabilities Australia - at the UN in

New York in 2000. Her formal qualifications are in the humanities and training areas. Donna has supervised, consolidated and developed the Gold Coast Men's Domestic Violence Education and Intervention Program over the past three years to ensure that its integrity has remained focused on and responsible to the safety of the women partners and their children.

Di Lucas is a feminist practitioner who has been the Counselling Manager at the Domestic Violence Prevention Centre Gold Coast Inc since March 2006. She has worked in the domestic violence field since the late 1980s, primarily in women's refuges and domestic violence services in the metro area of South East Queensland. Di has a Bachelor of Social Science (Human Service) degree from the Queensland University of Technology and has participated in collaborative research in the area of domestic violence since the late 1990s. She is the former Chair of Combined Women's Refuge Group South East Queensland and was appointed as Regional Member for the Gold Coast on the 2005–2007 Ministerial Advisory Council on Domestic and Family Violence.

Lesley McCartney has worked for four years as a women's advocate with women partners and ex-partners of men who are mandated to attend the Men's Education and Intervention Program at the Gold Coast. Lesley's tertiary education includes a Bachelor of Social Science. She has worked in the area of domestic violence for six years in various roles including refuge work, women's counselling, group work, children's worker and community educator within schools at the Domestic Violence Prevention Centre Gold Coast Inc and Macleod Accommodation and Support Service.

Susan Moore has co-facilitated the mandated Men's Domestic Violence Education and Intervention Program at the Gold Coast for five years and is currently coordinating the program and providing supervision for a team of facilitators. Susan's tertiary education includes a Bachelor of Applied Science in Psychology, a Graduate Diploma Further Education and Training and her current studies in Certificate 4 in Workplace Training and Assessment. She has worked in the area of counselling, risk assessment and management, career guidance and workshop/program facilitation for 14 years, across a range of environments. These include high and medium security prisons, the University of Queensland Student Support Services, Gold Coast TAFE Student Services, Southport Community Corrections, and the Gold Coast Domestic Violence Prevention Centre.

Patrick O'Leary is a social worker who has worked extensively as a researcher, educator and practitioner in gendered violence in numerous countries. He is currently based in the Department of Social and Policy Sciences at the University of Bath, United Kingdom, he also is a visiting Associate Professor in the School of Social Work and Social Policy at the University of South Australia.

Rosemary O'Malley (Bachelor of Arts in Criminology) has worked for Queensland Corrective Services (QCS) since 2003 as a Probation and Parole Officer. She has worked in various roles within the Agency including Assessment Officer for Drug Court; co-facilitator on Agency programs including: substance abuse, anger management, and sex offender programs; and Supervisor in the Southport District Office. She currently supervises a caseload of high risk offenders. Since 2005 she has been involved in the Gold Coast Domestic Violence Integrated Response co-facilitating the Male Perpetrators Program and in 2008 received a Queensland Corrective Services Excellence Award for her contributions in this role.

Joan Salizzo has worked for four years as a women's advocate with women partners and ex-partners of men who are mandated to attend the Men's Education and Intervention Program at the Gold Coast. Joan's tertiary education includes a Bachelor of Social Work and a Diploma of Applied Sciences Human and Community Services. She has worked in the area of domestic violence for ten years in various roles including refuge work, women's counselling, group work and court support at the Domestic Violence Prevention Centre Gold Coast Inc and Macleod Accommodation and Support Service.

Maggie Woodhead has worked with trauma, violence and abuse for the past twenty five years; as a trainer, academic, therapist, group facilitator and supervisor and has an academic background in Women's Studies and Counselling. She has worked with children, adolescents and adults who have been on the receiving end of violence and abuse, as well as working extensively with the perpetrators. For the past two years she has been the Family and Domestic Violence Consultant in the Department of Corrective Services, Western Australia. She has a particular commitment to the recognition of children as the hidden victims of domestic violence.

Introduction

Andrew Day

Domestic violence is widely recognised as a major social problem both in Australia and the western world. In Australia, around 5 per cent of the population is victimised in any one year (Access Economics Pty Ltd 2004), with international surveys have suggesting that around one-third of all adult women will at some point in their lifetime experience abuse perpetrated by an intimate male partner. Nearly half of all incidents involve physical injury and approximately two-thirds of all women who are murdered are killed by their husband or live-in partner. In Australia in 2005-2006, 66 of the 113 female victims of homicide had a current or past relationship with the offender (Davis and Mouzos 2007).

The consequences of domestic violence on victims are considerable. Domestic violence is considered to be in the top five risk factors for women's health in Australia (Access Economics Pty Ltd 2004), and many women experience ongoing difficulties in their physical and psychological health as a direct consequence of the abuse. The effects on families can be devastating. Studies have shown that children who witness domestic violence are adversely affected in a range of ways that impacts upon their healthy development (for example, O'Leary, Malone and Tyree 1994), and it has been estimated that domestic violence is accompanied by child abuse in around 50 per cent of all cases (Saunders 1984). Escaping domestic violence is the major reason for women's and children's homelessness in western nations (Chung et al 2001).

On a societal level, domestic violence produces significant direct and indirect costs to health and community functioning (Laing and Bobic 2002). Quantifying those costs is immensely difficult, but it has been estimated that domestic violence cost Australia $8.1 billion in the financial year 2002-2003, excluding costs associated with domestic violence prevention (Access Economics Pty Ltd 2004). Of this, $3.5 billion was estimated to be the cost of pain, suffering and premature death of victims.

There is clearly a need for the community to respond to this problem in ways that reduce the likelihood of violence occurring, and reduce the risk of known perpetrators committing further offences. Programs for domestically violent men began to emerge in the late 1970s and 1980s (Dobash and Dobash 1992), and there are currently hundreds of different programs offered around the world. Most of these early programs were influenced by the development of services for victims of domestic violence (for example, the women's shelter movement), with a consequent understanding of domestic violence in relation to issues of gender and power. Dobash and Dobash (2000) describe most programs as combining pro-feminist and cognitive-behavioural approaches. They suggest that the combination of these approaches reflects a "common view about the nature of the problem as generated within a context of gender relations, socialization and learning, and an orientation to treatment that focuses on changing behavior and ways of thinking" (2000: 380).

Men's use of violence is commonly precipitated by disputes relating to matters such as sexual jealousy, sense of ownership over the woman, household duties, childcare, and the distribution of household resources such as money and time. The approach to intervention thus focuses on changing attitudes towards women, and in particular intimate partners, and in developing new skills to manage interpersonal conflict in ways that do not involve aggression (Pence and Paymar 1993). For example, some of the attitudes that are typically targeted for change in treatment are those which imply that the man sees himself as central to the world and disconnected from his partner (for example, "I wasn't abusive, only angry and unhappy"), superior (for example, "there has to be a boss; my word is the last word"), and in some way deserving (for example, "she should appreciate what I do for her") (Russell 2002).

Despite the need for the development of effective community responses to domestic violence, support for the delivery of perpetrator programs is neither consistent nor universal. Some studies have suggested that many members of the community hold attitudes that tolerate domestic violence, and there is a widespread belief amongst both the public and professionals that women are at least partially responsible for their victimisation (for example, Davis 1984; Ewing and Aubrey 1987). The strongest community support for men's use of violence to female partners is if a woman is thought to have had sex with someone outside of the relationship. Such attitudes undermine the successful delivery of behaviour change programs in several ways. They reinforce the beliefs of perpetrators that they are in some way justified in their use of violence (thereby decreasing their motivation to engage in programs), or the beliefs of the judiciary and service providers that perpetrators are only partially responsible for their behaviour (and thereby do not necessarily need to be mandated to attend programs).

In this book we seek to describe and discuss the provision of programs and services that are designed to reduce the risk of domestic violence amongst known perpetrators. We will aim to voice a range of different perspectives about what might be considered to be an appropriate response to domestic violence, although our primary focus here is on the development and delivery of perpetrator programs. The book itself is the result of the ongoing development of an integrated service response operating in the Gold Coast region of Queensland, Australia, and an

Australian Research Council linkage project between the University of South Australia, the Gold Coast Domestic Violence Prevention Centre and the Department of Corrective Services in Queensland.

The Gold Coast Domestic Violence Integrated Response (GCDVIR)

The Gold Coast Domestic Violence Integrated Response (GCDVIR) is a community based integrated response to domestic violence that focuses on agencies working together to provide interventions which are coordinated, appropriate, and consistent within a justice reform model. The objective of the GCDVIR is to enhance victim safety, reduce secondary victimisation, and decrease the incidence of domestic violence through the enhancement and monitoring of interagency cooperation and collaboration. Through its advocacy and activism the GCDVIR also aims to hold perpetrators of domestic violence systemically accountable for their behaviour. The GCDVIR has been the recipient of the following awards:

- 2007 International Peace Star - PCVC - Chennai India
- 2006 Australian Crime and Violence Prevention Award - Certificate of Excellence
- 2006 Queensland Police Service Commissioner's Award
- 2005 Domestic Violence Prevention Award
- 2004 Gold Coast Community Safety Commendation
- 2002 Australian Crime and Violence Prevention Award
- 2000 Gold Coast Community Safety Commendation
- 1998 Gold Coast Community Safety Award

The GCDVIR sits within a dynamic region of Queensland, Australia, that is more representative of inner city Melbourne or Sydney in demographic make-up and cultural diversity, than a tranquil coastal holiday strip. It is a region that stretches from Coolangatta in the south, a border town with New South Wales, to the Coomera River in the north. The region is known for its high incidence of public crime, significant wealth, revolving door tourism and higher levels of homelessness than the State capital, Brisbane. Located in this area are two courthouses, Southport and Coolangatta; with Southport Magistrates Court identified as the busiest Domestic Violence Court in Queensland, recording the highest numbers of private and police applications for domestic violence and family violence protection orders. There are nine police stations in the region which are located at Coomera, Runaway Bay, Nerang, Southport, Surfers Paradise, Mudgeeraba, Broadbeach, Palm Beach and Coolangatta. The region also accommodates two offices of the Department of Corrective Services, one at Southport and the second at Burleigh, two funded women's shelters and one unfunded shelter, one Legal Aid Office, and one specialist domestic violence centre.

Structure of the book

In the first chapter, Donna Chung and Patrick O'Leary argue that programs which are delivered in the context of a coordinated systemic response to domestic violence are likely to be of greater benefit and safety than programs that are offered in isolation. In Chapter 2, Donna Justo describes the development of GCDVIR and the range of different services that are offered by the centre. This initiative was an early pioneer of integrated approaches in Australia, prompted by a number of domestic homicides in the region which brought to the fore the need for agencies to work together sharing information and developing effective practice protocols. Chapter 3 describes the experiences of some of the women who have accessed the centre, focussing on the particular role that the women's advocate plays in service delivery.

One feature that is critical to the success of any integrated response is the extent to which men's programs are able to combine an educational and therapeutic response with that of the criminal justice system. In Part II of the book we outline the perspectives of the police (in Chapter 4 by Patrick O'Leary and Laura Bahnisch), the magistrates (Chapter 5 by Annette Hennessy), and the community corrections officers (Chapter 6 by Rosemary O'Malley) on how the integrated response works in practice. It is apparent that all of these agencies need to work closely together if the risk of further violence is to be effectively managed.

Part III is concerned with the delivery of domestic violence perpetrator programs. Facilitating men's behaviour change groups can be a challenging experience. Facilitators have to balance inviting men to change, remaining respectful, and holding men accountable for their behaviour. The next three chapters discuss how programs work, on both a conceptual and therapeutic level. In Chapter 7 Sue Moore describes the Gold Coast men's program. This is a joint program managed by the Domestic Violence Prevention Centre and the Department of Corrective Services. The program is based on feminist models of intervention and aims to promote the safety of women and children by challenging men to take responsibility for their abusive behaviour and helping them learn how to form respectful relationships with their partners. An important feature of this particular program is that it is targeted solely at men who have been mandated by the courts to attend the group as a sentencing option for breaching a domestic violence protection order. In the next chapter (Chapter 8), Tony Fletcher provides some practice suggestions drawn from his understanding of feminist theory and his practice experiences in delivering groups in South Australia. In the last chapter of this section, Maggie Woodhead proposes an alternative approach to intervention, drawing on her experiences in program delivery and management in Western Australia (Chapter 9).

Part IV describes the outcomes of an Australian Research Council funded project to examine the effects of the Gold Coast program. First, in Chapter 10, Donna Chung and colleagues describe a series of case studies of people who have used the Gold Coast service. This chapter provides a vivid illustration of the type of challenges that are routinely faced by those who work in this area. The characteristics of program participants are described by Andrew Day and Adam Gerace (Chapter 11). It is particularly important to be clear about the men that access these services, and how they may differ from other groups of domestically violent men, such as those who volunteer for programs. This data also reminds us that not all men who are domestically violent are the same, and alerts us to the dangers of stereotyping male perpetrators in ways that can undermine program effectiveness. The specific problem of treatment readiness and engaging men in a change process is then discussed (Chapter 12 Patrick O'Leary, Andrew Day and Gary Foster), followed by an account of how men have changed over the course of program attendance (Chapter 13, Andrew Day, Patrick O'Leary, Gary Foster and Adam Gerace), and how women have experienced the program (Di Lucas, Donna Chung and Donna Justo, Chapter 14).

The final chapters of the book aim to provide a commentary on some of the key issues that currently face the sector. In Chapter 15 we discuss some of the broader theoretical issues around program delivery and how research might inform the further development of programs, and then in Chapter 16 Andrew Day and Ed Carson offer some thoughts about the different roles that facilitators can adopt in relation to the clients who are legally mandated to attend an intervention program. In the final chapter of the book (Andrew Day, Donna Chung, Donna Justo and Patrick O'Leary), we discuss the implications of this work for the future development of programs and services across Australia.

Our hope in writing this book is that it will provide a resource to practitioners and researchers alike that can usefully inform their work in this area, and ultimately assist in the development of programs and services that are successful in reducing the risk of known perpetrators committing further acts of violence towards women.

Part I

CONTEXT

Chapter 1

Integrated Response to Perpetrators of Domestic Violence: Good Practice Directions

Donna Chung and Patrick O'Leary

Historically, services for women in Australia have operated outside of government structures and have relied on a political activist framework to promote services for victims of domestic violence. At the same time the criminal justice system has dealt with domestic violence offenders in a separate context, viewing services for women primarily as an avenue for victim referral. Child protection responses to domestic violence in the past have mostly been autonomous, involving a third separate layer of response, as have the responses of a variety of other institutions that have also dealt with issues related to domestic violence, such as health and correctional services.

There has, however, been an increasing recognition that a number of different services deal with domestic violence and that a strategy is needed for these organisations to work together within a common ethos. Lessons learnt from the predominately disjointed response were that women's and children's safety was compromised and offenders were often not held accountable for the violence they perpetrated. Responses which are not well integrated tend to pay insufficient attention to the gendered nature of domestic violence, and its origins in imbalances of power between men and women in society. As the law tends to reflect societal values, domestic violence has consequently often been considered a private matter in which the criminal justice system should only minimally intervene. Acknowledging these aspects of domestic violence unavoidably brings a socio-political dimension to any response, requiring integration at both a functional and philosophical level amongst all participating agencies.

Coordination between these services has largely been a functional response to improve efficiency and protocols between key organisations dealing with domestic violence. However, this response does not necessitate a shared vision and value base because it does not arise out of a political activist frame. Integrated responses require a commitment from local agencies in the community to pursuing a common direction and outcome which is that of promoting women's and children's safety. This necessitates an approach to service delivery that is premised on an understanding of domestic violence as gendered violence and the violation of women's and children's human rights.

Integrated responses can be defined as "coordinated, appropriate, consistent responses aimed at enhancing victim safety, reducing secondary victimisation and holding abusers accountable for their violence" (Mulroney 2003: 2). This definition makes clear the important point that coordination is a means to achieve the primary goal of enhancing victim safety, and the secondary goal is increasing perpetrator accountability, rather than the key goal in itself. Confusion sometimes arises because the term "interagency coordination" is frequently used to describe both a *process* and an *outcome*. Coordination is an essential element of an integrated response to domestic violence. The emphasis on integration requires the following features:

- A shared philosophy and understanding of violence.
- Policies and procedures across participating organisations to guide the coordination.
- A formal structure for monitoring the coordination.
- A mandate.
- Other elements such as integrated case management, coordinated training and formal evaluation.
- A focus on process, particularly facilitating a respectful and inclusive culture between participating agencies.

The most common models of coordination have been developed in the United States, although in Australia services for women victims have developed into formalised integrated responses which locate perpetrator programs within a broader response to victims of crime. Australian approaches can be categorised into a number of models, based on the starting point for their development. (It is important to note that this approach to categorisation is only one way of approaching this material). These are:

- Coordinated responses.
- Criminal justice system reform projects based on a specialist Domestic Violence Court.
- Responses centred on policing initiatives.

Developing linkages between women's domestic violence services and the criminal justice system is the foundation to many of these models. These linkages are made frequently in the context of women's and male offender's contact with the courts. There are substantial barriers and challenges involved in delivering integrated responses, not least of which is the complexity of the system and debates about how to operationalise success and effectiveness. Key characteristics of integrated responses from the emerging body of practice and literature are:

- **Accountability to women** This requires looking at strategies to promote the safety of women and children as the primary goal and ensuring that programs are victim focussed. Strategies include: checking in with individual women partners and ex-partners and making sure they have access to support; involving women's services in various elements of the program such as content and facilitator practice which emphasises both the impact of domestic violence on women and children and their rights. Some programs have nights for women so they can find about the programs. The extent to which these activities are pursued by programs varies according to funding and organisational arrangements. These differences can reflect the various approaches to the place of perpetrator programs within an integrated response. (For further discussion of women's contact and support see Chapter 14.)
- **Processes for risk assessment and ongoing risk management.** This involves several components:
    - A process aimed at identifying the most dangerous men goes to the heart of interagency cooperation, as different agencies may hold information relevant to risk assessment, but it may not be shared or combined to provide the full picture about the degree of risk.
    - Screening and assessment for severe drug, alcohol and mental health problems, as these have been found to be associated with poor attendance, drop-out and reassault.
    - Assessment of risk should be informed by multiple sources (eg different service providers, child protection, male perpetrators' and female partners' and ex-partners' perspectives).
    - Ongoing risk management - risk assessment and risk management need to continue throughout the intervention period.
    - Programming to address the finding that the risk of reassault is highest when men are first in a program. This has implications for the frequency per week that the program is offered, the intensity of the men's correctional supervision and the level of support offered to women in the early stages of perpetrator programs.
    - Commitment to evaluation. Ideally this should be collaborative between stakeholders and independent evaluators, and should focus on the outcomes of the interventions and how effectively agencies work together in supporting the safety of women and children and stopping men's use of violence.

Development of Australian models of integration

The impetus for Australian models of integration has mostly been through feminist based domestic violence services for women. This has required a strong community base of political activism that has engaged key leaders in government and criminal justice systems. The evolution of Australian integrated models can be categorised into four main types:

- **Organically** in a manner consistent with general community development practices whereby one or two key stakeholders in the area take a lead role in engaging other relevant agencies and drive the model to fruition with ongoing maintenance and development.
- As a **catalyst** in response to dire consequences, such as a number of domestic homicides in an area or situations being exacerbated due to poor service coordination.
- A **top down** decision or policy initiative to implement an integrated approach in the jurisdiction at one or a number of sites as this is viewed as a successful approach in other areas.
- A **jointly supported decision** between policy makers or funders and local managers about the need to implement such an approach, as it is consistent with government policy directions and expected to be a more effective way of responding to domestic violence at the local level.

The first two categories represent bottom up approaches, the third a top down approach, and the fourth a totally different approach representing a negotiated position that involves both policy makers and local stakeholders collaborating to achieve better outcomes.

As models of integration have become more sophisticated, they have generally involved a greater range of agencies, and sought to develop and change local policies, practices and protocols to respond more effectively to domestic violence situations. The vision for many of these models is primarily effective intervention that maximises women's safety, although most also aim to deliver community education and prevention activities.

Critical milestones in developing Australian integrated approaches

Generally, integrated responses in Australia have the following characteristics and initiatives:

1. Limited geographical area

Integrated approaches to date have all had a limited geographical area as a starting point. Obviously each stakeholder agency may have differing boundaries so there needs to be agreement on the model's geographical limits, especially in the early days, as bringing together too large a group over a large area is unwieldy initially.

2. Involvement of initial agencies

The involvement of a women's domestic violence service (often this is the refuge or shelter) and the police as key stakeholders has often been a critical starting point. Without the involvement of these two key stakeholders the model is likely to be limited in its reach and impact.

3. Investment in gaining stakeholders' confidence

There is a need to sell the model by assuring agencies that involvement would make their work in domestic violence more efficient and effective. This aspect of development should not be underestimated in times when agencies often have long waiting lists and high demands for their services. The leaders of new initiatives need to be highly skilled negotiators, with a clear vision of what the new approach would look like and a detailed plan of how to achieve it, including the role of each stakeholder agency, to enable agencies to take time to develop a new approach.

4. Stable leadership and management commitment

Stable leadership and management commitment underpinned successful integrated approaches to domestic violence amongst the sites studied in our research (Chung, O'Leary and Zannettino 2003). If it is to grow, an integrated model needs stable leadership from one or two people attached to a lead agency. Leadership requires:

- the capacity to engage other stakeholders to commit to and actively participate in the integration;
- a vision which takes account of the broader environment, an openness to new ideas and the capacity for change;
- an acceptance that to some degree it is always a work in progress;
- the ability to inspire and encourage other stakeholder agencies' involvement.

Management commitment, as well as providing leadership, is also necessary to ensure the ongoing involvement of stakeholder agencies and their capacity to make changes to their practices. It is important to have senior managers involved in the integrated model in order to provide the authority and legitimacy to make changes at the agencies. A commitment to an open and reflective approach amongst agencies which actively encourages feedback and criticism can further improve the integrated approach.

5. Commitment to a common definition of domestic violence and associated practice principles amongst all stakeholder agencies

The importance of a shared commitment to a common definition of domestic violence and practice principles cannot be underestimated, and time needs to be devoted to ensure that agencies share the values and principles underpinning practice and understand each other's mandates. Shared understanding should move beyond statements that domestic violence is unacceptable, to understanding underlying issues such as gender inequity and perpetrator responsibility for violence and gaining agreement about how practice principles are implemented amongst the stakeholders. Definitions should emphasise that domestic violence has a gendered dimension of power and control, occurs in various forms (physical, emotional, psychological, social, financial and spiritual), and is mostly unreported to the criminal justice system. These fundamental concepts and practices should be annually reviewed to enable key changes in personnel and new knowledge and ideas to be incorporated into existing work.

6. Formal management structures

Integrated responses to domestic violence require funding to support a management structure at both interagency and intra-agency levels. To ensure cohesive and ongoing work in the development of the integrated response it is critical that there is accountability about its development from agency manager level through to service providers. This is essential to support integration at all levels. Meetings of stakeholder agencies should include appropriate participation of all levels of management.

7. Information sharing and limited confidentiality

Effective participation of agencies in integrated responses requires sharing information, especially in cases of high risk. This requires participating agencies to have limited confidentiality arrangements in their policies in regard to reporting information of concern for women and men. This can be a contentious issue requiring agreement on processes for information exchange that is guided by considerations of safety of women and their children as a primary goal of the integration. Interagency protocols for limited confidentiality are best established in policy documentation.

Central to any integrated response to domestic violence is setting up formalised meetings between agencies on subjects such as overall management, joint case conferences and reviews. Ongoing processes of information sharing are an essential component of integrated approaches in domestic violence. Practical examples of this component include:

- Regular case meetings amongst stakeholder agencies to ensure an exchange of information about cases. This can alert appropriate agencies to new proceedings that may be relevant. Safety and risk issues can be identified in addition to other information about community activities and education related to domestic violence.

- The formal process of regular information exchange between police and domestic violence services, so that services are alerted to information about those involved in police callouts and can take action as necessary.
- The Gold Coast Domestic Violence Integrated Response, where police share information with the Women's Domestic Violence Service regarding women who have consented to referral following a domestic violence callout from police. At perpetrator program level this involves facilitators advising the women's service of any concerns about men's violence.
- All relevant information about the perpetrator is kept on the victim's file for her safety and ongoing assessment of risk, whilst the perpetrator's file should not contain any information pertaining to the victim. This is to protect the victim in light of Freedom of Information legislation. Should information be requested from the perpetrator's file, there is no information available about the victim that could put her safety at risk.

8. Ongoing investment of time and resources

Ongoing investment of time and resources into the integrated model is necessary even when it is established - it does not run itself. In a climate of targeted funding for most agency activities, integrated responses require specific funding. It is not practical or sustainable to operate an integrated response to domestic violence without appropriate resourcing. However, many integrated services are not adequately funded and integration and coordination can be incorrectly conflated as an efficiency measure resulting in cost cutting. In contrast, as integrated responses gain momentum with agency partnerships become more sophisticated, greater amounts of time are needed, from management through to service delivery. This investment leads to a better quality of service provision for those affected by domestic violence and improved safety outcomes. However, without continuing active investment, the integration models are likely to become nothing more than information sharing.

9. Formalised structures and processes

Formalised structures and processes to guide the integration are essential to the sustainability of an integrated response. Whilst the formation of integrated responses requires individual leaders with passion and commitment, they should not rely solely on individual knowledge and participation. Formal agreements such as memoranda of understanding between stakeholder agencies are necessary to detail interagency protocols, for example, those related to agency commitment, information sharing and joint involvement practices in cases of domestic violence. Regular reviews of these documents are important to ensure they are responsive to a wide variety of situations of domestic violence. Such documentation should provide clarity and a mandate to the stakeholder agencies, and ensure that the model is sustainable - instead of being reliant on cooperative individuals. For example, a new manager commencing with an agency is less likely to decide the agency will no longer be involved if there are already signed commitments. The intention is for the interagency practices to become orthodox and not exceptional or individual practice.

Implementing male perpetrator programs as part of an integrated response to domestic violence

All agencies involved in an integrated response should work towards standards of practice and protocols. Each participating agency in an integrated response to domestic violence should provide a consistent message of its purpose, objectives and ethical stands taken. All agencies must give priority to the safety of women and their children so that it guides their work practices and how they assess the progress or otherwise of situations. Determining what defines successful outcomes and its measurement in perpetrator programs has been an ongoing debate. Ideally it is the cessation of violence by men against their female partners and children. However, as practice has evolved it has become evident that this is difficult to measure and not easy to achieve. A key aspect of perpetrator programs in an integrated response has been that they promote the safety of women and children first, and second that they bring about changes in attitude and behaviour amongst men in domestic violence perpetrator programs. Furthermore, men's participation in a perpetrator program is also a direct consequence of their criminal behaviour. This therapeutic approach to justice is often at odds with what men may view as a joint problem for which the couple should be held responsible. Most often this is addressed at the program. There is inherent hope that men will make sustainable changes to attitudes and behaviours central to their offending and much of this change is targeted through therapy and education. These two issues illustrate the tension that exists between punishment and therapy or rehabilitation. This tension is not easily resolved and there will continue to be differences of opinion about whether perpetrator programs should be run at all.

As a preferred model of practice, women's domestic violence services should be a key leader in the structure of perpetrator programs where they are involved in some or all of the following roles: group facilitation, observation, supervision and review. This should not be an added burden to the operation of women's services but specifically resourced in the integrated model. The purpose of this involvement is to ensure that the process involved in intervening with men who use violence against female partners is transparent, and allows the women's service to participate in and give feedback to the process at appropriate times. Involvement of women's services is an essential foundation to establishing gender accountability within integrated responses to male perpetrators of domestic violence.

Gender accountability

Gender accountability requires a coherent understanding of gendered violence and power needs. It is important to understand gender accountability as a process and not a finite goal. The process is based on mutual understanding and respect, and the belief that women as victims of domestic violence can be further disempowered if services do not reflect critically on their practices and processes. Accountability to women partners and women's services is more easily embedded and sustained within an integrated approach, as each key stakeholder is accountable through the integrated management and case conferencing processes. It provides an opportunity for dialogue about how to improve these developing areas of practice as there is an established forum or management structure for discussing such issues. At an organisational level the extent to which participating agencies have cultures which have historically been gender and culture blind can be considered in relation to how these issues are now addressed, so that organisational patterns do not mirror historical imbalances of power at the level of the integrated response.

A program for domestic violence perpetrators needs to have formal and informal processes that take account of imbalances of power between men and women in certain contexts. At the level of practice, gender accountability between male and female co-facilitators is an important aspect of working with men who use violence against female partners. This requires facilitators to understand the particular ways in which gender inequality and stereotypes can be reproduced overtly and covertly in the group practice and to make a conscious commitment to anti-sexist practice. Direct group observation by women's advocate workers can also provide gender accountability, as long as they are engaged after the group to contribute their ideas and views on what transpired. The micro practices of group work need consideration in various ways such as:

- The content of group activities and facilitators' responses being considered in terms of reflecting gender inequality and essentialism, and actively promoting gender equality.
- Male and female facilitators planning together practices to challenge the possible assumption of men participants that leadership roles indicate male authority.
- Use strategies that ensure joint leadership of the group is modelled - this includes non-verbal behaviour and how it portrays particular gendered images.

- Female facilitators not solely taking on traditionally identified feminine tasks such as doing dishes.
- Facilitators being confident and vigilant in their strategies to challenge male participants' stereotypical, sexist and essentialist comments about women, and not colluding with men by staying silent or joining in with such ideas.
- Where programs rely on casual or part-time facilitators, time needs to be specifically allocated to address gender accountability as part of the contractual agreement.

Engagement of child protection

In many parts of Australia, engaging child protection services in integrated responses has not always been actively sought or achieved. This can be attributed partly to the differing paradigms between the two sectors:

- Domestic violence services are non-statutory agencies whose primary clients have historically been the woman (and children who are also now counted as clients of such services, particularly in SAAP (Supported Accommodation Assistance Program) funded emergency accommodation). Where these services have had feminist philosophies they have guarded against approaches that focus solely on blaming mothers for their children's experiences of abuse, for example in relation to the concept of "failure to protect". An underlying assumption in feminist services is that where the mother can be supported effectively, this will improve her relationship with the child and the child's wellbeing in due course.
- Child protection agencies have a statutory responsibility for children's wellbeing and are expected to take action where child abuse and neglect is deemed to be occurring, with the child the prime consideration at all times.

In some areas these differing paradigms have resulted in limited dialogue between agencies. In other areas this has been seen as less conflicting and the two services have worked together alongside other agencies. Innovative practice in the area has included the police contacting child protection and undertaking joint visits where they are concerned about children's welfare in domestic violence, and reporting back to the integrated response meetings. In some cases police or child protection services have taken out an intervention order, on behalf of the children, against the male (father or mother's partner), which prevents him living in the family home. This takes the responsibility to take out the order away from the woman. Other innovative practices identified in the study include the domestic violence service participating in the child protection service case discussions.

Program logic and process with male perpetrators of domestic violence

The aim of an integrated response is to increase the safety of women and their children and to hold perpetrators of domestic violence accountable. The second element has often been difficult to operationalise where men's use of violence has not been under the scrutiny of the legal system, or when the legal system has been lenient in its response. Paradoxically what happens is that women and children doubly bear the brunt of the crime - initially in the home and then after escaping as they often have insecure and transient lives as a result of homelessness, interruption to employment and so on. Meanwhile the men are not seen to face any sanctions, or to take responsibility for their actions or have an impetus for changing their behaviour. Women and children are often the only target of intervention, for example, in child protection strategies. An integrated program needs to manage the tension of prioritising the safety and needs of women and their children while also overtly highlighting that these conditions have arisen from men's violence. These considerations should be evident in the integration of program logic and goals of male perpetrator programs that are not restricted to men's individual change but also reflect circumstances and opportunities that may increase safety and desired change for women and their children. This of course does not preclude or deny that there are often associated problems such as substance abuse or poverty that co-exist alongside problems of domestic violence.

The mandatory continuum

Reviewing perpetrator programs across Australia as either court ordered or voluntary may be a false dichotomy (O'Leary, Chung and Zannettino 2004). Very few men enter such programs of their own volition. Men may see attending a program as a way of avoiding undesirable outcomes in court or in other forums. Or their motivation may have little to do with taking responsibility for violence, for example, a female partner may leave if the man does not get help. Therefore most men attending domestic violence programs can be placed along a mandatory continuum. At one end is a social mandate (expectations from family, friends, socially sanctioned), at the other a legal mandate, where attending a program is a condition of their sentence after committing a criminal offence (usually assault).

Social Mandate←--→Legal Mandate

This also provides a way of articulating further the different types of mandatory attendance - is it diversionary and therefore avoiding criminal charges, part of bail conditions, or part of sentencing?

The mandatory continuum is an attempt to reflect more accurately the different pathways to such programs, however participants are not dichotomous groups and this work with men requires dealing with their various resistances to involvement.

Difficulties recruiting and retaining quality staff

Information from program providers across Australia has consistently indicated difficulties in recruiting and retaining staff with necessary knowledge and skills to run programs for male perpetrators of domestic violence. This is both a workforce capacity and resource issue. The work with male perpetrators does require specialist knowledge of domestic violence, the power dynamics which operate and the practice styles and approaches appropriate to working with this group of men.

Program purpose

In terms of program purpose, capturing an accurate measure of women and their children's safety cannot rely solely on men's self-reports. For example, men's attendance at the program may result in increased scrutiny of his behaviour resulting in a lull in his perpetration of violence, allowing a window of opportunity for separation and/or for the woman to attend a victim focussed service. In this instance men's behaviour change may not be sustainable but his involvement has enabled women and children to access specialist services. Men's behaviour change is in this sense a secondary purpose. Changes or effectiveness need to be considered at a variety of levels. Levels of effectiveness can be seen, for example, by increasing court awareness and referral of men to domestic violence education and intervention programs. Mandated attendance cannot guarantee attitudinal or behaviour change, but it does allow offenders to be placed under greater scrutiny and provides an opportunity for engagement with women and their children to access services that may assist with safety plans. These considerations of effectiveness cannot be underestimated in an integrated response.

In our prior research (see Chung et al 2003; O'Leary et al 2004), the majority of agencies providing programs viewed domestic violence as related to gendered power relations and the abuse of male power. However, there was often a disjuncture between philosophy, explanations and group program practice with men. Most group practice is aimed towards men taking responsibility for their use of violence. Nevertheless, facilitators also need to be sensitive about how they communicate and interact with the men in the group so that they do not condone comments which are indicative of female and male stereotyping, homophobic or racist attitudes. These are examples of an obvious fissure between stated philosophy and practice. It is thus critical that integrated responses monitor perpetrator program practice as part of a commitment to continuing quality management.

Key elements of a program for men who use violence against their female partners

As a minimum standard of practice, men's programs should have established links with a domestic violence service for women. Domestic violence programs for men should be conceptualised as having their primary emphasis on ending domestic violence, which should not be conflated with making them into better men. Our research has highlighted that, at a minimum, programs for men who use violence against their female partners should include:

- an individual assessment of the man for suitability to the program;
- a program for men that is a minimum of 12 weeks in duration;
- a written contract with the man about the conditions of participation which include contact with his partner or ex-partner;
- ongoing documented risk assessment of the perpetrator from a number of sources - facilitators, self-assessment and the female partner;
- contact with the woman partner by a female worker (women's advocate or co-facilitator) at the beginning, middle and end of the program, unless she deems it unsuitable.

An anticipated outcome of increased community intolerance of domestic violence is more court-ordered and mandated programs for men, as entry into the criminal justice system is more likely. This would then change the balance of programs over time in Australia towards a greater number of legally mandated programs.

Contact with women partners

Programs should always include contact with female partners or ex-partners. Partner contact can occur in various ways:

- A women's advocate, other than the group facilitators, regularly contacts the women by letter and telephone to check safety, and provide support, safety planning and referral to services as needed. The advocate could come from within or outside the organisation that provides the men's group.
- A female co-facilitator regularly contacts the women by letter and telephone to follow up her safety concerns.
- A facilitator contacts the women intermittently as resources are scarce.

As discussed later in this book, partner contact is a difficult task as women respond in various ways. Often women do not wish to have contact. In other instances women's contact support can be difficult as women are in -

crisis and transient, making regular contact unlikely and the situation highly changeable. However, it is imperative to monitor women's and children's safety and provide appropriate support if needed.

Conclusion

A long history of fragmented responses to victims of domestic violence has heralded the need for direct focus on male perpetrators in an effort to stop domestic violence. Part of this evolution has identified the need for intervention with perpetrators of domestic violence to be included as part of an integrated response - not only for reasons of efficiency but also for enhancing safety, stopping domestic violence, and gender accountability. Integrated responses require an intersectoral approach to domestic violence and should always incorporate clear interagency agreements on understandings, values and practice positions. In this regard, integrated responses to domestic violence are both a legal and social intervention that evolve according to changing social environments, emerging knowledge and increasing community intolerance of gendered violence.

Chapter 2

The Gold Coast Domestic Violence Integrated Response to Perpetrators of Domestic Violence: Political Activism in Practice

Edited by Donna Justo[1]

This chapter describes the work of the Gold Coast Domestic Violence Integrated Response (GCDVIR). The GCDVIR is a community based integrated response to domestic violence that focuses on helping agencies to work together to provide interventions which are coordinated, appropriate and consistent with a justice reform model of service delivery. The overarching objectives of the integrated response, as it is known colloquially, are to enhance victim safety, reduce secondary victimisation, and decrease the incidence of domestic violence through the enhancement and monitoring of interagency cooperation and collaboration (Mulroney 2003). Through its advocacy, activism and by benchmarking standards, the integrated response also aims to hold perpetrators of domestic violence systemically accountable for their behaviour.

Responses to domestic violence have changed considerably over the past 30 years. Women's shelters, first established in the 1970s, provided the first, and for many years the only, option for women wanting to escape from the abuse that they experienced. Ardent lobbying from shelter workers and women's advocates was significant in bringing about legislative reform, leading to the funding and development of specific domestic violence policies and programs.

The Gold Coast Integrated Response developed from a broad-based community forum held in 1996. Discussions at the time focused on the high incidence of domestic violence and domestic homicides in the area

1 This chapter is based on work conducted by all of those, past and present, who have an association with the GCDVIR.

- Southport Magistrates Court consistently records the highest number of applications for domestic violence protection orders in Queensland. The catalyst for change for the Gold Coast community, however, was a period in 1997 in which there were eight domestic homicides in a 12 month period. In some instances, the murdered women had told more than one agency of the threats against her.

Eight years later in 2005, the then Director of the Gold Coast Domestic Violence Prevention Centre, Betty Taylor, was instrumental in leading a major political protest outside Parliament House in Brisbane (alongside women from other agencies across the State) highlighting the need for significant systems reform. They called for the funding and establishment of a Domestic Violence Fatality or Death Review Board. This board, as it was envisaged, would review systems and interventions, monitor systems of service delivery, identify gaps and provide support to close them. A defining feature of the integrated response in the Gold Coast, then, is the way in which political activism has helped to shape and guide the development of services.[2]

Guiding principles

The safety of the woman victim (and her child or children) is central to the development of any initiative implemented by the integrated response. The guiding principles which underpin the development and implementation of the GCDVIR all reflect the understanding that victim safety is of paramount concern at all times. These principles are that:

- perpetrators of domestic violence must be held accountable for their behaviour;
- domestic violence is a crime that needs a criminal justice response;
- everyone has the right to a life free from domestic violence;
- the cultural diversity of society requires that strategies and programs are inclusive and culturally appropriate;
- victims of domestic violence are entitled to access services which are immediate, consistent and which work together to lessen the occurrence of secondary victimisation;
- domestic violence needs to be understood in the political, social, cultural and economic context which creates unequal power between men and women.

2 Other programs which have also provided inspiration and content have been the Quincy Court Model and the Duluth Domestic Abuse Project (both in the United States), and the Hamilton Abuse Intervention Project, New Zealand. These programs, while differing from each other in important respects, all have the core elements necessary for the establishment of a successful multi-agency approach to domestic violence.

The ways in which these principles have been implemented are central to the goals of program delivery, the means by which systems hold perpetrators accountable for their behaviour, and the mechanisms of interagency support that have been developed as part of the integrated response. These are described below.

Operationalising the Guiding Principles

The specific goals of the program are to enhance the safety of women victims and their children by:

Ensuring timely, appropriate and consistent interventions

Providing adequate legal protection

Providing on-going support

Providing an integrated response which promotes best practice principles

Providing information to victims which will assist them to make informed choices regarding welfare, health, counselling, medical and legal needs

Providing services to victims which treat them with compassion, courtesy, respect and in a manner which is responsive to age, ethnicity, culture and linguistic differences or any disability or other need

Involving victims of domestic abuse in the program development, monitoring and evaluation.

To hold perpetrators of domestic violence systemically accountable for their behaviour by:

Interventions which recognise the criminality of domestic violence and promote the utilisation of the Criminal Code in responding to domestic violence

Interventions which are timely, appropriate and consistent and which prioritise the safety of victims and their children

Providing programs which challenge perpetrators of domestic violence to accept responsibility for their abusive behaviour

Providing individual contact with men to assess lethality and suitability for programs

Providing a Domestic Violence Offender Program (a fully court-mandated group program for men who are convicted of a breach under the *Domestic and Family Violence Protection Act 1989*)

Providing programs or groups which adhere to the Best Practice Standards for Men's Groups developed by the Queensland Department of Communities in consultation with the NGO sector.

Benchmarking practice statewide, nationally and internationally.

To provide a multi-agency response to domestic violence on the Gold Coast by:

Further developing collaborative working relationships across agencies working with domestic violence to ensure more comprehensive responses

Developing protocols within and across agencies

Continuing to seek funding for the project

Monitoring, evaluating and reviewing activities and interventions undertaken by the Domestic Violence Integrated Response Project

Providing training across agencies as well as within the community

Identifying gaps in services and responses

Lobbying for law reform.

Governance

Building an integrated response to domestic violence takes time, energy, commitment and a vision that things can be done better, more safely and more efficiently. The motivation for doing things differently will change from community to community - for some it may be a tragic event that brings the community together, whilst for others it may be scant resources, lack of community cohesion around domestic violence responses, or broader community concerns about crime and safety. The history of service responses in Queensland shows that programs and policies have mostly developed in isolation from each other. Often there has been little coordination between different services. The Gold Coast experience, for example, showed that client confidentiality, which some agencies had prized so highly, could result in harm and death.

The programs of the integrated response are constantly evolving. There is significant planning and dialogue behind each new initiative and in consultation with other GCDVIR members at the monthly Gold Coast Domestic Violence Integrated Response meetings. Considerable work has been undertaken between 1996 and the present time on the development of clearly articulated principles, aims and protocols, both within participating agencies as well as across agencies. This is regarded as critical to the sustainability of the integrated response and is based on representatives having the authority to act and influence change within their own agency. This has been achieved while keeping the women (victims) central to the process and to the decisions that are made regarding their safety and further risk of harm.

The Gold Coast Domestic Violence Integrated Response (GCDVIR) Committee meets monthly and holds an additional planning meeting at the commencement of each year to establish three priority focus areas for the coming year. Key personnel in each participating agency sign protocols and cross-agency agreements, and regularly review these. This gives all members input into the establishment and ownership of the priorities, and ensures their support and financial commitment where relevant. Membership of the committee is described below.

Committee Structure of the GCDVIR

GCDVIR Committee

GCDVIR Director; Manager-Integrated Response; Manager-Counselling

Queensland Police Service Inspector District Support Services; Officer-in-Charge Police Prosecutions; District Domestic Violence Liaison Officer; Inspector Communications and Operations, Superintendent of Police

Department of Corrective Services Zonal Manager of Gold Coast District; Manager Probation and Parole Southport; Manager Probation and Parole Burleigh Heads

Department of Communities Manager; Community Resource Officer; Senior Resource Manager; Regional Manager

Legal Aid Queensland (Manager, Southport).

Southport Magistrate's Court Registry Coolangatta Court Registrar-Southport Court; Quarterly Magistrate or Acting Magistrate

Macleod Women's Refuge Manager

Majella House Women's Refuge Coordinator

Sanctuary Seven Women's Refuge Coordinator

Department of Child Safety Managers and Team Leaders; Labrador Child Safety Service Centre; Nerang Child Safety Service Centre; Mermaid Waters Child Safety Service Centre

Department of Housing Regional Manager

Centacare Men's Court Information Service; Men and Family Violence Service

---

The committee is divided into seven subcommittees (see below) which take responsibility for different areas of activity. The subcommittees meet twice monthly, or as required. Most commonly the Gold Coast Domestic Violence Prevention Centre Inc acts as secretariat to the process through the role of the Integrated Response Manager who coordinates these meetings and the feedback and information sharing process. It is through subcommittees that specific processes, protocols, risk assessment and case management occur. They are also the vehicle for developing new forms and risk assessment tools as part of the evolving nature of the DVIR.

Subcommittee Structure

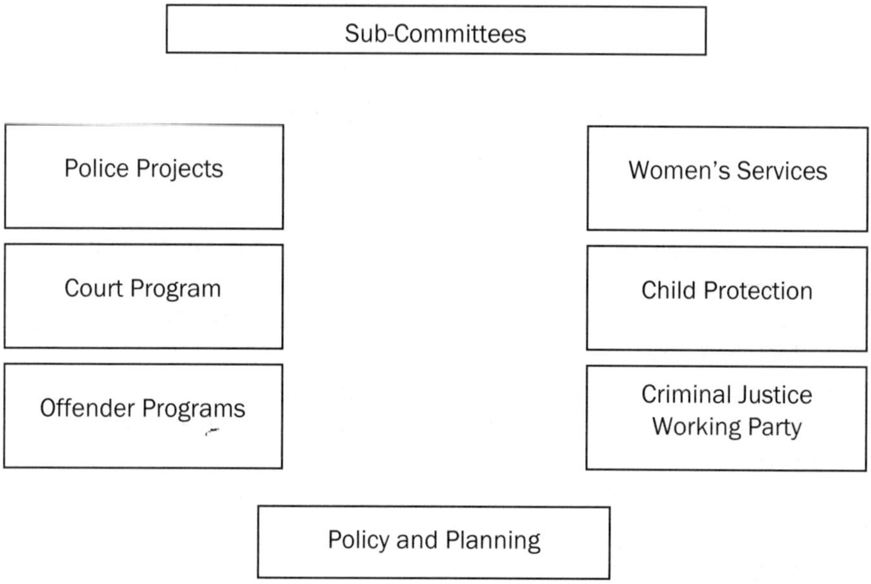

Key programs

The following programs operate under the Gold Coast Domestic Violence Integrated Response:

Domestic Violence Court Support Program

In an endeavour to find ways in which the Domestic Violence Court could become safer, more efficient and better coordinated, discussions began between the Domestic Violence Prevention Centre Gold Coast Inc and the Southport Courthouse in 1993. This resulted in the establishment of one of the safest and most innovative domestic violence court support programs in Australia. The location of a specific program within the courthouse has greatly enhanced access to legal protection for victims of domestic violence by providing: information about legal and court processes and applications for protection orders or variations to existing orders; safety planning; pre-court visits and orientation; help in preparing evidence; support in the courtroom; referral and advocacy.

An example of the integrated response process in 2008 has been the scanning of protection orders at court, which are then emailed to the relevant police station in the region and subsequently served on the perpetrator or offender in very quick time, hence enhancing the safety of the woman and potentially reducing further risk of harm.

The Domestic Violence Court Support Program

The Domestic Violence Court Support Program, through the court support workers, provides immediate support, information and assistance to victims of domestic violence. Staff can provide the following services:

- Assistance with new applications
- Assistance to revoke or vary an existing application
- The provision of information about the Domestic and Family Violence Protection Act 1989
- Pre-court information
- Support in the courtroom and post-court debriefing
- Referral for legal information
- Referral for counselling and support
- Safety planning

Integration within the court is achieved with Police Prosecutions, Court Clerk, Domestic Violence Court Support and Registry staff continuing to meet to discuss issues that impact on the smooth running of the program.

Court Support Program Staff participate in the State-wide Domestic Violence Court Assistance Network (DVCAN) throughout the year and attend the DVCAN conferences and other relevant training and professional development, when available.

Safety 1st Project

The Safety 1st Project aims to increase the safety of women and children who have been accommodated in a women's refuge in the Gold Coast area. The project involves sharing important information between local women's refuges and the Domestic Violence Prevention Centre about safety and security needs. With her consent, when a woman leaves a refuge, a referral form is completed which includes her current safety plans. The form is then faxed or emailed to the Domestic Violence Prevention Centre. This information helps the counsellors to form a comprehensive approach to women's safety on the Gold Coast, and to undertake an assessment of the risk of future harm. The information is not shared with anyone outside the women's refuges and the Domestic Violence Prevention Centre unless the client gives consent.

Police Fax-Back Program (high risk intervention) or 'Police Assisted Referral'

The fax-back program is a mechanism for responding to victims of domestic violence following a police callout. It is an assisted referral process for victims of domestic violence where investigating officers offer the victim support and assistance. This applies to all incidents of domestic violence. With consent, police fill out a referral form on arrival back at the station and fax it through to the Domestic Violence Prevention Centre on a pre-programmed number. A counsellor from the Domestic Violence Prevention Centre then telephones the victim to offer support, assistance, information and counselling. The project also aims to reduce the number of police "repeat calls for service" by providing timely intervention, information and assistance. The fax-back program was first developed in 1998 as a project of the integrated response. This partnership has continued to strengthen and develop over the past 10 years, during which time both organisations have undergone a process of education about issues faced by each organisation and have developed a joint problem-solving approach. There are four key elements to the project:

Interagency collaboration

The project directly involves police. The fax-back worker liaises closely with the Domestic and Family Violence Court support workers and is able to provide information about any matters before the court. Communication with the domestic violence offender program and women's counsellors provides a critical component of the project.

Hospital fax-back

This process enables the hospital social work team (with the woman's consent) to forward a fax to the Gold Coast Domestic Violence Prevention Centre to enable support to be provided to the woman during or after her stay in hospital

Information sharing

Regular meetings provide a mechanism for information sharing and problem solving. These are conducted with domestic violence liaison officers from all Gold Coast police stations and the district domestic violence liaison officer in conjunction with staff from the Domestic Violence Prevention Centre. Police station performance is reported on a monthly basis.

Police training

Ongoing training is provided to police of all ranks by the Domestic Violence Prevention Centre regarding domestic violence issues and the fax-back program. Training topics have included: Investigating Domestic Violence; Using Risk Assessment Tools; Investigating Attempted Strangulation; and Identifying the Predominant Aggressor.

Police Involvement

Queensland Police make between 600-700 referrals each year to the Domestic Violence Prevention Centre. Data consistently shows that approximately 75-80 per cent of victims referred are new clients to the Domestic Violence Prevention Centre at the time the referral is made. Approximately 91 per cent of victims are female. As part of the process of building positive relationships with operational police and the station Domestic Violence Liaison Officers (DVLO) the Domestic Violence Prevention Centre makes regular police station visits. The purpose of this is to make contact with the DVLO, give feedback to each station about the number of referrals made, supply resources including brochures, posters and forms and to discuss any other issues associated with domestic violence.

Project SAFER (Safety Assessment for Every Response)

Project SAFER - Phase 1 and 2 was a joint project between Queensland Police, Gold Coast District, and the Domestic Violence Prevention Centre Gold Coast Inc. The project was developed in response to local needs and issues and draws on international experiences from the United States and Canada. The first phase of Project SAFER was developed in 2003 and was piloted at Southport Police Station from August 2003 until November 2003 as an initiative of the Gold Coast Domestic Violence Integrated Response. It is described in Chapter 4 of this book.

Men's Domestic Violence Offender Education and Intervention Program

The Men's Domestic Violence Offender Education and Intervention Program is a joint project between the Domestic Violence Prevention Centre Gold Coast Inc and the Department of Corrective Services: Probation and Parole Gold Coast. The program has been operating since 2000. The program runs for 24 weeks and is based on the Duluth model that looks at challenging men to take responsibility for their abusive behaviour and to work towards changing their behaviour and forming respectful relationships with their partners. The men have all been mandated by the courts to attend the group as a sentencing option for breaching a domestic violence protection order. The program requires considerable management and monitoring and complies with the statewide practice standards for working with male offenders developed by the funding body of the programs - the Department of Communities. A part-time coordinator manages the considerable work and monitoring involved in the program, in 2008 the program extended to two group programs. From a management perspective the risk and safety of the women partners and their children is the significant aspect of the monitoring process. This program is explored more fully in Chapter 7.

Women's safety has been paramount in all aspects of the program including a pre-group assessment process which aims to determine risk factors and the men's suitability for the group. Pre-group sessions were held with the women to give them information about the purpose and structure of the group, the role of the Domestic Violence Prevention Centre Gold Coast Inc, issues of confidentiality and to work with them to develop a safety plan.

Moving forward

It is an exciting time politically for Australia, in that Federal and State Governments appear to be focussed on reducing violence against women and their children. In March of 2008, the Queensland Premier Anna Bligh stipulated that she wanted to see a reduction in the number of women being injured and dying at the hands of their male partners. This type of public identification of the ongoing severity of the problem ensures commitment across government and non-government or not for profit agencies in their quest for a violence-free Australia.

It is critical at this stage of development in the Gold Coast integrated response that time and resources are dedicated to consolidate and review all aspects of the program, and to ensure that protocols and procedures are in place to sustain the response. It is also imperative to consolidate all aspects of the infrastructure to ensure it is solid and focussed. One of the greatest challenges for the integrated response, however, has been to retain a feminist agenda and develop services in accordance with the philosophical underpinnings of the feminist approach.

As part of moving forward comes a vision for the future: a Gold Coast Family Violence Justice Centre. How do we get there? Our activism suggests that it is via the introduction of a criminal justice pilot project to establish model parameters, protocols and timelines for full implementation, beginning with the funding of a specialist domestic violence court based at Southport Magistrates Court. The proposed project would seek to reposition domestic violence crimes within a reformed criminal justice system that addresses and supports the safety needs of victims while holding perpetrators of violence systemically accountable. An outline of the project is set out below. The funding for additional resources to the project is likely to be offset with cost savings in reducing the number of repeat police callouts, reduction in court hours, more effective management of offenders and safer communities.

Components of the Proposed Criminal Justice Project

The Criminal Justice Project as part of the ongoing work of the Gold Coast Domestic Violence Integrated Response has the following aims:
To provide a proactive criminal justice approach to domestic violence interventions
To provide clearer pathways through the criminal justice system for victims of domestic violence
To provide a specific framework for the management of domestic violence cases within the criminal justice system
To provide for the establishment of a specialised domestic violence court using the principles of therapeutic jurisprudence
To hold perpetrators of domestic violence systemically accountable for their behaviour

Considerations for the Project are:

Victim Support
Investigation / Evidence Gathering
Prosecution
Court Processes
Sentencing Options
Offender Accountability - Monitoring
Development of Multi-agency Responses
Law

Criminal Justice Project Partners:

Domestic Violence Prevention Centre Gold Coast
Queensland Police Service - Gold Coast
Justice Department - Southport Magistrates Court
Legal Aid Queensland - Southport
Department of Corrective Services, Southport and Burleigh Heads

Proposed Outcomes of the Visions for the Future:

Perpetrators of domestic violence are systemically held accountable for their behaviour through criminal justice interventions
A cost effective judicial management of domestic violence cases
An integrated multi-agency strategy to coordinate the criminal justice response to domestic violence

The experience of model programs both overseas and in other jurisdictions in Australia has demonstrated this can be achieved:

Without clogging the courts
Compromising the safety of victims
Or the requirement of continued escalating costs.

Conclusion

This chapter has presented an overview of the structure and services offered through the GCDVIR. It is the courage, hope and resilience of the many thousands of women survivors of domestic violence who continue to drive the motivation and momentum for this political change. In the first 15 years of operation of the centre there have been more than 219,000 contacts from women who have experienced domestic violence. The series of case studies described in Chapter 10 establishes further why it is essential that the voices of women continue to inform the development of the GCDVIR, and that their experiences, their reality and, most importantly, their safety and that of their children, are upheld by all service systems responses to their experiences of domestic violence, (for example, police, courts, child protection systems).

Chapter 3

What's in it for the Women?

Donna Justo, Di Lucas,
Joan Salizzo and Lesley McCartney

Over the past 10 years the political agenda in relation to appropriate community responses to domestic violence in Australia has been influenced both by lobby groups advocating for men's interests, and by large general human service agencies which compete for government funding. The results have, in many ways, been disastrous for women and their children. In Queensland, for example, changes to the *Family Law Act* (and the push for children to spend equal time with both the perpetrators and victims of domestic violence), and welfare reforms (which have forced women to return to work and affected their ability to negotiate or afford suitable housing and childcare), are both factors which have contributed to women remaining in situations in which they are at serious risk of harm and even death. In our view such measures reflect beliefs and values that blame the victims of domestic violence. They reflect a view that women who have been abused should be expected to be able to function as productive members of the community, despite their physically and emotionally traumatic experiences.

At the heart of this debate is the question of whether the development of programs for men diverts much need funding from victims' services. This is vigorously denied by those who allocate funding, but women's services who support victims and their children remain sceptical, particularly when faced with the response that there is "no money" to develop victim support services. In addition, doubts remain about the effectiveness of programs for men. As Gondolf (2002) states, feminist practitioners and activists constantly question whether working with men will make them take responsibility for their violent behaviour and increase the safety of women and their children. In this chapter, we consider broader issues of domestic violence service provision from the perspective of women.

A Personal Perspective: Di Lucas

As a feminist practitioner with over 20 years experience in working in the domestic violence sector I find I am wondering how the focus moved from having the work of domestic violence intervention and prevention, focused on the safety of women and their children who have been victims of men's violence, to looking at men's violence as an independent entity. How did gender slip off the agenda?

I am not sure when the "new hype" about working with perpetrators infiltrated and hijacked the agenda but the response validates my thoughts that it is still a patriarchal society that still focuses on looking after males by trying to change them – even if they don't want to be part of the process. Whilst many women live in hope that their violent partner will change they are still receiving the message that reinforces the stereotype that they are responsible for what happens within their intimate relationships. This can often contribute to decisions to stay in abusive and violent situations that are unsafe.

Child protection

The child protection system presents by far the most significant challenges to the provision of effective responses to meet the needs of victims of domestic violence. Women are often terrified that their children will be removed, and as a consequence may choose not to seek outside assistance and support (including from the police and the criminal justice system). Others who have had contact with this system have had a negative, and often punitive, experience.

In some ways contemporary practices developed by the Department of Child Safety in Queensland along with changes to the child protection legislation can be seen as holding women responsible for a "failure to protect" their children, rather than focusing on those who are responsible for the abuse. Indeed, it has been suggested that the child protection system and its workers may be over-focused on the responsibility of women to protect their children (The Australian Domestic and Family Violence Clearinghouse 2007). Burke (1999) goes as far as to state that an "invisible man syndrome" exists which excludes men (as fathers) from taking any responsibility for the protection of their children. Put simply, the notion that if a woman leaves a violent partner then she and the children are safe is still ingrained within the culture and practices of the department. This is a myth that can have serious consequences – our experiences have shown that the time of separation is often the most dangerous for women and their children.

In Queensland, notifications to the Department of Child Safety are automatically made by the police if they attend a domestic violence incident and children are present. However, no risk assessment is undertaken, and this in itself contributes to children being removed from the care of their mother, even if she is willing to, or has left, a violent partner. Ideally a child safety response that is focused on the safety of both women and their children is required. Regardless of changing gender roles and family law that promotes shared equal time, women are usually the primary carers of their children, even if they are working or studying. This must be acknowledged and enshrined in child safety legislation and policy. The development of practices such as departmental child protection officers taking out domestic violence orders requesting the removal of violent men, rather than the children, from the home would help to overcome these problems. This is not rocket science - there is enough contemporary evidence and research to indicate that such an approach could have better outcomes for victims and their children. There just needs to be a common sense approach and the political will to make it happen. The following case study illustrates how a traumatic, hostile and negative experience with the child protection system resulted in the victim taking action to protect herself and her child.

Case Study: Lisa[1]

A child health clinic nurse made a referral and attended a crisis appointment with Lisa and her three-year-old son, who has a disability. Lisa was too frightened of her partner to take out a domestic violence order, even though he was physically, psychologically, sexually and financially abusive and had the capacity to access and use weapons. Lisa decided to take no action, but because the nurse was a mandatory reporter, she made a notification to the Department of Child Safety.

When her son was admitted to hospital there was an incident that resulted in hospital security ejecting his father from the premises. The Department of Child Safety began an investigation and a child safety officer told Lisa that she had to take out a domestic violence order and leave her partner, or the child would be removed from her care. This response is typical in many cases. Lisa reported that the departmental worker did not provide any support or show empathy or compassion for her situation particularly considering her child's unique care requirements. It is highly probable that her son's disability would have made it difficult to place him in alternative care, and may have contributed to the decision for him to remain in her care.

Lisa contacted the Gold Coast Domestic Violence Prevention Centre and was provided with court assistance to obtain a domestic violence order. Lisa found alternative accommodation and her child was eventually discharged from hospital into her care. Lisa's ex-partner, who is a wealthy man, undertook a campaign of using the system to further harass and intimidate her. He tried

1 Names have been changed to ensure anonymity.

to coerce Lisa to drop the domestic violence order as the Department of Child Safety had closed the case because of the separation and the perception that the child was therefore safe.

Lisa began counselling and during the process was able to identify that she and her child were at serious risk of harm. She would not have left because she feared that her ex-partner would kill her and her child. Her counsellor encouraged her to view the intervention by the Department of Child Safety as leverage to continue to have a domestic violence order, in the face of her ex-partner's constant endeavours to get her to drop the matter.

Lisa had experienced significant trauma over many years, and the impact affected her physical and emotional health and wellbeing. She stated that she would still be in the situation if she had not been forced to make the decision to leave by the Department of Child Safety. She became stronger but faced the ongoing struggle to cope with the legal matters in both Domestic Violence Court and then the Family Court (proceedings are still ongoing two years later).

Whilst there was a positive outcome, eventually, in this matter that resulted in the victim remaining as the primary carer for her child, Lisa reported that her experience was almost as traumatic as the violence and abuse that she had experienced from her ex-partner.

Continuous revictimisation

In many ways legislation that was designed initially to protect women and children can also be used to revictimise them. For example, when the police are called to an incident and there are conflicting stories about who the victim is and what happened, they are often inclined to take out cross-applications against both parties. There have been many instances when women victims have been taken to the watchhouse and charges against them have been filed. When this happens, women report that they believe that the system is against them and there is no justice. Jill's story is an example of how her ex-partner was able to use the system to continue his abuse.

Case Study: Jill's Story

It started slowly and before I knew it, it was a regular occurrence. And not once did I ever get an apology from him. What I did get was two years of Family Law court proceedings, police and Department of Child Safety people investigating me because he was such a good liar. He accused me of being everything that can be imagined and boy did some of those accusations hurt. Even though I knew they weren't true and I eventually disproved him, they took their toll, and my life as a young mum, with a gorgeous young child, was stripped from me, temporarily, yet still lost.

I only have two positive things that I have gained from all of this turmoil, tension and abuse. The most important one, first and foremost, is my gorgeous son. Secondly it would have to be the help I have received from the Domestic Violence Prevention Centre.

I have had a lot of bad experiences with people like the Queensland Police, Department of Child Safety and even the Family Law courts. The Department of Child Safety is a huge crock of S#*T. They started out on my side by putting myself and my son in a refuge, yet after speaking with my ex, the abuser, they turned on me and did everything in their power, like the abuser, to try to make me crack. I was, and still am, too strong for them. They do nothing but destroy families when they should actually be helping the families and the children that need them. Not interfere and take side with the abusers as in my case and so many others that I have heard about. The Queensland Police aren't much better. Most of the male police officers take the male's side and told me I must have deserved to be hit considering I was so upset! They told me I was the aggressor even though they had the photographic and physical evidence to show I was the abused.

The last thing I have to say is if you know someone who is being abused; do NOT just let it happen. Stand up for them. Help them escape the vicious cycle and let them move on with their lives. And introduce them to the Domestic Violence Prevention Centre.

The role of the women's advocate

The women's advocate role monitors the safety of women and their children who may be past or current partners of the men who have been mandated through the courts to attend the men's program. Men who attend the program have breached their domestic violence orders (often multiple times) and have typically been assessed as high risk to their partners. Ongoing risk assessment is a key component of the women's advocate role. Women are asked to rate their perception of current risk level. This is often challenged if current levels of abuse are incongruent with their rating. It may also fluctuate during the life of the program. The women's advocate role enables women participants to have a voice that previously has been silenced, to be heard, valued and noted within the program. For example, Ann told the women's advocate that she had been walking down the street when her ex-partner stopped his car and got out, approached her and grabbed her by the throat then threw her to the ground resulting in injury and bruising. The incident was witnessed by passers-by who encouraged her to go to the police, which she proceeded to do. However she stated that she could not go into the police station and report the breach because of fear of reprisal from her ex-partner (as this had occurred on several occasions previously). Ann said to the women's advocate that "*I now feel like I have a voice and am able to speak of this freely and know that I will be safe and heard by the women's advocate who will inform the facilitators of the men's program*".

At times the women's advocate engages with two different women for one perpetrator. Having established a supportive and helpful relationship with the women's advocate, women often reconnect with the centre after the program has been completed. One woman recently commented, "*I have no-one else to talk to or help me who really understands my situation*". Women also feel comfortable to discuss safety issues or concerns, regression of abusive behaviour, legal issues or seek referrals to other agencies or organisations. Having an already established relationship enables them to do this easily.

Effective engagement with women is paramount to establishing and facilitating a safe and trusting environment in which dialogue and relationships can be developed for ongoing support. The quality of information received from women also depends on the relationship that develops between participants and the women's advocate. Building rapport and establishing relationships can take some time, and often depends on the quality of the relationship formed in the first face-to-face session. The level of engagement is also often influenced by whether or not women are with their partners or separated. For example, if women are separated from their partners they may decide not to take part in the program for many reasons including:

- They have moved out and on with their lives.
- They may be in another relationship.
- They may not want to remember past abuse.
- They may have continued contact with perpetrators through family law orders and be concerned about reprisals.
- They may have had extensive interaction with various systems, for example, Department of Child Safety, justice system, police, and courts and be resistant to further systems interventions.
- They may be fearful of further abuse.
- They may have moved to a safer location and feel participation would impose further risk.
- Whether or not women are separated from abusive partners or continue to live with them, there is often still a strong level of perceived power over their lives and decisions.

For women who remain with their partners engagement can be limited due to the following factors:

- High level of real risk to women and children.
- High level of perceived risk to women and children.

- Desensitisation that results from living with domestic violence.
- Minimisation of risk to women and children.
- Normalising of abusive behaviour.
- Lack of understanding about domestic violence.
- Guilt, shame and self-blame.
- Avoidance tactics.

The program content and process is explained to the woman in an initial phone contact and she is invited to be involved. Participation is not mandatory, although some women may feel an initial obligation to take part in this process because they are hopeful that the program will bring about the desired change in their abusive partners. Alternatively they may feel they have to participate by default because they were the victim of the perpetrator. Throughout the process the women's advocate is mindful about the replication of unequal power dynamics in this process where further systems intervention could make them an unwilling participant. Once again the aim is to work with women in respectful and meaningful ways that allow them to be in charge of their process.

Some women report that perpetrators blame them for having to attend the program and can get particularly angry on the night that they attend. Some men may continue throughout the program with a high risk rating, taking no responsibility for their behaviour, and continue to blame the woman for their attendance at the program. Quite often for the duration of the program men will show some signs of improvement in their behaviour, modifying the level and intensity of abuse, which seduces women back into cyclical patterns of hope and denial. Women's advocates often seek to challenge unrealistic expectations or false thinking that women may hold about the ability of perpetrators to effect lasting, permanent or dramatic change -whilst acknowledging small steps and advances that are possible.

Conclusions

The conclusion from this chapter is that the systems that become involved following a notification of domestic violence, be they police, courts, or child protection, are central to providing safety in high risk situations. Often women are coerced at these critical points of engagement to accept orders that are inappropriate and/or to drop criminal charges that should proceed regardless. Federal and State legislation, policies and programs must deliver domestic violence prevention and intervention responses that focus on victim safety as paramount.

It is also clear that funding for domestic violence programs for men must include a dedicated component that is specifically for women partner contact work (O'Leary, Chung and Zannettino 2004). The women's advocate has a critical role to play in supporting women through their contact with these agencies, aiding their understanding of the programs that their partners attend, monitoring risk, and empowering women to make effective decisions. Political will and commitment is required to implement change and to provide funding for a criminal justice response that operates to ensure that the systems that are supposed to protect and increase the safety of victims work. There has been enough research, consultation, and rhetoric – action is required.

Part II

SYSTEMS RESPONSES

Chapter 4

Progress and Challenges in the Development of Police Responses to Domestic Violence: The Project SAFER Experience

Patrick O'Leary and Laura Bahnisch

Police responses to domestic violence deliver an important community message to victims and offenders about the unacceptability of violence against women. Resulting charges and consequences can deter potential offenders as well as impact on repeat offenders. Police provide a critical portal for access to safety, justice and services for women, men and children who are affected by domestic violence. As such, police are integral to any integrated response to domestic violence.

Police agencies around Australia have often been the target for considerable criticism in relation to the relatively low number of arrests, prosecutions and convictions for domestic violence offences. Sometimes this criticism does not fully take into account the broader social context of policing, community attitudes and resources. At other times the criticism rightly questions what appears to be a reluctance to pursue criminal charges against domestic assailants compared to other criminals. Thus critiques have heavily focused on the inappropriate use of police discretion in pursuing domestic violence offenders. Some critics have seen this as devaluing women's safety, and the impact of violence on their lives, thus, ensuring a status quo in condoning violence against women.

When police officers are asked about jobs that evoke both fear and irritation, many will cite responding to domestic violence incidents. For police on the front line this consumes a considerable amount of their time. Police officers are also at risk of being victims of violence when attending incidents, particularly given that some perpetrators see this violence as a private matter. Underlying this view is a broad community attitude that women provoke the violence and are thus in some way culpable. Over the last two decades, however, criminal justice agencies have increasingly seen the need for greater police action and specialised intervention in relation to domestic violence. Numerous initiatives have been implemented such as mandatory training in domestic violence for all police cadets, civil court orders to protect victims, and referral to social support agencies. Police forces across Australia now have specialised officers dealing with domestic violence cases, while others have implemented specific standing orders to deal with domestic violence incidents.

This chapter aims to underscore the point that police agencies have a fundamental role to play in any integrated response to domestic violence. It provides a basis for understanding a variety of possible police strategies and initiatives within an integrated community response to domestic violence and to highlight proactive strategies. This is done by giving an overview of police responses to domestic violence internationally and in Australia and reporting the results of a project from the Gold Coast Domestic Violence Integrated Response.

Policing domestic violence: a complex task

It is widely acknowledged that the majority of domestic violence incidents go unreported to police. Victims can be reluctant to call police due to factors such as shame, guilt, minimisation of the seriousness of the violence, fear of confidentiality, past negative experiences of police or experiences of inaction in regards to past complaints of domestic violence and fear of the prosecution or imprisonment of the offender. Outsiders such as neighbours or other family members may also be reticent to contact police due to common community attitudes and myths concerning the seriousness and responsibility for domestic violence. When police attend they do so with a specific focus on the current domestic violence incident, yet there almost always is a history of non-investigated offences.

Domestic violence incidents can be complex. Difficulties arise in how the incident is minimised by the offender or presented in terms of "normal" relationship conflict. Often offenders are reluctant, or unable, to clarify what has taken place, especially where intoxication is present. Both parties in a domestic violence incident can make complaints against each other – often clouding who is the victim or offender. It is also likely that when police are called to a domestic violence incident it is unlikely to be the first occurrence and nor can it always be considered to be the most serious incident. It has been found, for example, that for every one police callout to a domestic violence incident, there are more than 12 unreported incidents (Buzawa, Austin and Buzawa 1995). As a result police are often informed of past acts of violence that are difficult to verify legally, but can be important indicators of future risk. Further complexities exist when children witness domestic violence and are deemed to be at risk. Finally it is widely recognised that police can have heavy workloads that present competing demands for direct intervention, placing time constraints on their attendance at some incidents. An important consequence of this is that police officers cannot assume that domestic violence can be self-identified and requires officers to determine whether a domestic violence offence has taken place.

Women are now much more likely to report victimisation than they were 10 years ago, although a considerable imbalance between the number of complaints of domestic violence and charges and convictions remains. A United States study identified three major barriers to calling police for help and proceeding with prosecution: the victim's personal circumstances, her negative experience with police and the victim's fears of negative repercussions through involvement with the police (Wolf in Crime and Misconduct Commission - Queensland 2005: 15). If police fail to arrest despite a victim's wishes, this can add to the negative cycle of a woman not calling police because of previous dissatisfaction with the results. The percentage of women who experienced physical assault by a male perpetrator who contacted police in the previous 12 months increased from 19 per cent in 1996 to 36 per cent in 2005 (Marcus and Braaf 2007: 6). Victims' first contact with police presents an important opportunity for both legal and social intervention by assessing risk and ensuring links with social support agencies. This can provide victims with a proactive intervention that has the potential to prevent ongoing violence. Early police intervention can also provide offenders with clear incentives for behaviour change before serious criminal charges are required. However, both these issues require police officers to appropriately balance their role of law enforcement and social support. Police officers also have an important role to play in assisting victims to seek assistance and justice, while also prosecuting offenders and connecting them to rehabilitative opportunities.

Police responses: Internationally and in Australia

International developments in domestic violence policing have been closely watched in Australia. The last decade has seen a strong international and national trend towards interagency approaches to domestic violence in which police occupy a central position. This has ranged from pro-arrest policies in the United States, where evidence shows that a community approach by a number of agencies reduces the level of domestic violence (Shepard 2005: 3). In the United Kingdom, policing is a key focus of government policy (Hague and Malos 1998: 1), for instance with some police departments working alongside non-police staff such as child protection agencies (Humphreys et al 2005: 13). New Zealand, the United States and Canada have also seen the adoption of restorative justice approaches in domestic violence policing (Coker 2004: 1344).

Reform in criminal justice responses to domestic violence to improve police investigative and prosecutorial processes needs to be cognisant of the broader social context. It is not possible to enter into reform without considering community attitudes and political commitment to bring about possible change in policing domestic violence. Thus it is not possible to entirely separate the criminal justice and social service responses to domestic violence even in the most practical analysis. Critical debate continues in the United States in how to balance police roles in both criminal and social intervention in domestic violence. This highlights the need for clear interagency collaboration in determining the intersections of criminal, civil and social jurisdictions of intervention. Research indicates that community integration of services has seen higher rates of arrest, better evidence collection, more convictions, and better enforcement of court orders protecting victims (Zweig and Burt 2003: 270).

Mandatory arrest

The United States has seen a variety of changes in the policing of domestic violence over the last two decades. These were facilitated by federal law changes in 1994 effectively encouraging state law enforcement agencies to adopt a zero tolerance approach towards domestic violence in return for generous federal government grants. Police agencies have adopted prosecution policies irrespective of victim participation. This change has seen a dramatic improvement in evidence collection procedures and liaison with partner organisations (Ellison 2002). These changes have been closely scrutinised in Australia and the United Kingdom with a view to implementing similar initiatives (Holder 2001). However, the approach does not translate easily into the Australian context because the legislation is different, thus requiring careful consideration of overseas techniques that can be adopted in the local context. Despite these difficulties, all jurisdictions have one thing in common - successful prosecution ultimately hinges on the evidence available in each individual case. The question then, is how to maximise the effectiveness of both the collection and the later use of evidence. The international experience clearly demonstrates that there are both specific and systemic answers to that question. Here we will examine mandatory and pro-arrest policies, evidence gathering, police culture and training.

Some Australian States have made legislative changes designed to gather better evidence for court and to better protect victims. Tasmania instituted the *Safe at Home* initiative in 2004. It includes a 24 hour telephone hotline, extension of legal aid, court support, counselling and other services for victims, children and offenders (Government of Tasmania 2004: 2-3). In Queensland, police roles and court funding have also increased, to implement the pro-arrest, pro-prosecution response. Police officers at the rank of sergeant or above now have the authority to issue a police family violence order and service this at the time the offence is committed (Crime and Misconduct Commission - Queensland 2005: 81). The order is valid for 12 months.

The Australian Capital Territory Family Violence Intervention Program (FVIP) was the first coordinated interagency response to domestic violence in Australia, beginning in 1997. The proportion of incidents where police took legal action increased from 27 per cent to 47 per cent over nine months and 86 per cent of family violence matters resulted in convictions in a two year period. Changes have been primarily due to early evidence gathering by police, pro-arrest and pro-prosecution (Holder and Mayo 2003: 10). Reviews in Western Australia, New South Wales and Queensland have also recommended giving police officers above a certain rank powers to issue immediate temporary or full protection orders (Crime and Misconduct Commission - Queensland 2005: 82). Aside from legislative change, it is worth examining in detail how police operate in the current climate and how this relates to overseas trends.

Evidence at trial

There are two main contentious areas regarding the rules of evidence and their suitability in domestic violence trials. These are the use of a victim's prior statements if she does not testify at trial, and the admission of prior acts of domestic violence to show propensity (not as similar fact evidence). In the United States, the rules of evidence have been specifically modified in domestic violence cases to allow for these two types of evidence to be far more easily used at trial. As Ellison (2003) points out, differences in the United States rules of evidence mean that adopting the specific changes made for the United States rules would be counter-productive and unnecessary for England and Wales. Australia's rules of evidence, sourced in English common law, are similarly less amenable to the United States-style adaptations because of legislative restraints.

The potential for reform in this area lies in understanding how probative evidence of prior acts of violence is likely to be. Again, much research has been done in this area, suggesting that conceptual rather than factual similarities are far more probative in domestic violence offences than for other offences (Ellison 2003). Patterns of domestic violence behaviour are often present and identifiable, although expert evidence may be needed, particularly regarding the cyclic nature of the offending given its underlying causes. One prior incident of domestic violence is thus likely to be far more probative than a single incident of other violence, for example.

Evidence gathering

Victimless prosecution

Successful police action to secure legal sanctions against offenders requires a creditable basis of evidence. One of the most commonly reported difficulties in domestic violence prosecutions is being able to rely on victims to maintain testimony consistent with their initial complaint. The underlying dynamics of domestic violence often result in victims being pressured by the offender to drop charges or minimise the severity of the offence. This can lead some women to change their original police statements, or in some cases appear as a defence witness. When this has happened the majority of prosecutions cases have been terminated. Sometimes this has been a justification for police not to pursue particular domestic violence cases. This can influence the investigative process if officers involved perceive an individual witness as likely to withdraw from the process at a later stage. Police who believe the case is likely to be dropped may be disinclined to pursue wider evidence gathering, at which point their belief is likely to become a self-fulfilling prophecy, since a successful prosecution depends on strong evidence: "anticipation of victim withdrawal and discontinuance can be seen to prompt a police response that promotes that very outcome" (Ellison 2002: 837). Conducting an investigation without an emphasis on the availability of the complainant's testimony avoids such Catch 22s.

The strategy of "victimless prosecution" has been used in the United States in an attempt to remove reliance on victim's testimony in prosecution cases. This strategy requires police officers to investigate domestic violence in a manner that renders the victim's personal testimony superfluous to the trial - as occurs in the prosecution of murderers. Victimless prosecution thus removes the dependence of the prosecution case on the victim's testimony and willingness to proceed with criminal charges. In San Diego, the victim is not asked whether they want to press charges; the prosecution automatically does so if the evidence is sufficient. The FVIP, Duluth (on which it is based) and indeed most other programs incorporating a broader evidentiary focus proceed similarly. In Queensland, police asking the victim if she wanted a formal complaint laid was identified as an inhibitor, especially if asked in the presence of the perpetrator (Douglas and Godden 2003: 8). Ellison notes that "reliance on victim support in domestic violence cases in England and Wales is such that victims effectively exercise a power of veto over the prosecution process" (2003: 840). Reducing this reliance by broadening the evidence base used at trial sidesteps all of the above problems.

Holder and Mayo (2003) argue that placing prosecutorial discretion with the prosecutor, rather than relying on the victim's cooperation, is in the interest of the victims, despite some concerns that it takes power away from an already disempowered victim (Alcoff 2000). However, the concept of victim disempowerment needs to be assessed in the light of her level of empowerment in reality, with particular regard to the level of control exercised over her by the perpetrator, and her emotional state. These dynamics are closely related to the debate over compelling victims to testify - victimless prosecutions avoid the issues surrounding such compulsion (Ellison 2003).

In San Diego 70 per cent of cases are victimless prosecutions with 90 per cent resulting in a conviction (Gwinn 2004). Ellison acknowledges the need to treat statistics on victimless prosecutions with caution due to a lack of general research, but emphasises a "predictably clear" link between superior evidence gathering and successful prosecutions even where there is no testimony from the complainant (Ellison 2003: 842). Given that victimless prosecutions hinge by default on corroborative evidence, the initial investigative process is crucial. It is around this area that the majority of police training programs, manuals and instruments have been developed.

Use of photographs

Taking polaroid photographs of injuries and crime scenes has become standard practice in relevant United States jurisdictions. One study of factors relating to guilty verdicts in domestic violence cases suggests that the availability of photographs increases the likelihood of conviction (see Cramer 1999). Photographs are also routinely used in Australian programs such as the Australian Capital Territory's Family Violence Intervention Project. There are ongoing debates about the court's acceptance of digital photos, which have been disputed by defence counsel. A final reading on the accessibility of these processes is important for future evidence collection procedures.

Domestic violence instruments

On a practical level, a number of United States programs such as Duluth and San Diego use standard forms for evidence collection, including diagrams of the body on which to note physical trauma, detailed questions for the officers to ask and issues to address, and post-arrest information, including follow up photographs. Victims sign the completed forms and this includes consent to the release of medical records and referral to associated services. Australian police forces have tended to rely on non-specific instruments for domestic violence incidents. The use of instruments specific to domestic violence cases has been advocated to minimise police discretion and maximise a standard approach. This has occurred in a context where police decision making in domestic violence cases has been the subject of significant critique. Later in this chapter we look at a police trial of risk assessment instruments as an initiative of an integrated response to domestic violence.

Decision making behind police responses to domestic violence cases

Besides legislative and policy initiatives, there are many factors that may influence the successful implementation of a consistent response to domestic violence policing. The way police make decisions about whether or not to arrest domestic violence perpetrators include demographic, organisational, attitudinal and situational factors. Despite the pro-arrest policies in the United States, rates of arrest on domestic violence remain low (Buzawa, Austin and Buzawa 1995: 444). In Australia, although police powers to deal with domestic violence have been strengthened, the approach tends to remain civil not criminal, with low arrest rates (see, for example Crime and Misconduct Commission - Queensland 2005: 13; Victorian Law Reform Commission 2005: 4; Western Australia Ombudsman 2003: 19, 23).

Demographic factors

There are demographic differences affecting arrest rates that relate to police as well as to victims and perpetrators. In the United States, researchers have found that older or more experienced officers made fewer arrests than younger officers (Robinson and Chandek 2000: 20). In the Crime and Misconduct Commission (2005: 50) on policing domestic violence in Queensland, results of a survey on police officers' responses indicate that more experienced officers did not place as much importance on the victim's wishes, due to a belief from their experience that the victim would change her mind and not support a charge. While a United States study shows that male police officers were more likely to make arrests than female officers (Robinson and Chandek 2000: 31), there was no difference based on gender in Queensland charges (Crime and Misconduct Commission - Queensland 2005: 50).

Differences in police perception can be demonstrated by a comparison with higher charge rates in assaults by strangers. A United States study shows that as the level of intimacy in the relationship between parties changes from more to less intimate, arrest becomes more likely (Buzawa, Austin and Buzawa 1995: 452). Also, in assault cases involving strangers, there is less reliance on witness evidence and more compliance with the victim's wishes (Buzawa, Austin and Buzawa 1995: 456). This indicates that domestic violence may not be taken as seriously as other crimes.

Organisational influences

While official organisational policies have been changing within the police force, the unwritten rules of actual practice can differ dramatically. In the United States assaults by strangers are more likely to be viewed as a breach of the peace, justifying a call to police, despite the fact that domestic violence tends to be more severe and to reoccur more often (Buzawa and Buzawa 1993: 560-561). The Crime and Misconduct Commission found that there are four key factors that police use to decide whether to apply a protection order: whether violence was likely to recur; the victim's willingness to cooperate; perceptions that the victim is at fault; monitoring of police actions. This is despite Queensland Police Service operational procedures that the wishes of the victim should not be a determining factor in the officer's decision to seek a protection order (2005: 45). Administrative factors, such as the amount of paperwork and the time taken to attend an incident, discourage officers from acting (Crime and Misconduct

Commission - Queensland 2005: 47-48). A call to a domestic violence incident that occurs towards the end of an officer's shift might mean police were less likely to act (Crime and Misconduct Commission - Queensland 2005: 48), which concurs with United States research (Robinson and Chandek 2000: 31).

The Victorian Law Reform Commission also found a tendency towards police inaction due to organisational culture. Police do not approach a family violence incident as they would a crime scene, often failing to gather evidence, and not applying for intervention orders or not enforcing orders until there have been multiple breaches. The term "domestic" in police culture, and sometimes as used more broadly in society, conjures up images of a relatively trivial or annoying incident. Victims and agencies thought that police stereotyped women, assessing if their claims were genuine or exaggerated and were more likely to respond where the person subject to violence seemed "fearful, not angry" (Victorian Law Reform Commission 2005: 15-16). In Western Australia again police action varies from existing policy, with attitudes such as victim-blaming around the "type" of woman who became victims leading to reluctance to charge perpetrators (Western Australia Ombudsman 2003: 19, 21). This parallels discriminatory attitudes in the United States, where arrests are less frequent if the victim's lifestyle is seen as including violence as "a normal way of life" (Buzawa and Austin 1993: 610).

In addition to thorough training, support by senior police administrators may affect police actions (Buzawa and Austin, 1993: 622). Recently, the number of inquiries and reviews into police action on domestic violence in Australia shows that governments and police departments are serious about tackling the problem. The Queensland Police Service sees the monitoring of its actions as a significant influence on its decisions, which could be beneficial (Crime and Misconduct Commission - Queensland 2005: 46). In regards to reluctance to take action towards the end of an officer's shift, clarification about the availability of overtime by managers could counteract this (Crime and Misconduct Commission - Queensland 2005: 48).

Situational differences

Domestic violence can occur in many different situations and this can be a major factor in decision making. United States research shows that arrests are more likely when witnesses are present; if the suspect and victim are living together and less likely if the suspect has left the scene (Robinson and Chandek 2000: 30). Arrest is more likely according to the seriousness of the victim's injury and whether a weapon is involved (Buzawa, Austin and Buzawa 1995: 455). Queensland evidence also emphasises tangible factors, such as injury, use of a weapon and violence against police (Crime and Misconduct Commission - Queensland 2005: 50). Police are influenced by the commission of an indictable offence and the breach of a protection order; yet the victim's desire for an arrest is the least influential factor for most officers (Crime and Misconduct Commission - Queensland 2005: 48).

Attitudinal factors

It is recognised that police attitudes to domestic violence will be representative of community values. In Australia police officers may not consider domestic violence cases to be "real police work" (Crime and Misconduct Commission - Queensland 2005: 17). Therefore it stands to reason that some of the variance in police action is attributed to believing myths concerning domestic violence, along with personal experiences that may bias decision making. This underpins the importance of monitoring police action in domestic violence and the ongoing need to have training and accountability processes that reflect the community stand on issues such as domestic violence.

The way victims act towards police is another influential factor. If the victim is drunk, disruptive or abusive to officers, arrest is unlikely; while the views of rational, undemanding or deferential victims are given more weight (Buzawa and Buzawa 1993: 566). Arrest is much more likely in cases when suspects are hostile to police, in order for police to avoid personal injury and regain control of the situation (Buzawa, Austin and Buzawa 1995: 447). In Queensland surveys, police saw domestic violence cases that involved verbal arguments arising from socioeconomic factors, relationship skills and substance abuse as grey areas that were more the responsibility of social welfare agencies than the law enforcement agencies (Crime and Misconduct Commission - Queensland 2005: 56). The tendency of police to consider domestic violence as not serious and not part of their role as law-enforcers, and the propensity to judge and stereotype are alarming aspects of the decision-making process.

Training and managerial support

Possible causes for the lack of action on domestic violence are the context of the incident, the victim's wishes and the process of collecting evidence. In general, an assault by a stranger can be isolated to one incident, with evidence drawn relating to that particular time and place. In contrast, a domestic violence incident must be viewed in the context of the history of the relationship and must include a risk assessment of future threats. As we have seen, police officers need to understand the cyclic nature of domestic violence in order to understand evidence relating to propensity.

For instance it has been suggested that Queensland police often fail to respond to breaches of protection orders due to what they see as insufficient evidence, particularly if the victim does not cooperate (Crime and Misconduct Commission - Queensland 2005: 68). Domestic violence agency workers feel that police fail to act on breaches not understanding that what may seem minor harassing behaviour in isolation, can be serious and fearful in the context of years of abuse (Crime and Misconduct Commission - Queensland 2005: 75). A follow-up survey of victims found that offenders were charged with assault in only five of 17 cases where women sought medical attention for their injuries (Crime and Misconduct Commission - Queensland 2005: 76), a clear example of police inaction despite corroborating evidence. The Commission found that there is "strong evidence" that officers' decisions to arrest and charge offenders continues to rely on victims' testimony as their primary source of evidence. Thorough investigation and evidence collection is vital to ensure the best results for victims through either civil or criminal action (Crime and Misconduct Commission - Queensland 2005: 79). Other States also stress the need for training on the dynamics and nature of violence (Victorian Law Reform Commission 2005: 10) and the need for proper forensic evidence collection and refresher training for existing officers (Western Australia Ombudsman 2003: 27). The disregard of victims' wishes by more senior officers shows the importance of regular retraining.

Another factor that greatly affects police decision making is their ability to make a thorough risk assessment of the domestic violence incident. This can help officers judge what action to take based on the seriousness of the incident in the context of its history, relationship and other factors and its likelihood of reoccurrence. A number of risk assessment tools have been used in different contexts, which are revealing about police responses to domestic violence incidents.

Developing innovative police responses in Australia

Police responses to domestic violence continue to go through significant reform. There is considerable pressure for integrated responses to domestic violence to improve the role of police in intervention and prevention. Overarching this is the need for a consistent response that maximises victim safety and proactively deals with offenders at the earliest stage. Not least of these difficulties is the complexity of domestic violence, which requires police to make different assessments than they would make in other criminal investigation cases. At a basic level it requires police officers to identify who are the victims and who are the offenders. Without a specialist understanding of domestic violence this could be problematic in cases where both parties have injuries or make counterclaims of assault or intimidation. These considerations include the collection of evidence, and understanding past acts of violence and ongoing risk to the victim and her children. Police attendance might be the first opportunity for victims to be referred to social support services. Likewise it may also offer opportunities for early intervention with offenders.

In an attempt to address this situation and to directly monitor police responses the Gold Coast Domestic Violence Integrated Response

(GCDVIR) initiated a project – Safety Assessment For Every Response (SAFER) – to trial an instrument that prompted proactive police assessment of domestic violence incidents. In this section we examine key learning from Project SAFER. This is done by exploring the use of risk assessment tools for police and the implementation of the SAFER instrument. Key results from the evaluation are explored detailing the impact of the project on police action along with key characteristics of cases encountered in the project.

Characteristics of risk assessment tools

Risk assessment instruments are designed to assist police to determine levels of ongoing risk to victims when they attend an incident, and to aid victims to do the same, especially if they are not aware that certain behaviours or factors indicate a tendency toward escalating levels of violence. There is also some potential for risk assessment instruments to assist the courts to determine appropriate sentencing and/or treatment options for offenders.

Laing (2004) emphasises the need for caution in the level of reliance placed on the risk assessments alone, partly because study of the predictive ability of most instruments is in its early stages. Campbell, Webster et al (2003: 16) suggest using risk assessment tools as a guide in the process. However, it is clear that such instruments can significantly assist personnel to respond appropriately to situations of domestic violence, particularly if carefully and deliberately implemented.

Testing the accuracy of risk assessment tools' predictions is a difficult task, and much depends on the methodology used. The literature to date indicates that a large number of variables needs to be taken into account, such as differently weighted items, combinations of factors that may have a cumulative effect when not assessed in isolation, the previous history of suspect and victim, and the effects of court actions and sanctions on reoffending (Goodman, Dutton et al 2000). Laing recommends "multiple methods and sources" be used in studies of the reliability of risk assessment tools (2004: 14). Weisz, Tolman et al note that risk predictions for survivors were made following a comprehensive review of the history and nature of the violent relationship (2000). This suggests that risk assessment is most helpful when used with specific details of the circumstances. Despite these notes of caution, it is clear that risk assessment tools do provide valuable information to police and other workers to support decision making in their response to domestic violence.

Project SAFER's list of risk factors is similar to that used in the Dangerousness Assessment Scale (DAS) (Goodman, Dutton et al 2000); the SPECSS+ Risk Assessment Model, developed by the Metropolitan Police in the United Kingdom (Humphreys et al 2005: 8) and the Domestic Violence MARACs (Multi-Agency Risk Assessment Conferences) for Very High-Risk Victims in Wales (Robinson, 2004: 7). The 15 factors are:

- Prior history of domestic violence.
- Prior police callouts.
- Increase in frequency and/or severity of domestic violence.
- Threats of homicide or suicide.
- Any hostage taking.
- Any strangulation attempt.
- Violence to victim while pregnant.
- Violence towards children.
- Rage towards police or others.
- Abusing pets.
- Obsessive/possessive beliefs.
- Abuser's perception of betrayal by the victim.
- Prior or additional criminal activity.
- Increasing drug or alcohol use.
- Access to weapons.

Apart from the checklist, there are three questions asked of the victim:

- How frequently does he or she intimidate, threaten or injure you?
- Describe the most frightening event or worst incident of violence involving him or her.
- How has his or her past and current behaviour impacted on you and your children's feelings of personal safety?

Effectiveness of risk assessment tools

As would be expected, the DAS is more predictive than assessment based on violent history alone (Goodman, Dutton et al 2000). For this reason, SAFER uses many of the DAS risk assessment items. Its role is to "enhance victim safety, manage lethal situations, make better use of intelligence, and to increase the standard of the investigation and supervision". Thus it was designed to be about "prevention not prediction" and "risk assessment and risk management", emphasising the need for action (Humphreys et al 2005: 9-10).

It is clear that risk assessment tools are only as good as their implementation. Care must be taken not only in adopting or varying a program's individual risk assessment tool, but also in its day-to-day use. The SPECSS+ study indicates that training, high levels of supervision, commitment and leadership at the senior level are essential to improving intervention responses (Humphreys et al 2005: 57). Laing (2004) emphasises the need for workers to have a clear understanding of the reason they are including a risk assessment component in their domestic violence response in order to make the most of both its predictive and informative potential. Domestic violence responses are best seen as an ongoing process, and the literature thus far on risk assessment tools indicates that risk assessment "should not be seen as a single static event" either (Laing 2004: 14). Risk assessment tools can do much to aid officers in making informed decisions, especially in their aim of protecting victims from future violence, given that risk assessment tools are designed to help manage the risk faced by victims on an ongoing basis (Laing 2004: 15).

Combining risk assessment tools with predictions from victims is seen as a more comprehensive way of assessing an offender's potential to reoffend. Studies indicate that risk assessment tools are no more accurate than victim predictions. Weisz, Tolman et al (2000: 87) state regarding their study: "The results suggest that when a survivor predicts danger, it must be taken seriously even when other markers fail to identify a risk". They recommend that both methods be used concurrently for the best results. The DAS is now used in this way by directly asking the victim whether she believes the perpetrator is capable of killing her, although it does not ask for her perceptions of other future dangerous behaviour.

Common to all literature in the area is the warning to use risk assessment tools in a case context, to allow for some factors to be more heavily weighted than others and not approach checklists mathematically. This warning is important when testing the tool's validity, and more so in making an interpretive assessment of the risk of future violence faced by any individual victim. For example, Strauss uses a checklist of 18 factors for risk assessment, yet the presence of three or more of those factors indicates a risk of future violence warranting further action (Weisz, Tolman et al 2000). Campbell, Webster et al (2003: 19) indicate that an average score for abused women on the DAS is only three out of 15. A score of four or more indicates "the need for great caution and protective action", and a score of eight or more indicates very grave risk, with the average score for murdered women being just under eight out of 15 (2003: 16). It is crucial that any person administering a risk assessment checklist knows how to interpret the result.

Apart from assisting officers to make informed decisions regarding arrest and other responses to callouts, there is a further reason why assessment results must be interpreted accurately. Whilst many women are able to make accurate assessments of their own risk, some are not. Some victims' perceptions of their situation and consequent ability to predict violence may be adversely affected by factors such as trauma, memory impairment, or if they are minimising the danger to themselves as a coping mechanism. Additionally, they may doubt their own judgment if they have been subjected to ongoing emotional abuse (Weisz, Tolman et al 2000: 76). Campbell, Webster et al's (2003: 16) study of homicide risk factors indicated "almost half of the murdered women studied did not recognise their risk". Risk assessment tools have a strong educative value, which in turn may indirectly prevent violence by better informing a victim of the objective risk she faces. However in order to do this, the results must be correctly interpreted with the victim.

The highest risk factors within the DAS were identified by Campbell et al (2003) in a study on risk factors for intimate partner homicide. They found that women who were threatened with murder were 15 times more likely to be killed and those who were threatened or assaulted with a gun or other weapon were 20 times more likely to be killed. Additionally, threats to kill, attempted strangulation, severe jealousy and forced sexual activity indicated a higher level of risk than the presence of alcohol or drug abuse. This supports the inclusion of forced sexual activity in risk assessment checklists. It also demonstrates the importance of ensuring that officers receive training about the relative risk weighting for factors such as threats to kill and threats or use of weapons. Strangulation is unique as a risk factor and as an injury since it can cause potentially fatal damage despite a lack of visible injury (Maryland Network Against Domestic Violence 2002). For this reason, officer training in the United States recommends that police inform victims that it can be difficult to tell whether damage has been done without medical assessment and advise victims who have experienced this kind of injury to seek such assessment even if they do not feel unwell (Block 2003; Maryland Network Against Domestic Violence 2002).

Block (2003) identified further points of note for officers and workers responding to domestic violence callouts. She analyses a Chicago study of women experiencing domestic violence, as well as reviewing case files of intimate partner homicides whether the woman was the victim or offender. Contrary to some expectations that such homicides occur at the end of a long course of domestic violence, she found that the homicide or life-threatening incident of violence occurred on the first occasion of violence from their partner for as many as one in five women. For those who had experienced prior violence, "the number of days since the last act of violence was an important risk factor" as half of the women killed had been subjected to violence 30 days prior to the homicide. An additional high risk factor identified by Block is an attempt by the woman to leave the violent relationship. She notes that such an attempt was a triggering factor in 45 per cent of homicides, and that "three quarters of homicide victims and 85 per cent of women who had experienced severe violence had left or tried to leave in the past year" (2003: 6).

These considerations influenced the design of the SAFER instrument as a risk assessment tool, prompt for evidence collection, information resource for police and referral device. Data from this instrument was used in our analysis.

Evaluation of Project SAFER

Evaluation was based on data collected with the project SAFER instrument. This was analysed using the software program SPSS. Existing police data was also used for comparative analysis with areas that did not use the SAFER instrument.

Characteristics of domestic violence incidents

An important aspect of resource allocation for police and related services is to understand key characteristics of incidents of domestic violence that police attend. This includes information on common times when domestic violence callouts occur.

Time of Arrival at Callouts

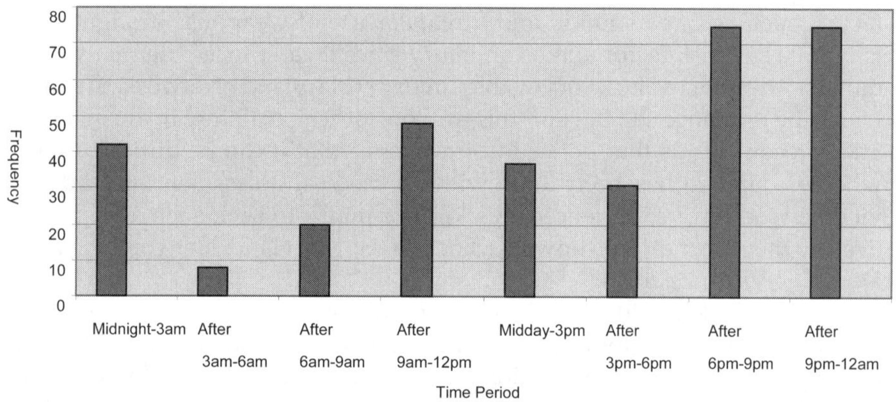

The above graph highlights that domestic violence incidents requiring police attendance predominantly occur after 6 pm. Furthermore 72.2 per cent of incidents occurred between 3 pm and 9 am. Results also showed that 34.1 per cent of incidents occur on Saturday and Sunday. These results largely support popular perception that domestic violence occurs during times that households are more likely to be together such as evenings and weekends. It is also at these times that people are more likely to be engaged in substance use (alcohol and illicit drugs), a known exacerbating factor in the occurrence of violence (People 2005: 5-6). We have seen that incidents occurring towards the end of shifts can mean that police are less likely to act (Crime and Misconduct Commission - Queensland 2005: 48). This reinforces the importance of timing shifts in line with times of peak need. This should be a consideration in roster systems to ensure that officers with domestic violence expertise are available at these times.

The majority of calls (66.6 per cent) to police were made by the victim of domestic violence. These figures highlight the ongoing responsibility of victims to take action and the low likelihood of community members contacting police on the victim's behalf. It also reinforces the fact that in the majority of cases, police are the first line of response to domestic violence incidents, putting them in an ideal position to inform victims of their options (Western Australia Ombudsman 2003: 28). The majority of victims who were asked if the police could refer them to the Gold Coast Domestic Violence Prevention Centre consented. This referral role is also a central component of any integrated community response to domestic violence. It is recognised by the Gold Coast Domestic Violence Prevention Centre that a substantial number of victims referred through Project SAFER had not previously considered a self-referral to a support service.

Identification of offender and victim

Consistent with most studies on domestic violence, offenders identified in Project SAFER were mostly men (84.7 per cent). There appeared some inconsistencies in how police identified victims. This is evident in gender differences in injuries, emotional state and fear observed in victims and offenders. For example, sometimes police identified men and women as both offender and victim because both claimed to be injured by each other. When this is looked at in more depth it was observed that more women who are identified as suspects report serious injuries than do men who were suspects, in some cases up to six times the rate of men. These injuries observed in women suspects were more likely to be bruising and fracture and these are indicative of assault and defence injuries

More than 35 per cent of victims were observed by police to have physical injuries. Most commonly this was bruising, redness, swelling or complaining of pain. There was a wide continuum of injuries observed, some of the more serious including stabbing punctures, fractures and unconsciousness. More women reported internal injuries, such as strangulation, bruising and pain that may necessitate a higher level of medical intervention than was evident in injuries reported by identified male victims. The higher rate of injuries to female suspects and the different nature of injuries evident in female victims gives strong indication that there is some inconsistency in appropriately identifying the predominant aggressor and consequently the offender.

Victims' emotional state was also observed by police. Mostly this was general distress such as crying, shaking and other signs of emotional turmoil. Other emotions of victims were anger towards police and psychological states consistent with intoxication. Emotional states such as crying, upset, fear, nervousness and shaking were more likely to be displayed by women. Female victims (19.2 per cent) were less likely than male victims (40.8 per cent) to be intoxicated. It is also notable that only 28.3 per cent of women were considered by police to be calm at the time of callout compared to 60.7 per cent of male victims.

One of the most important findings is reports of fear. Fear was observed by police, while victims and suspects were also asked by police about their fearfulness of the other party. Victims' responses to the police question "Are you fearful of him/her?" showed that 11.6 per cent of women and 45.5 per cent of men reported never, while 51.3 per cent of women and 15.2 per cent of men reported past and ongoing fear. Both these results were statistically significant ($p < .001$). Police observations support this with fear observed in 71.1 per cent of women victims and 41.3 per cent of men victims.

Further evidence of women's fear of offenders can be seen in the risk assessment questions asked by the police. For example, women victims were asked whether the offender was capable of carrying out threats to kill them or their children - 50.8 per cent (n=295) of women and 26.7 per cent (n=45) of men believed that the offender was capable. Other known indicators of risk of further violence were asked in risk assessments. These included: past false imprisonment - with 50.8 per cent (n=327) of women and 16 per cent (n=50) of men reporting this occurrence; and past incidences of sexual assault - with 19.4 per cent (n=325) of women and 4.2 per cent (n=48) of men reporting this occurrence. All of these indicators of gender difference amongst victims were statistically significant ($p<.01$). These risk factors have been shown to be predictive of future violence (Weisz, Tolman et al 2000: 87). According to a study on risk factors for intimate partner homicide, some indications of high risk included threats to kill, attempted strangulation, severe jealousy and forced sexual activity (Campbell, Webster et al 2003: 16). The significance of these factors, particularly for female victims, is important for determining the predominant aggressor and areas for further investigation.

Police action with Project SAFER

The overriding aim of Project SAFER was to increase police action. More specifically it was hoped that victims would be accorded official and protective measures to uphold their safety and more offenders would be held criminally accountable for their violence. In broad terms the project did deliver positive results, with police who used the SAFER instrument showing a decrease in "no action" and a substantial increase in the number of protection orders. However, the project did not see a substantial increase in criminal prosecutions or convictions for domestic violence offences. These results need to be seen as a positive step. The project is an important element in a comprehensive approach towards policing domestic violence. In this section we explore these results and point towards further enhancements in any future initiatives.

To illustrate the positive impact of Project SAFER on policing, the following two graphs compare two stations in the Gold Coast region: Southport and Broadbeach. Southport trialled the SAFER instrument from 2003 until 2006 and Broadbeach had no specialist domestic violence risk assessment instrument.

These two graphs show that over time the level of action at Southport rose consistently and the level of "no action" fell correspondingly. At Southport this trend may have started as a result of the pilot SAFER in 2003, reinforced by SAFER 2 in 2005-2006. Sixty-five per cent of cases that

2003-2006 – Southport Compared to Broadbeach

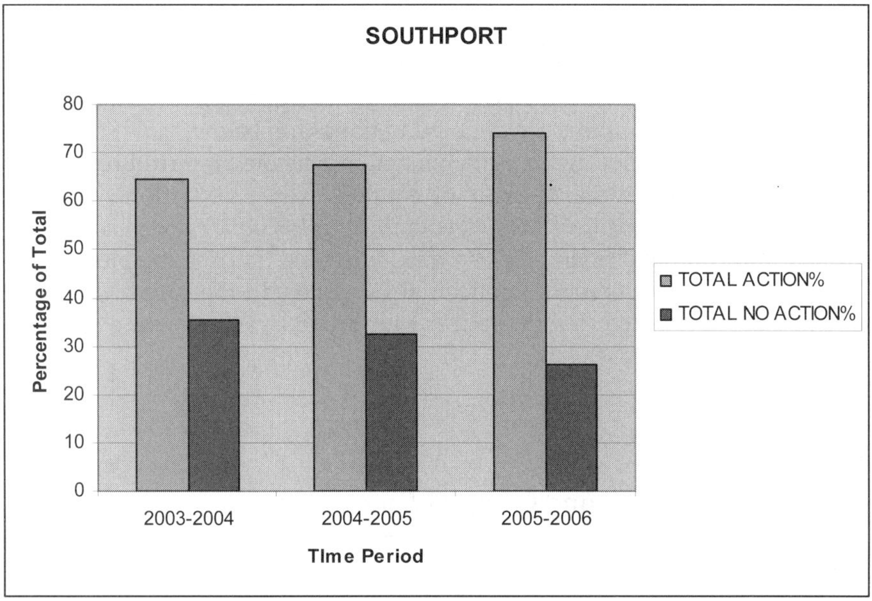

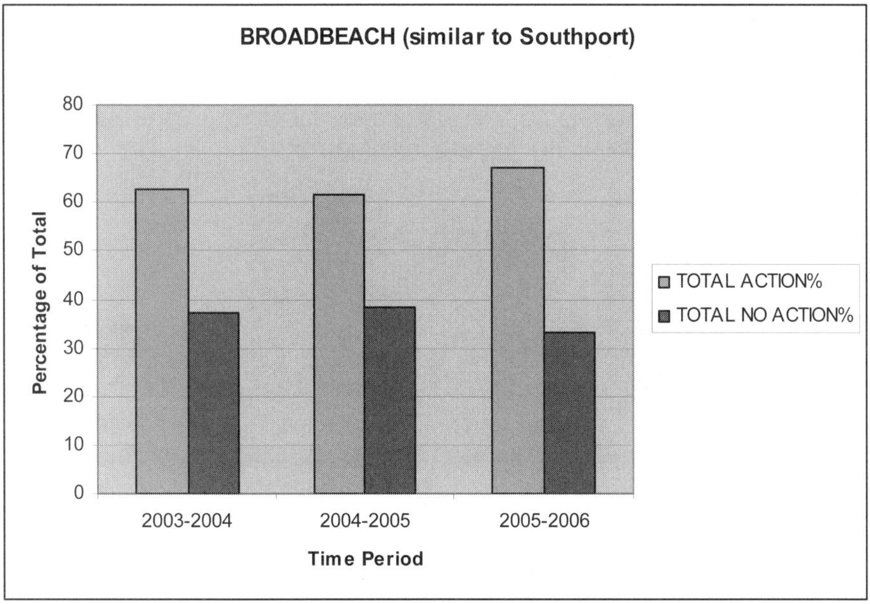

were actioned at Southport in 2003 compared with 74 per cent in 2005. In contrast, in Broadbeach there was little overall change to action or no action over the same three year period, with only a 4.3 per cent increase overall (62.7 to 67 per cent).

Closer examination of the type of action taken by police using the SAFER instrument indicates a strong preference towards civil action through either a police or joint victim and police application for a protection order. The results of this are detailed in the graph below.

The graph shows again that civil action was the preferred response but also that a substantial number of callouts were "no action" or "no domestic violence". This indicates a general trend for police not to consider joint civil and criminal action. These results can be partly explained by a relatively low level of evidence collection by police. In the cases where at least one injury was recorded by police at the scene, evidence was collected in only 35 per cent of cases.

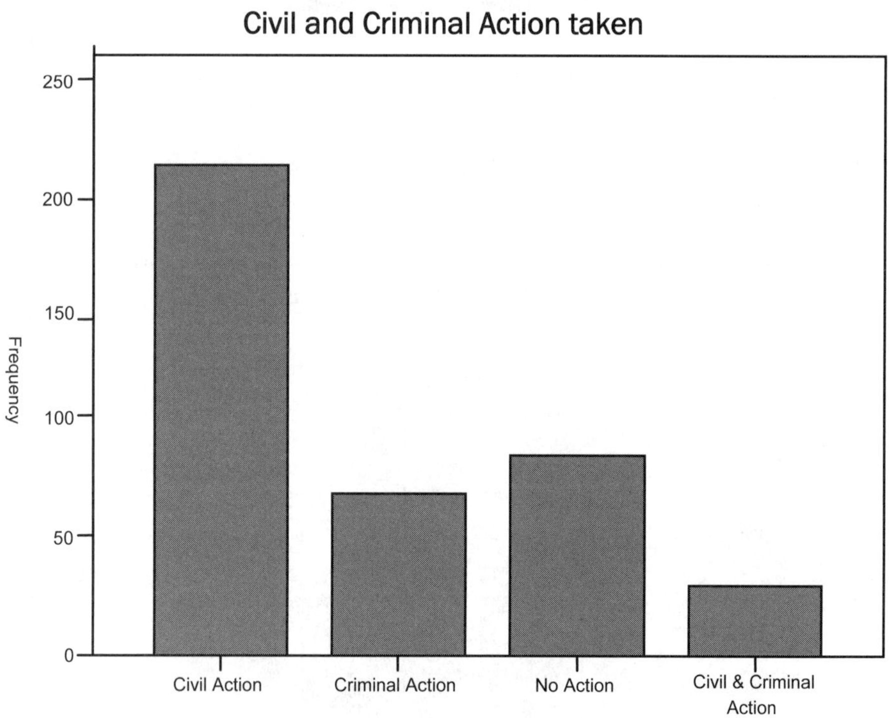

Key learning from Project SAFER

There have been numerous lessons learned from Project SAFER. The evaluation has shown some progress in the project achieving its aims and objectives. There has been an overall increase in police action, primarily civil action in the form of protection orders. Analysis indicates that there have been inconsistent decision-making processes in determining the most appropriate action. The research indicates that in response to domestic violence, criminal action against offenders is rarely pursued in the first instance. This is despite information that indicates that further investigation and evidence collection may result in criminal charges.

The project showed that a structured instrument specific to domestic violence does increase the overall level of action taken by police. Conclusions beyond this are more complex because the degree to which police discretion and decision making accurately reflect the most appropriate action is problematic and contentious. Police may be more accountable and therefore take action, but this action is not always commensurate with the incident. Therefore the impact of Project SAFER is that police are more likely to pursue some type of action, but not necessarily the most appropriate action.

Important data has emerged from the research that will help with understanding the nature of domestic violence incidents requiring police attendance. There is a consistent pattern regarding the timing of domestic violence incidents, with most occurring in the evening and on weekends. This should be considered when allocating rosters for specialist domestic violence officers.

Some patterns also emerge regarding the manifestation of injuries and fear reported by men and women. These issues indicate likely power imbalances helpful in assessing impending risk, as well as identifying the victim and offender in cases of counterclaims.

Thorough and regularly updated training for police officers at all levels is one of the clearest needs for optimum decision making in domestic violence cases. Police need an understanding of broad social factors, such as risk indicators, the cyclical nature of domestic violence and the effects of gender and power on relationships. Also, they need specific training in evidence collection methods, the purpose of risk assessment tools and how best to work with other social agencies in determining appropriate responses.

Another important conclusion from Project SAFER and other similar programs is that any changes to legislation or practice should be matched with proper funding and human resources, to avoid prejudice from staff. Adequate shift changeover times and allowances for proper follow-ups would help to mitigate the time pressure that police officers frequently report. Before introducing widespread changes like Project SAFER, the process of changing the rules of evidence should be pursued strongly. Duplication of paperwork was another common complaint about the new tool. Similarly, as police officers in Queensland are unable to place restraining orders themselves, unlike in some other States, this could act as an impediment to action.

Conclusion

Moves within Australia have shown that improving police responses to domestic violence is a priority for governments. Integrated responses to domestic violence require police participation to provide a visible sign of formal community action for both victims and offenders. Innovative processes such as Project SAFER give a shared foci for agencies to respond collectively with police. What is apparent is that these initiatives in Australia are still evolving. These responses are also highly dependent on legislative reform and police resources. Local and overseas models show that police responses are more effective if they are backed up by legislative change and court action. In the absence of significant legislative change, the role of police remains a critical area of development for integrated responses to domestic violence. Results from Project SAFER demonstrate police commitment to being a central player in integrated responses through increased action and referral to social services. Guiding the most appropriate police action through training, resourcing and development of tools remains an important initiative in the operation of integrated responses to domestic violence.

Chapter 5

Specialist Domestic and Family Violence Courts

Annette Hennessy

This chapter looks at the development of specialist domestic and family violence courts, the need for this type of court process in Queensland, and the benefits of such specialist courts. The aim of the chapter is to detail the initial efforts in the Queensland Magistrates Court to work towards developing a specialised domestic and family violence court.

The development of specialised domestic and family violence courts – a brief history

Specialist domestic and family violence courts have been operating overseas (in the United States, Canada and the United Kingdom) and in some Australian jurisdictions since the 1990s. These courts developed out of recognition that traditional adjudicative approaches were not working particularly well, and that there could be benefits in adopting a more holistic approach. Specialty courts represent a move towards a model of justice that recognises the behavioural and environmental factors that contribute to offending, and the judicial systems' capacity to deal with these problems (Freiberg 2001). Legislation is enacted or amended in circumstances where a marked shift in the role and power of the court is required, although courts established under existing legislation can be developed (Payne 2006).

Most specialised domestic and family violence courts use a problem-solving approach with a tendency towards therapeutic jurisprudential processes. Problem-oriented courts seek to use the authority of the courts to address the underlying problems of individual litigants, the structural problems of the justice system, and the social problems of communities (American Bar Association 1996). Common elements of the approach include re-engineering the criminal justice (and societal) response to a social problem, judicial monitoring, interdisciplinary collaboration, and developing non-traditional roles in the courtroom. There is a focus on tangible case outcomes (Berman and Feinblatt 2001; Carney 2000). The main objective of a specialised domestic violence court process is to ensure victim safety (Eley 2005).

Overseas initiatives

The development of specialised domestic and family violence courts began in the main in the United States and Canada in the 1990s. Some of the initiatives in this area in Australia and overseas are described below.

The first specialist domestic violence court opened in **Brooklyn** in 1996 for felony level criminal cases. The court is presided over by a single judge, with a fixed prosecutorial team and enhanced staffing to monitor defendants and provide assistance to victims (Mazur and Aldrich 2003). Victim services are accessed by the victim advocates provided by the court. The services offered include safety planning for victims, counselling, information about the court process, emergency shelter and food, job training, immigration services, child services and programs directed to improving self-sufficiency. There are strong relationships between the court and service providers, continual monitoring of defendants and service providers by the judge, separate lists, modified courthouses to provide safe places for victims, and specialised domestic violence education and training for all staff.

The **Santa Clara** Domestic Violence Court in California is an integrated court dealing with all aspects of family conflict arising from domestic violence. It provides a combination of criminal, juvenile and child safety courts, and is coordinated with the Family Court. Protection orders are used in conjunction with probation orders for offenders (including children), with programs for offenders being virtually mandatory. Probation orders are monitored by the court until successful completion, with the protection order conditions becoming part of the conditions of the probation order. Frequent review of offender progress on the programs is considered an essential element of the process (Hyman 2006).

The **Winnipeg** Family Violence Court in Manitoba, Canada, was established in 1990 to deal with child, spouse and elder abuse cases. The process required a social and cultural change in participants and workers involved with the court in an environment of a creative response to challenges. The process involved a mandatory arrest policy where there was evidence of a crime, irrespective of the victim's wishes, with a specialised prosecution team which attains a higher conviction rate than similar offences prosecuted in other settings in Canada. Protection orders seek to achieve the immediate safety of victims which remains the focus throughout.

There is also a policy of rigorously prosecuting offenders without revictimising the victims. This is achieved by a massive increase in the funding of victim support services. Orders for criminal offenders focus on treatment and Corrections has developed specialised programs in the community and prison system. Domestic homicide rates fell significantly as a result of the court initiative. There has also been a reduction in recidivism and earlier and more frequent reporting of violent offenders to police (twice the national average), leading to more arrests (Ursel 2006).

The K Court in **Toronto**, Canada, includes elements of local justice community coordination, enhanced investigation by specially trained police, coordinated prosecution led by trained crown attorneys, fast tracking cases, victim support programs and a pro-charge policy. The specialised domestic violence court demanded changes to police practices to focus on collecting corroborating evidence which includes a detailed description of the crime scene, including any broken furniture for instance, seizure of exhibits, photographs of the scene and of injuries to the parties, identification of witnesses and the obtaining of statements at an early stage.

Matters are handled by the same prosecutor for the duration of the matter to provide greater continuity for the victim and witnesses, which enhances the likelihood of their cooperation. Victim assistance is offered as soon as possible after the incident of violence. This includes referral to services and the provision of material about the court process. Probation and parole services have dedicated treatment places in programs to ensure fast tracking of rehabilitation services. Judicial leadership in management of court time, agencies, offenders and service providers, and case processing expediency are also features of K Court.

The Australian experience

Domestic and family violence courts were first developed in Australia in South Australia in 1997. Later, initiatives of varying styles were undertaken in all mainland States except Queensland. Domestic and family violence courts operate primarily in an adversarial, non-therapeutic environment in Australia.

The **South Australia** initiative was developed without a legislative base and involved four distinct court sessions on the one day in an effort to link the separate jurisdictions related to family violence. Treatment programs were offered to all offenders, victims and families which were supervised and monitored by the Department of Corrections. There are dedicated magistrates, police and advocates for all parties.

In **Western Australia**, the Joondalup Family Violence Court was launched in 1999 with aims to improve the criminal justice response to family violence, make perpetrators accountable for their behaviour, support victims in the criminal justice system and ensure their safety and reduce the incidence of family violence in the Joondalup district (Final Report 2002). Civil matters for restraining orders and all criminal matters related to family violence are dealt with in the integrated Magistrates Court process. There is a special police domestic violence investigation unit which investigates all incidents and has a proactive role in targeting high risk offenders through early intervention. Formal risk assessment tools are administered at an early stage in relation to victim safety and offender risk of further offending. The victim support area is located in the courthouse. Victim impact statements are received by the court. The court utilises sentencing options with an emphasis on intervention with the offender. There is close supervision of offenders through bail based programs which are taken into account in the sentencing process. The 2002 evaluation report on the process recommended a rollout of the process throughout Western Australia.

In **Victoria**, a pilot project in the Magistrates Court of a Family Violence Division (2005-2007) provided for all legal matters associated with family violence, including family law issues, to be attended to in the one jurisdiction. Court staff were trained in family violence issues and separate support persons (called liaison officers) were provided for parties. Their role was to explain the court processes to the parties, risk assess each of the parties and develop safety plans, make referrals to outside agencies providing counselling and programs and also to housing, financial, employment and support services. Counselling programs of 20-25 week duration to address violent behaviour can be ordered as a condition of the intervention order. Magistrates are required to inquire as to the welfare of children in the proceedings and are empowered to make orders relating to children on their own initiative.

In some areas, other initiatives provide a solid base for specialised court services. In Queensland, the Gold Coast Domestic Violence Prevention Centre has, for the last nine years, in conjunction with the Southport Magistrates Court, operated a community based integrated agency response to domestic violence. The response focuses on accountability of the offender and includes a 24 week perpetrator program which the court can access as a sentencing option for breach charges.

Is a specialised domestic and family violence court needed in Queensland?

> There can be no doubt that domestic and family violence of this level affects the victims, their children, their family and friends, employers and co-workers. It also has repercussions for the quality of life in a local community. It affects people of all ages, cultures, backgrounds and life experiences. There can be far reaching financial, social, health and psychological consequences. The impact of violence can also have indirect costs, including the cost of the community bringing perpetrators to justice or the costs of medical treatment for injured victims. (Irwin 2005)

The Rockhampton experiment, as it is known, came about following the Australian Institute of Judicial Administration (AIJA) (as it then was) conference in Adelaide in February 2006. The Chief Magistrate, Judge Marshall

Irwin, subsequently approved an initiative to develop a model for a specialised court in Queensland, and to identify the resources required to effectively operate such a court. Judge Irwin considered that the court process could deal with all matters arising from family violence, rather than merely responding to the outcome of the violence. Some of the issues that were considered in the development process were:

The extent of the problem

In the first year after the 2003 amendments to the *Domestic and Family Violence Protection Act 1989* (the Act),[1] there was a 24 per cent increase in applications for protection orders to the Magistrates Courts, an increase which was largely maintained in the following financial year (Irwin 2005). There has been an overall increase in domestic violence applications to the Magistrates Court in Queensland of 38.2 per cent in the last five years (Irwin 2007). In the year ended 30 June 2007, the Magistrates Court heard 24,626 applications for protection orders. 12,666 temporary protection orders were made and 15,863 protection orders were granted. There were 4082 variations made to those orders and 263 orders were revoked. It is apparent that domestic violence is a significant area of work for the Magistrates Court.

The role of the court

At present, issues of domestic violence in a family may lead to the family becoming involved in an application under the Act (civil closed jurisdiction), criminal charges (criminal open jurisdiction) and child protection proceedings (children's court closed jurisdiction). Of these three jurisdictions, the two closed jurisdictions are closed to all other jurisdictions.

A respondent may be subject at the same time to a protection order, bail conditions and directives under an interim order under the *Child Protection Act 1999*. Given that these orders are generated from different jurisdictions and cannot be determined simultaneously, there is enormous potential for conflict between the orders. At the present time, court processes are not harmonised or coordinated internally to detect any such conflicts.

A family facing these issues is likely to be dysfunctional and is probably unfamiliar with the legal processes involved. The parties may also lack legal representation in one or more of the proceedings or legal representation may vary in the various proceedings. In these cases the parties are unlikely to be able to detect or resolve any conflict in orders. A respondent may become confused as a result of such conflict (or deliberately abuse the confusion caused by the conflict) and is therefore much more susceptible to breaching orders and being exposed to further criminal charges.

---

1 The Act significantly extended the categories of relationship coming within the jurisdiction of the Act, for instance, to include informal care relationships and dating relationships.

A more coordinated court process is the only reliable way to address the potential for conflict or disharmony amongst orders in any of the three jurisdictions. Further, the integrated court process allows parties to navigate one court system for all matters relating to domestic violence. This amounts to the provision of better access to justice and improves fairness to parties, particularly self-represented persons, by making the process easier, quicker and more immediate.

Underlying issues

The making of a domestic violence order does not address the underlying causes of the violence or the dysfunction in the family or relationship contributing to the domestic violence. It has long been possible to make a condition of a protection order which requires a party (usually the respondent) to attend a program or counselling. Parties may also be referred to counselling by the court during adjournment periods of applications.

Such orders not only depend on the willingness of the party or parties to attend to address their issues, but also depend heavily on the availability of appropriate, effective and affordable counselling and programs in the community in which the parties reside. Of course, the safety of the aggrieved person must remain the highest priority in this process and this in itself can militate against the structure of some forms of programs being practical or appropriate.

It is essential to address the underlying issues and causes of the domestic violence and the sooner the better. Early intervention with the respondent party tends to increase accountability for their actions at a time proximate to the aberrant behaviour and can encourage behavioural change which increases the safety of the aggrieved and associated persons.

Risk factors for domestic violence perpetration include being a childhood victim or witness of violence, controlling behaviour, tendency to violence outside the home, abuse of alcohol, repeat victimisation, pregnancy of partner, time of day and day of the week (evenings and weekends are peak times), location in a regional or rural area, low education and income of male partner, personality disorders, and Indigenous background (Makkai 2006). Witnessing domestic violence has been said to endanger the emotional wellbeing and development of children (Suderman and Jaffe 1999) in a number of ways including predisposition to committing violence in adulthood.

Breaches of orders

Unfortunately, domestic and family violence protection orders are often breached by the person whose behaviour it seeks to modify. Criminal charges for breach of orders can be laid by police, with or without complaint by the aggrieved person. The Magistrates Court deals with charges of breach of domestic violence orders, although associated charges of common assault, assault occasioning bodily harm, making threats, stalking and more serious offences of violence can also accompany the breach charge. The incidence of domestic violence within a family unit may also lead to the intervention of the Department of Child Safety in the family's life and consequent applications to the court regarding the children. There may also be criminal compensation applications or less often civil proceedings for damages arising from the violent conflict.

Capacity to deliver

Queensland Magistrates Court has an illustrious history of initiating and implementing problem-solving and therapeutic court approaches, including Drug Court, Murri Court, Homeless Persons Court Diversion Program, Special Circumstances List, QMERIT (referral into treatment program), some of which have been developed within the current resources of the court. The development of a specialised domestic violence court would dovetail with these other initiatives and the court has demonstrated its capacity to deliver justice services in this manner.

Many courts have had facilities developed to assist parties to attend court without confrontation or unnecessary trauma by providing appropriate and separate waiting facilities. Newer court buildings such as Brisbane, Thursday Island and Caloundra have been built with specialised facilities which provide separate access to the courtroom for aggrieved and respondent persons, waiting lounges with en suite facilities in secure areas, and separate play areas for children that reduce the exposure of children to discussions regarding the court process. Facilities vary from court to court but the initiative is at the forefront of the development of new courthouses and the redevelopment of existing buildings.

Counselling and assistance is provided to aggrieved persons in Queensland courts by trained court assistance workers from the Domestic and Family Violence Court Assistance Service funded by the Department of Communities. In some courts, services are provided for respondent persons by DV Connect or other service providers. Counselling is available through various service providers in many centres at all stages of the court process with some areas having access to treatment and support programs. The availability of such programs is heavily dependent on the funding available through non-government organisations. Some programs can be directly accessed by the courts through a referral process.

In some centres, police have developed procedures which include providing information on services and programs to parties, particularly the respondent person, at a very early stage in a situation of conflict. On some occasions, when appropriate, this may be done before an application for an order is taken out. In the absence of any formal evaluation of the effectiveness of this approach, it can only be a positive move especially if the party takes up the opportunity for intervention at this early stage.

The benefits of specialised domestic and family violence courts

There a number of benefits in specialised domestic and family violence courts. The four major benefits are:

- **Victim assistance, support and improved safety** There are many benefits to this other than obvious protection from further harm for the victim and children: improved understanding of the legal process which can assist a victim to stay in the process until the conclusion of the issue, building stronger members of the community who are able to become self-sufficient, empowering victims and supporting them to improve their situation in life.
- **Increased accountability of offenders and fast tracking of offenders to programs and counselling** Programs can be offered to offenders on a number of bases: voluntarily either in conjunction with a protection order or otherwise; as a condition of a protection order; as a bail-based program pre-sentence; or a post-sentence condition of a community based order for criminal offences. The earlier in the process that an offender faces their violence and takes responsibility for their behaviour, the better the prospects for behavioural change and victim safety.
- **Potential to deal with complexity of cases across jurisdictions** A more integrated approach to all of the legal issues facing a family which has been the subject of domestic violence will help to ensure consistency in orders, remove obstacles to the family from the system which is otherwise segmented and lengthy, provide more timely resolution of the legal issues through dedicated lists, and improve safety through timely intervention with the family.
- **Greater consistency in sentencing compared to prosecution of domestic violence cases in other courts** (Clark, Burt, Schulte and Maguire 1996) A more consistent approach by the courts to the issue of sentencing increases the likelihood of offenders becoming more accountable for their actions.

There is no universal model for specialised domestic violence courts but most courts involve certain processes which include specialised investigation and prosecution processes, a high level of collaboration between the court and agencies, an integrated approach from the courts across jurisdiction types and support for victims and offender behaviour change through service providers and programs.

The Rockhampton experiment

Goals of the Rockhampton Specialised Domestic and Family Violence Court

The vision of the Rockhampton experiment was to develop a procedure to meet the following criteria within the current framework of the courts, without extra funding and along the lines of the Australian and international models of specialised domestic violence courts. There were areas where the absence of resources negated the possibility of adopting some processes. The goals were (in no particular order):

- **To reduce the number of unnecessary appearances** required by the parties in applications for domestic and family violence orders by having applications, hearings and breach proceedings heard on the one day in the one court.
- **To ensure maximum access to domestic violence support workers** for the aggrieved person in relation to applications for protection orders on a temporary and final basis. Previously hearings of applications were listed at various times through the court list and could not be attended by the support workers.
- **To enable the court to receive victim impact information** by allowing an aggrieved person to attend court for breach charges should they wish to do so.
- **To improve information available to parties** to applications at the earliest opportunity. This includes information about the court process and support services.
- To **improve prosecutorial knowledge** of the matters through specialisation of prosecutors and prosecutors having continued access to the parties.
- To improve child protection outcomes by improving Department of Child Safety comprehension of the domestic violence court system, the contents of orders made and providing an opportunity for the department to inform the court of issues impacting on the making of orders relating to particular parties. The Child safety callover is listed on the same day in the same court as domestic violence matters.
- **To reduce conflict or inconsistency amongst various orders** from different jurisdictions affecting the same parties.
- **To provide the opportunity to refer offenders to perpetrator programs** or counselling during bail periods prior to sentencing on breach charges or as a condition of a community based order.
- To **provide further safety and comfort** for aggrieved spouses when attending court.

Early achievements

Stakeholder meetings established the links between the court and service providers and stakeholders from the outset. The meetings were convened at the request of the magistrate by the Queensland Police Service domestic violence liaison officer (DVLO).

Early on, the court was able to arrange for some minor remodelling to the existing facilities attached to Court 1 (the major arrest court). The domestic violence support room was moved into another office and was modified to provide access to Court 1 by a private corridor which permitted direct access to the courtroom (rather than through the public entrance) to avoid unnecessary distress for the aggrieved person and significantly reduce the potential for confrontation with the respondent person or persons associated with or supporting either party. The facility provides a comfortable waiting area in a supportive environment.

Unfortunately, one downfall is that the facility still opens into the main foyer where respondent spouses are waiting and where there is full public access, necessitating the aggrieved person to run the gauntlet of potential contact coming and going from court. In other courts it has been possible to provide such a facility away from the main public areas (such as Yeppoon) which further improves the comfort and safety of the aggrieved person. Alternately, a separate waiting area for the respondents would be beneficial as exists in some courts.

A number of other issues were easy to address and changes were quickly made in the following areas:

- **Changes to the listing arrangements** for domestic violence matters in 2007 - two dedicated domestic violence days per month were arranged with application mentions (9 am), breach charges (9.30 am), hearings on applications (10 am) and child safety matters (2 pm) listed on the one day.
- A **dedicated prosecutions team** was created by the Queensland Police Service with the DVLO (a sergeant) prosecuting first return mentions of applications each morning and a prosecutor (with the assistance of the sergeant) prosecuting all domestic violence matters on the dedicated day. Police inquiries office personnel (responsible for serving applications and orders and taking statements in support of applications) appear to support and instruct the prosecutor on each occasion.
- **Domestic violence support officers** attend court to support aggrieved persons on each domestic violence day as well as on the first return mentions each morning.
- **Improved written material about and referrals to service providers** are provided to parties to applications, and appointments to provide statements to police are made at court, increasing the likelihood of the necessary preparation for hearing being achieved.

- **Improved communication and liaison** between the court and all interested parties in the system through regular meetings and co-ordination of processes.
- **Police changed their procedure** to facilitate breach charges being returnable on the dedicated domestic violence court days.
- **Concurrent police follow-up and call-back program by DVLO**. Repeat calls for service were addressed by police. Families that police are called to more than three times in a six month period are case managed, with serious offences being managed by a senior officer, normally a sergeant. DVLO (a sergeant) will attend on families that are already known to her but otherwise a sergeant from the local police station will follow up. When attending the family, referrals to services for the aggrieved, the respondent and children if necessary are given. At appropriate times, a domestic violence worker attends with the police officer. The anecdotal evidence from DVLO is that despite attempts to engage the family in the process, attendance at referred services is not high, and even those who do attend tend not to engage in a meaningful way with the service, attending once or twice but then falling away.
- In Rockhampton, one third of domestic violence callouts are to Indigenous families. **Police liaison officers** are Aboriginal and Islander officers who also attempt to engage with families who have issues with domestic violence. They attend at houses where an incident has occurred a couple of days after the incident and encourage the respondent (and family members if appropriate) to attend the Indigenous Healing Centre - Helem Yumba.

Stumbling blocks

Some changes were more difficult to achieve and are still being developed:

- Difficulties around the availability of perpetrator programs through service providers, the intermittent nature of the funding arrangements for programs, the lack of sufficient places in programs dedicated for court use, and confidentiality issues regarding the provision of information about offenders to service providers and the reporting back of information from service providers to court.
- Lack of **legislative support** for a bail-based treatment program, and reliance on local police attitude to the laying of potential breach of bail charges where offenders fail to answer bail conditions to attend programs.
- Difficulties occasioned by the removal by Department of Corrective Services of **Indigenous focused post-sentence perpetrator programs** available through the Probation and Parole Service. The

excellent program of Ending Family Violence was operating effectively but is no longer available in the new suite of programs.

- **Delays in engaging** with the process by Department of Child Safety.
- Effectiveness of police liaison officers' actions in attending on families. **Domestic violence training** for those officers and coordination with other services may be needed.

Later achievements

At the commencement of the pilot arrangements, Relationships Australia, Centacare, and Anglicare were all running domestic violence programs of varying descriptions. Further, Helem Yumba (Indigenous Healing Centre) offered domestic violence counselling for Indigenous people which extends beyond the respondent and includes assistance for the aggrieved and other members of the family in a holistic approach. Currently, only Relationships Australia and Helem Yumba run dedicated domestic violence perpetrator programs.

An approach which was attempted earlier in the pilot arrangements has finally come to fruition. An arrangement has been made with Relationships Australia (RA) and Helem Yumba for referral of offenders to attend a domestic violence program post plea but pre-sentence. Both services are funded to provide services for male offenders only. The RA program is free of charge to the offender, is of 15 weeks duration (three hours per week) and three programs will be run per year. RA has agreed to be flexible as to the entry time for the offenders, enabling them to start up to four weeks into the program. Helem Yumba will run a 12 week program. Consent to the release of information by the service providers will be signed by defendants and they will be provided with a copy of the facts of the incident, the subject of the charge before the court, and their criminal history to provide to the program convenor. Court appearances of the defendant at regular intervals during the program will enable the court to monitor the progress of the defendant with feedback information being provided to the court. Completion of the program can then be taken into account by the court in sentencing the defendant.

The same programs may also be available to be referred to as a condition of a community based order as the Department of Corrective Services offers no domestic violence programs.

Challenges for the development of specialised domestic and family violence courts

- The Rockhampton court arrangements are presently operating without funding.

- Magistrates have to provide time for the development and operation of the program within the constraints of the list and other demands on the court. Court time needs to be made available to integrate the various jurisdictions (to improve access for the parties and avoid conflicts in orders) and time is needed to monitor the supervision of offenders on programs. A liaison officer would meet the need for continuing communication between key services and the court, as well as provide a resource for evaluating and monitoring the development of the process.
- Appropriate facilities need to be available at courts to provide for the safety of the victim while attending court and appropriate housing of the respondent. Victim services need to be available and readily accessed by the victim, preferably at any early stage in the proceedings.
- Queensland Police Service may need to devote further resources to ensure the increased focus on evidence gathering and early intervention initiatives with families at risk of domestic violence as well as providing specialised prosecutorial and follow up services.
- Funding needs to be available to providers of treatment and counselling programs to run those services in a sustainable and ongoing way, with provision to enable information sharing between the service provider and the court, and to provide court-dedicated places in the programs.
- Legislative support is needed for a bail-based treatment regime which would improve offender uptake of such programs without risk of further bail-based charges. Depending on the approach favoured by government, legislative change may be necessary to address the difficulties in working amongst three jurisdictions to integrate court matters.
- Training for all staff of the court and service providers would facilitate effective and appropriate communication with parties.
- Depending on the approach favoured by government, increased availability of legal representation for parties, particularly in applications for protection orders, would assist parties.

Conclusion

Specialised courts of this nature seek to achieve a therapeutic outcome for the parties (Freiberg 2001). Respect for victims needs to be at heart of the process, with a view towards improving safety and empowerment of victims through referral to appropriate services and support mechanisms being available at the court. At the same time, a focus needs to be on offenders taking responsibility and accepting accountability for their behaviour. This can best be achieved through the use of court ordered programs for criminal offenders with supervision of progress by the court.

The process will best be achieved through high level cooperation and collaboration between court, service providers and stakeholders, including a mutual understanding of the response of the various agencies to domestic and family violence issues. The development of a more user-friendly environment at the court through moving away from traditional procedures, integrated court lists, case management subject to judicial monitoring, and the physical surroundings of the court ensures that victims in particular will be more likely to engage with the process. The lead agency needs to ensure coordination and monitoring of processes and data collection.

It is clear that domestic violence is an issue which has a marked impact on the community and it has been shown in other jurisdictions that through a moderated court process the issue can be influenced in a positive way. If the will is there to assist the community to become safer and less violent, and the resources are made available for this purpose, the court can deliver justice and safety outcomes for families subject to domestic violence in a realistic and sustainable way.

Chapter 6

The Probation and Parole Perspective

Rosemary O'Malley

The core business of Queensland Corrective Services (QCS) is risk management and community safety. In 1996, the Southport and Burleigh Heads District Offices of the Probation and Parole Service joined the Gold Coast Domestic Violence Integrated Response (GCDVIR) Group for the purpose of using the strength of a multi-agency approach to enhance the safety of women and children in the local community. This chapter will: explore QCS participation in, and commitment to, the GCDVIR; the challenges of supervising domestic violence perpetrators; the advantages to probation and parole officers (PPOs) of being part of an integrated model; the case management of offenders after completing the program; and areas of future focus for QCS and other stakeholders involved in the GCDVIR on how better to respond to this particular group of offenders.

Prior to involvement in the GCDVIR the standard interventions recommended by the judiciary for domestic violence offenders were that they complete an anger management program and undertake some form of relationship counselling. However, research has shown that these interventions are likely to be ineffective in addressing the criminogenic needs of domestic violence perpetrators (see Dobash, Dobash, Cavanagh and Lewis 2000). Dr Brian Sullivan (O'Sullivan 2006) describes domestic violence as anger that is controlled and controlling; it is neither impulsive nor the result of poor self-regulation. Sullivan gives the example of an offender who stated that during a cocaine-induced rampage he attacked all of his partner's belongings with a machete. When asked what he destroyed of his own property, he acknowledged that none of his belongings had been damaged. This is controlled anger and not the kind that is generally addressed in anger management programs. Sullivan (2006) further notes that relationship counselling where domestic violence is a factor has been described as dangerous, unethical, and ineffective. Furthermore, it may not take into account the power imbalance that exists within violent relationships, and situations in which women may not feel safe to disclose violence, or there may be adverse consequences if she does (see Dobash,

Dobash, Cavanagh and Lewis 2000). Requiring the female partner to participate in relationship counselling also implies that she is in some way responsible for the violence, when in reality it appears that women's behaviour has little effect in changing the course of an abusive episode (Misso 2004).

The men's program

In March 2000, QCS agreed to fund one of the two facilitators required for the 24 week men's perpetrator program and to provide a venue for the program at the Southport Probation and Parole District Office, as well as to provide security personnel for the program. However, the intangible resources that are intrinsic in this commitment are even more significant. QCS employs an Integrated Offender Management (IOM) model for the supervision of offenders. The five principles of the IOM model relate to risk, need, responsivity, professional discretion and program integrity. These principles are based on research and best practice in the field of corrections. The model is offender centred, focuses on reducing reoffending, includes a robust assessment of risk, provides integrated process for an offender's progression through the system, and emphasises the individual responsibilities of the offender (Queensland Corrective Services 2006). The structure of the model, as well as the skills and experience of Probation and Paroles Officers (PPOs), boded well for the Probation and Parole Service being a valuable member of the GCDVIR.

When the men's program commenced, Southport Probation and Parole was providing a service to the Southport Magistrates Court. In this role PPOs were in a position to perform an initial assessment of which offenders were likely to be suitable for the program and to recommend to magistrates that the men's perpetrator program be placed as an additional requirement on their probation orders and intensive corrections orders. This additional requirement is necessary as the offender has to agree to pay the fees for the program. This mandated aspect of the men's program is one of its most important features. Sullivan (2006) suggests that it is not always realistic to appeal to a man's better nature as he may not have one. But if one appeals to his self-interest there is the possibility of exerting more leverage that also provides him with the opportunity to change his behaviour. The offender's goal or self-interest may be *"I don't want to have contact with the criminal justice system"*, and through the men's perpetrator program he learns how to modify his behaviour and develop new strategies for addressing his power and control issues that underlie his use of violence and thus to reduce his contact with police and the courts.

Other advantages of having the program mandated include the increased scrutiny and surveillance of the offender through normal QCS case management and supervision practices. If an offender fails to participate appropriately during the program, he may be returned to court and be fined for breaching his order. If offenders fail to attend the program or are excluded from the program they face being returned to court, having their order revoked and being re-sentenced on the original breach of domestic violence order (DVO) offences, and this may result in a term of imprisonment.

Mandating the program does not only occur through the court process where offenders are placed on community based orders such as probation or intensive corrections orders. It can also occur for those offenders sentenced to terms of imprisonment and released to either board ordered or court ordered parole. Instead of the men's program being a special condition on their order, the offenders are given a written lawful instruction to commence and attend the program. If they fail to comply with this lawful instruction they breach their order which may result in their parole being suspended or cancelled and them being returned to prison.

Assessment

Effective supervision and case management of offenders begins with thorough assessment. During the assessment phase individualised offender management plans (OMPs) are developed that identify all of the offender's criminogenic needs and the interventions to address these needs. In addition to the normal assessment process that occurs for any offender commencing a community based order, offenders with the men's perpetrator program additional requirement on their order (or who have been identified as requiring this intervention on their OMPs) also undergo a specialised assessment for the program. This assessment includes:

- The Assessment Questionnaire (Male);
- Abuse Behaviour Inventory (Male);
- Dangerousness Checklist;
- Group Participation Contract; and
- Authority to Release, Exchange and Disclose Information.

The assessment officer collates information from a variety of sources. Through the Queensland Police Service (QPS), Probation and Parole Officers (PPOs) are provided with the facts of the offences (QP9s) and their criminal histories (including interstate criminal histories). Psychological reports are frequently provided by the court or defence lawyers, and PPOs also have access to the offender's custodial histories through the QCS integrated information management system. This may include exit reports from programs they completed while incarcerated or were supervised on previous community based orders. Thus the offender's self-disclosures during the assessment phase are challenged or corroborated by the collateral evidence provided by independent sources.

Another important aspect of the assessment phase is identifying responsivity needs. These may include the offender's level of motivation and other factors that may affect his participation in the program such as underlying drug, alcohol, mental health issues, or medical conditions such as frontal lobe damage. Dr Edward Gondolf (Gondolf 2001) states that the abusive man who abuses alcohol does not have a problem, he has two problems. Sometimes the underlying issues such as alcohol dependency have to be addressed before the offender can effectively participate in the men's program.

It should be noted that competing paradigms impact upon the assessment phase and ultimately upon the case management process. Offenders often report to probation and parole directly from court after being placed on a probation or intensive corrections order and are still making statements that work in the court paradigm. The common denial phrase of *"I only pleaded guilty because my lawyer told me to"* is one of the great frustrations for PPOs. Additionally, they can cite verbatim the submissions made by their legal representative that minimise or justify their offending behaviour. It is, of course, the role of defence lawyers to advocate on behalf of their clients, and to make submissions that may reduce the penalty that might otherwise be imposed. For example on 15 April 2008 the *Courier Mail* (see Gregory 2008) reported on a Supreme Court trial involving a man stabbing his wife to death (inflicting 20 stab wounds). The headline read *"Wife-killer 'provoked' by affair"*. The defence barrister admitted that his client had killed his wife but went on to argue that he was *"provoked"* which could lead the jury to a verdict of manslaughter. The solicitor further submitted that his client's wife had made him *"lose control of his mind for a brief time"*. Whilst this may be an effective legal argument, apportioning blame to the victim inhibits the offender taking responsibility and being held accountable for his decisions and offending behaviour. These justifications and minimisations do not work well for the offender in the Corrective Services paradigm as they increase the offender's assessed risk level and are identified as cognitive distortions and a criminogenic need that requires intervention.

After the assessment phase is completed the offender's file is brought to the joint meeting of the GCDVIR which is attended by representatives from Probation and Parole, the Domestic Violence Prevention Centre (DVPC), and the program facilitators. This meeting determines the offender's suitability for the program and the proposed induction and commencement date for when they will roll into the program. If an offender is deemed suitable to participate in the men's program his supervising officer issues him with a written reasonable direction (or lawful instruction) to commence and complete the 24 week men's perpetrator program. He then attends an induction session for the program where the conditions of his group participation contract and consequences of not complying are again explained to him by a representative from Probation and Parole. The PPO also ensures the offender is aware he may be randomly breath tested or urine tested before any program session to ensure he is not attending the program under the influence of alcohol or illicit drugs. The offender is reminded that he is required to pay his program participation fees within a specified time frame.

At the induction session the role of the DVPC is also explained to the offender and he is made aware that his partner or ex-partner will be contacted and offered support from this service. The program facilitators also attend the induction and explain the Duluth model and the Power and Control Wheel concepts. They answer any questions and address any concerns or apprehension that the offender may have regarding participating in the program. The offender usually rolls into the program the same evening as the induction session or the following week.

Case management

Once offenders commence participation in the program their PPOs begin receiving weekly feedback in the form of the Sessional Risk Assessment Form which includes information on their attendance, participation, attitude, skills level, and most importantly their current risk level. This feedback then becomes the blueprint for case management during office visits. PPOs can note deficits or improvements in the offender's participation particularly in relation to their levels of minimisation, denial, and blame. There is also a section that makes specific recommendations or actions that require follow-up by the PPO. On this feedback form the program facilitators assess the offender's risk of acting in a violent or abusive manner in the coming week based on their disclosures and participation in that week's program session. This risk rating is also greatly informed by the level of risk the offender's victim has provided on the women's feedback forms. The Sessional Risk Assessment Forms are faxed to the DVPC after each program session so that DVPC counsellors and the manager of the DVPC are immediately made aware of any increased risk to female partners or ex-partners.

These Sessional Risk Assessment Forms are given to the supervisors in the Southport and Burleigh Heads District Offices, and those offenders assessed as being at a high risk of acting violently in the coming week are discussed with district managers. The PPOs of those offenders are instructed on what action to take to address this level of risk. This may include directing the offender to report more frequently or earlier than his next scheduled appointment; increasing urine and breath testing of the offender; giving the offender written reasonable directions regarding restricting or prohibiting contact with his partner or ex-partner; liaising with the QCS intelligence officer who in turn will seek assistance from the police; liaising with local police to arrange for welfare checks to be conducted in the coming week. High risk offender profiles are also provided to police at monthly joint meetings so these offenders also remain high on their surveillance and communications systems. Supervising offenders who have been convicted of breaches of DVOs can be a confronting and difficult experience for a PPO. These offenders can be amongst the most resistant to attending interventions and the potential to act violently as a coping strategy is higher than for other offenders on PPOs' caseloads.

Sometimes the power and control issues that are central to this type of offending manifest during the case management process as demonstrated in the following example:

A participant was being excluded from the men's program for inappropriate participation. He had attended sessions under the influence of alcohol, had been aggressive towards facilitators, and had also not shifted in his denial stance despite participating in the group for several weeks. He knew he was being returned to court for breach action and began bringing pressure to bear on his PPO. He brought in photographs of his children and had prepared a long speech which focused on the effect his possible incarceration might have on his family. At one point during this discussion he said to his officer "*look what you're doing to my children*". He also attempted to collude with his officer by stating "*you know what women are like, I didn't do anything, this is all about money and property settlements*". He worked very hard on image management trying to convince his officer that he was "*really a nice guy*" who had not previously had a problem with any other woman apart from his ex-wife. When all of this failed to sway his officer he eventually became aggressive and intimidating. His whole cycle of manipulation, control, and intimidation was clearly demonstrated over a 45 minute office visit.

In situations such as this it is often useful for officers to debrief with colleagues to ensure that they are not being seduced by the offender's script and are remaining objective (Sullivan 2006). This incident also demonstrates the necessity for thorough and appropriate training for PPOs supervising this type of offender. The advantages for PPOs of being involved in the GCDVIR include greater surveillance, weekly collateral checks, and more people assessing the level of risk of these offenders. The PPO does not have to rely solely on their own observations during office visits, and subsequent collateral checks; but also has the ears and eyes of two very experienced facilitators providing feedback and identifying risk markers for the program participants. Additionally, partner feedback through the DVPC provided on a weekly basis is perhaps the best indication of their level of risk and that the behaviour of these offenders is changing.

Inconsistency between what the offender reports regarding his relationship and what his victim reports is one of the most important risk markers. Inconsistencies between what the offender discloses during office visits with his PPO and what he discloses during program sessions may also indicate increased risk. Offenders have been known to disclose during a program session: being fired from a job; being evicted from their usual address; ending a relationship, or using illicit drugs – but fail to disclose this to his officer in the case management process. The reverse situation also occurs. For this reason close liaison between PPOs and facilitators is essential and occurs on a weekly basis at the Southport office where the program is held, enabling facilitators to talk to PPOs as they prepare for the program. Additionally, it occurs more formally on a monthly basis at the facilitator DVIR meetings when offenders' participation, progress, and risk levels are discussed with supervisors (or district managers) from the Southport and Burleigh Heads District Offices, program facilitators, women's counsellors and the manager of the DVPC.

While the offender is participating in the program the PPO also reminds offenders to make regular payments towards their program fees. Sullivan (2006) states that by paying these fees offenders are taking responsibility for their violence. He suggests that they may have to forgo buying cigarettes or alcohol to fund their participation in the program and this is a good indication of their commitment to addressing their offending behaviour. PPOs may also issue the offender with a written reasonable direction to commence a payment plan to pay these fees.

Assessing change

As per the terms of the Group Participation Contract an offender's progress in the program is reviewed after six weeks. The review occurs during the offender's scheduled office visit and is attended by his PPO and a program facilitator. If the offender is participating appropriately and making progress he continues on the program and he is next reviewed at 12 weeks. If he is not participating appropriately and has not begun to shift in his levels of minimisation, justification, and denial he is cautioned and warned that his participation will again be reviewed in six weeks. If, after 12 weeks in the program, the offender is still not participating appropriately and continues to minimise, justify, or deny his behaviour, breach action may be initiated by the PPO.

When breach action is approved by the supervisor the offender is issued with a written warning regarding his unsatisfactory participation and he is removed from the program for a three week stand down period during which time his responsivity issues are addressed through the case management process. Motivational interviewing is utilised to assist the offender to move to the stages of change (Prochaska and DiClemente 1992). If, after the three week stand down period, the offender has made progress in addressing his responsivity issues and verbalises a motivation to continue on the program, he restarts the program from week one. Participation is reviewed after six weeks and if he is still maintaining a denial stance and has not made any further progress, he is excluded from the program. At this point formal action is taken and the offender is returned to court for breach of his community based order.

The offender may also have to restart the program if he has three approved absences, that is, absences that have been approved by the supervisor at a District Office upon the offender providing a medical certificate, a letter from his employer, or any other written collateral evidence that provides a reasonable excuse for his not attending a session of the program. Additionally, if an offender has one unapproved absence, that is, failing to attend the program without providing a reasonable excuse, it may result in the matter being returned to court or he may have to restart the program.

The decision to exclude an offender from the program is canvassed thoroughly with each party involved. The GCDVIR is aware of the research that indicates that those who start but do not complete intervention programs are at a higher risk of reoffending than those who do not commence programs at all (McMurran and Theodosi 2007). However this must be balanced with the effect that the behaviour of these participants has on group dynamics and other participants in the group. Often offenders who are minimising, justifying, and denying their domestic violence, are also white-anting the group before, during, and after sessions. Additionally, if there are no consequences for inappropriate participation or absences, then a strong message may be sent to other men in the group that this behaviour is acceptable.

The role of the PPO after an offender has been excluded from the men's perpetrator program is critical given these offenders are at a higher risk of reoffending. Increasing reporting frequency and home visits during this time; ensuring breach action is initiated as quickly as possible; maintaining liaison with the DVPC to ensure the victim is remaining safe; and flagging these offenders as high risk during joint meetings with the police is the focus of supervision for offenders excluded from the men's program.

Program completion

To this point the chapter has focused on compliance issues and what happens if an offender does not make the most of the opportunity afforded him by the court to address his domestic violence issues. However, the majority of offenders who complete the program state that participating in this intervention has been a positive experience. Most participants also make shifts in the core beliefs that support their domestic violence and are able to verbalise how they are applying their new skills in their interactions with women. For some men the support they receive from the group is the most positive experience of their adult lives. Sullivan (2006) notes that for participants who are isolated, attending the men's program can be like reconnecting with society, and they value the time they spend in the group.

During the program some offenders reveal they are overwhelmed by the realisation of the damage they have caused in their intimate relationships. In 2006 one offender, after attending a session run by a guest speaker (a counsellor who works with children who have witnessed domestic violence), realised the full extent of the pain he had caused. He presented to his supervising officer in the midst of an emotional crisis which resulted in a relapse into cannabis use and depression. He was excused from attending the program while these issues were addressed and after he stabilised he rejoined the group and completed the program.

When asked why he had reacted so strongly to the counsellor's presentation he stated *"I didn't get it before. Then seeing those pictures the kids had drawn, it hit me. If you don't get it and feel that intense level of pain over what you've done, then you really haven't got it. I'll never forget that pain and I never want to forget it, it's what drives me to keep working on this stuff"*. This example demonstrates two things. First, the program contributes significantly to some offenders experiencing significant shifts in their core belief systems. Second, there is sufficient flexibility in the model to enable the offender to be stood down from the program to address his responsivity issues (through the case management process), and then re-enter and successfully complete the program.

Post-program the role of the PPO is even more significant. The focus of case management during this period of supervision includes ensuring recommendations noted in the program exit report are followed up; monitoring any new relationships that develop; liaising with the Department of Child Safety regarding management plans for offenders with children; and encouraging the offender to develop a safety plan. Offenders with children may be referred to parenting courses after completing the men's program. Sullivan (2006) notes that 50 per cent of men who abuse their wives or partners also abuse a child - this is seven times the rate of non-violent men. He suggests the starting point for improving their fathering skills should be challenging them to move from child management to exploring "What sort of relationship do you want to have with your child?"

In the months following the program the offender's PPO will continue to request that the offender verbalise and demonstrate how he is applying the concepts and skills learnt during the program in everyday life and relationships. It is easier to change behaviour than to change a belief structure (Sullivan 2006), and the offender's core beliefs continue to be challenged through the case management process.

An authority to disclose and exchange information is current throughout an offender's order, which means that a PPO can continue to liaise with the DVPC after an offender completes the program. They can confirm that the offender's victim does not have any concerns and ensure he is complying with his DVO, particularly if a no-contact clause is part of the order. Monitoring risk markers and surveillance becomes the responsibility of the PPO after the offender completes the program.

Future directions

One area for future focus for QCS is specialised training in the supervision of domestic violence perpetrators. New officers are often unsure how to supervise offenders with domestic violence issues and a common concern is knowing how to effectively manage these types of offenders. These offenders can be intimidating and controlling in an interview situation and as previously noted they can be very resistant to attending intervention.

Staff from the Southport and Burleigh Heads District Offices have the benefit of supervising domestic violence perpetrators within the context of the GCDVIR, and other offices around the State are now considering adopting the integrated model.

The need for a maintenance group after the treatment program is completed warrants further investigation. Other QCS programs, such as substance abuse and sex offender treatment groups, are followed up with maintenance groups during which their relapse prevention plans are revised. In the maintenance group the offender is provided with the opportunity to fully develop or further refine relapse prevention plans. After the treatment program some offenders feel lost without the support of the group and need to be weaned from the intensive intervention rather than kicked out of the nest. In Chapter 15 it is suggested that some domestic violence offenders require 100 hours of face-to-face contact. The current men's program runs for 48 hours, therefore the balance could be accumulated in a maintenance group over the period of the order. The offender could roll in and out of this group according to increased risk, or need for revisiting their relapse prevention plans: for example if they commence a new relationship, lose custody of their children or present with any changes in dynamic factors that may increase their of risk of reoffending.

Gondolf (2006) asserts that "the system matters", and QCS is one component working within the criminal justice system (CJS). The investigative (police) and the adjudicative (courts) components of the CJS are two of the major stakeholders in the GCDVIR, and how they deal with domestic violence perpetrators can ultimately have implications for how QCS supervise these offenders. When the police component of the CJS charges an offender who assaults his partner or ex-partner with the offence of breach of domestic order rather than assault, this may reinforce to the offender and his victim that his behaviour is not treated seriously by the CJS. This has been borne out from women's stories through participation in the integrated program.

Victims have approached PPOs stating that their partners have wrongly been charged with assault by the police. When PPOs ask for more details regarding the incident, the victims often relate details of being punched, kicked, being dragged along hallways and having their heads pushed through walls, and being burnt with cigarettes. When PPOs note that these incidents of violence are probably the basis of the assault charge, victims are frequently surprised and do not equate this violence with being assaulted. The system appears to have taught these victims that when their partners punch or kick them he is breaching his DVO, but it is not assault.

The system also appears to have taught the offenders the same lesson. One of the impediments to offenders making progress in addressing their violence is the establishment of core beliefs the offender has developed from his experience of being arrested and charged for domestic violence offences and how these matters have been dealt with through the adjudicative process. Sullivan asserts it is through the criminal justice system that a society defines what it is prepared to accept (Sullivan 2006). If the penalty of choice employed by the courts to address the breach of domestic violence orders is the widespread use of fines, this may reinforce the message that the CJS views violence perpetrated against partners as less serious than violence perpetrated outside of an intimate relationship.

Research indicates that before they come before a court, domestic violence offenders are likely to have had a long history of violence and abuse that has never been reported (see Dobash, Dobash, Cavanagh and Lewis 2000). The structure of the legislation guiding Magistrates Courts, namely the *Penalties and Sentences Act 1992* indicates a progression from fines, to community based orders, to imprisonment. However, for breach of DVOs, offenders may be fined for a considerable length of time before being placed on a community based order. Therefore, it would appear desirable that offenders be placed on a community based order (with the men's perpetrator program as an additional requirement) as early as possible in their offending cycle to prevent the pattern of violence escalating over a long period of time.

The program has great potential for growth and expansion. Potential restrictions to this expansion include the number of referrals from the courts, resourcing factors such as the availability of qualified facilitators, and securing the physical space to accommodate numerous programs being run simultaneously. Individual treatment for these offenders is possible and available, but change needs to occur at the societal level and through regular review of current practices within the criminal justice system.

Part III

BROADER PRACTICE APPROACHES

Chapter 7

The Gold Coast Domestic Violence Offender Education and Intervention Program for Male Perpetrators

Susan Moore

The program and model

The model currently being used as the basis for the Men's Domestic Violence Education and Intervention Program as part of the Gold Coast Domestic Violence Integrated Response is the Duluth Domestic Violence Program Model, "Creating a Process of Change for Men who Batter" designed by Ellen Pence and Michael Paymar (revised edn 2003).

The Duluth model was designed to be applied within an integrated framework, based on information exchange and participation of key stakeholders in the community. Within the Gold Coast Integrated Response these stakeholders include the Domestic Violence Prevention Centre Gold Coast Inc, Gold Coast Women's Refuges, Gold Coast Hospital, Corrective Services, including Southport and Burleigh Heads Probation and Parole, Southport and Coolangatta Magistrates Court and the Queensland Police Service, Gold Coast.

Pence and McDonnell (2000) in discussing the feminist influences on policy and protocol around the Duluth program, emphasise that the model advocates for collaborative policies and procedures to improve the safety of women and children. The women partners of men on the program are contacted and are offered regular contact, counselling and support, by women's advocacy workers at the DVPC, while their partners or ex-partners are completing the program. Those who consent to be part of this process are contacted, either weekly or fortnightly, to assess support needs and to clarify any concerns about safety or changes in their circumstances. A summary of this contact is then sent to the facilitators of the program to consider when assessing risk rating and risk management strategies, as part of the weekly risk assessment process for each participant. This information can be helpful in scheduling specific topics and areas of focus for intervention. It is important that facilitators use this information carefully in order not to breach confidentiality or potentially escalate an area of risk.

The Duluth program aims to address denial, and to encourage ownership and responsibility in the participants. Gondolf (2007: 7) endorses the cognitive behavioural therapy aspect of the program in that it "addresses excuses, rationalisation, and justifications that are often tied to one's attitudes, belief system and cognitive scripts".

There are 26 possible sessions in the Duluth model with session outlines, tools, exercises (vignettes, role plays, discussion, skills practice), strategies and video scenarios for each topic. The delivery of the program at Southport is condensed to 24 weeks. There are eight main topics in the model with three weeks spent on each topic. If a recent incidence of violence is disclosed, this would be processed in precedence to the topic at hand. These topics are part of the Power and Control Wheel, which was originally designed by consulting over 200 women victims of domestic violence. The topics relate to the most common clusters of behaviours reported by victims, and reflect women's experiences of financial, sexual, emotional, mental and physical abuse. Most of the men relate to many aspects of abuse named on this wheel. The videos are acted scenarios that demonstrate common domestic violence situations, and illustrate the various obvious and subtle tactics that perpetrators use to exert power and control. There is consistently positive feedback from the men about the usefulness of these videos and watching incidents being played out. The men are removed enough from the scenario to examine the contents objectively, even to the point of identifying what the victims may be experiencing. They often say they see themselves in the scenes. The scenarios are a valuable teaching which can be creatively used to promote discussion and to encourage the development of insight and empathy. The videos illustrate how to deconstruct, scene by scene, participants own incidents of domestic violence.

The Power and Control Wheel (Pence and Paymar 2003) represents the most commonly experienced clusters of domestic violence behaviours that women report. Each theme on the Power and Control Wheel is discussed and work is done with participants over three weeks towards changing behaviours towards non-violent respectful choices. Themes overlap and the constant issues of minimisation, denial and blame surface in most sessions, as does the use of intimidation and threats. The themes are:

- Violence versus non-violence;
- Using intimidation versus non-threatening behaviour;
- Using emotional abuse versus demonstrating respect;
- Using isolation versus providing trust and support;
- Minimising, denying, blaming versus being honest and accountable;
- Using children versus responsible shared parenting;

- Using male privilege versus shared responsibility (includes sexual respect);
- Using economic abuse versus economic partnership;
- Using coercion and threats versus negotiation and fairness.

One of the videos contains discussions generated by a group of women (previous victims) who speak about what it was like to experience a particular controlling or abusive behaviour from their partner and how it made them feel. This is another way of ensuring that the experience of victims remains a central part of the program and is not lost amongst the program's processes and aims.

Under the topic of responsible parenting, the Gold Coast program has employed a child counsellor to attend one half of one session to present information about how abuse affects children. Part of the presentation includes describing the mental, emotional and physical effects on children of witnessing and experiencing violence and also includes a PowerPoint presentation of photos of children's artwork and sand play expressions. These images speak for themselves about the pain, trauma, anger and helplessness children experience. Though many men deny abusing their children, in recounting their stories of domestic violence it is apparent their children are present, and in the very least have heard or witnessed abuse of their mothers. At least half of all abusive partners also batter their children (Pagelow 1989), and these sessions provide a time to discuss with and inform participants of the undeniable traumatic effects of domestic violence on children. The three parenting sessions often raise issues of the men's experience of violence and abuse as children. The presentation exposes their experience as victims when they were growing up and provides excellent opportunity for validation, and for exploring how they may want their children's experience to be different from theirs. A question often asked is "What kind of a relationship do you want your children to have with you?" and "What kind of a father do you want to be?" It is noted by facilitators that these sessions often provide a place for empathy development, insight and motivation towards change.

Assessments

The pre-program assessments for the domestic violence program are administered by probation and parole assessment officers. The Assessment Questionnaire (Male) gathers information about personal particulars, partner contact details, childhood experience, violence in current and previous relationships, health and lifestyle, relationship with the law, and support networks and goals. The Abuse Behaviour Inventory measures frequency of particular domestic abuse behaviours. The Dangerousness Checklist is completed by the assessment officer who gathers information that is already available to rate the risk of violence to the victim. At the time of the assessment the men sign a program contract which includes all aspects of what is expected during their attendance at the program including session times, rules, reporting of absences etc.

Included in the assessment package is a copy of the community based order, for example, probation order, parole or suspended sentence, a copy of the Queensland Police Report (QP9) (which details the domestic violence incident, including injuries to the partner, and the men's behaviour at the scene), and a copy of any available criminal history from Queensland or any other State in which this person may have resided. If there is an indication of a psychiatric illness or an acquired brain injury, then other supporting documentation from appropriate professionals is requested in order to make a decision about the suitability of this person for group work. If someone is found to be unsuitable for the program, an alternate recommendation is made to the probation and parole officer for an appropriate program through Mental Health, one-to-one counselling, or other intervention. There are occasions when a person has understated their use of drugs or alcohol and this becomes apparent when they attend the sessions under the influence or are randomly tested for drug and alcohol use.

Despite a thorough assessment process, approximately 10 per cent of participants find their way into the group with undisclosed drug or alcohol dependency that is evident in group sessions. Consistent intoxication is disruptive to group processes as well as limiting the man's comprehension of program content. It also undermines the seriousness of the group program and the fact that men have been ordered to do the program by a court. When a person tries to participate in the group but is under the influence of drugs or alcohol, they tend to disrupt, over disclose, overreact, or be excessively drowsy or agitated. If they have not been drug or breath tested the person is asked to leave the group when this behaviour is exhibited, and this is reported on their session assessment for follow-up. In consultation with the probation and parole officer, a decision may be made to stop attending so they can address this issue before restarting the program at a later date, although generally men who fail to meet the requirement not to be intoxicated by drugs and alcohol respond after initial warnings. The impact on the group when someone attends under the influence and is immediately asked to leave is that the men see that they are accountable to the group and the group contract, and are responsible for their decisions. It is explained to the group that to be attending under the influence of a substance is counterproductive to the aims of the session and does not allow that person or the other members of the group to work productively. This problem appears to remain a constant issue, but does not appear to be increasing in frequency.

The completed assessment package is sent to the Men's Domestic Violence Education and Intervention Program coordinator and the manager of the Domestic Violence Prevention Centre Gold Coast Inc (DVPC) for perusal. A decision is made as to the suitability of this person for the program and a date for induction and commencement is decided.

Because the men in the program are on various kinds of community based correctional orders, they are constrained to attend and to comply with the conditions on their particular order, including being assessed for the program and successfully completing. For example, a typical condition stated on a probation order by a magistrate would read "must be assessed for suitability to attend, and if deemed suitable, then satisfactorily attend and participate in the Men's Domestic Violence Education and Intervention Program and not attend under the influence of alcohol or drugs". If they fail to attend they face the consequences of breaching the order and returning to court for resentencing, which may result in a term of imprisonment or another community based order.

Induction

Before men begin the program they attend an induction session which is attended by a probation and parole officer (PPO), two facilitators and a representative from the DVPC. The purpose of the induction session is for the facilitators to meet the participants, provide clear information about the program, how it works, and to field any questions participants may have. The facilitators explain briefly the aims of the program, the DVPC representative explains the role of the agency in supporting the women partners while the men are on the program, and the PPO explains the compliance issues stated in the contract around attendance, use of drugs and alcohol before a group, absences and reporting. The men are invited to ask questions, or discuss what they will be asked to contribute and how they, their partners and children may benefit. The induction thus sets in place clear expectations and requirements of participation in the program. Importantly at this session the participation of other agencies such as the correctional services and the women's service provide a clear message that the man's responsibilities extend beyond the program itself.

Facilitators

The program employs a team of experienced professional facilitators who are trained in working with perpetrators of domestic violence. The training and qualifications of facilitators adhere to the Queensland Department of Communities Practice Standards (Working with Men who Perpetrate Domestic and Family Violence 2007). These standards outline the unacceptable, essential and optimal professional practice standards of men's domestic violence programs in Queensland, covering facilitator qualifications and training, staff safety, roles and responsibilities, professional development, program structure and operation, program accountability, client's rights, safety and risk assessment, advocacy work, reporting, course content and structure and external review and evaluation.

Quality training and consistent support and supervision of facilitators are crucial to the program and contribute to the retention of qualified program staff. Each facilitator is required to undertake specific domestic violence training regarding the experience of victims. They possess bachelor degree qualifications, and many have post-graduate specialisations and experience in generalist counselling, plus experience delivering behaviour change programs, with an emphasis on having worked with mandated clients.

Before commencing in a group, facilitators observe three sessions including the planning phase and the assessment process at the conclusion of the sessions. Facilitators then co-facilitate with an experienced Level 3 facilitator for three consecutive sessions. These sessions are supervised by a Level 3 facilitator, who observes all aspects of the session delivery and assessment and provides feedback to the facilitator in training.

All group programs are conducted with a male and female facilitator with one of the facilitators employed by Probation and Parole, the other by DVPC. As well as all the challenges involved in facilitating a men's domestic violence group, they are responsible for demonstrating equality and respectful interaction to group members in all aspects of program and session delivery.

Facilitators must have thoroughly reviewed their own beliefs about equality, gender and control. They must have a solid understanding of the complex and subtle dynamics of domestic violence and be able to demonstrate this through their co-facilitation. They must be able to engage the men in critical dialogue. To be effective, facilitators must operate as a team. If control is displayed by the male or female facilitator towards each other, the process, or group members, this could result in collusion, condescending behaviour or power struggles. Consequently the session may be ineffective, but more importantly, this may serve as a subtle reinforcement to perpetrators' distorted beliefs about equality and respectful relationships between men and women. According to Ellen Pence and Michael Paymer (2003), there are six roles facilitators are responsible for:

- participating in an interagency effort to hold participants in offender classes accountable for further acts of violence and, when necessary, for failure to complete the rehabilitation program;
- keeping the class focused on the issues of violence, abuse, control and change;
- facilitating reflective and critical thinking in the class;
- maintaining an atmosphere that is compassionate, challenging and not colluding;
- providing new information and teach non-controlling relationship skills;
- facilitating a positive and affirming class experience.

Facilitators need to have a plan of action for various scenarios. Although not every incident can be anticipated, discussing some general responses can be useful. If a participant suddenly reacts (for example, when he has consumed alcohol before the group), and becomes physically agitated, verbally abusive and disruptive, it is important that facilitators have a plan of action to manage this. It is not always appropriate to stop and process this type of incident, as some men will not calm themselves so this can occur.

As a case study example, at the end of the first hour of a session a participant, who had consumed alcohol before the group became agitated, angry and controlling by standing and gesturing to the group. This appeared to be in response to the issues that were being discussed. Facilitators handled this by acknowledging what was going on and encouraged the participant to use the ten minute break as a time out and to use self-calming techniques before re-joining the group for the second hour of the session. All other group members came back in after ten minutes, but this person was late back and appeared even more agitated. One facilitator believed it would be more beneficial to this person and to the group if he left the session. The other facilitator was trying to process his behaviour and calm him with no result. Very quickly the facilitators consulted each other and it was agreed that he should be asked to leave the premises. He was respectfully and firmly asked to leave the group and did not respond the first time. He was asked again to leave, which he then did.

Participants need to know facilitators can manage the group and any disclosures or incidents that may occur. The technique of immediacy, where facilitators can stop the process and briefly discuss and decide on a different direction or agree on an action to be taken, is another necessary tool for effective facilitation.

The role of facilitators is to hold perpetrators accountable by continually inviting and challenging them to take responsibility for their domestic violence and the effects it has had on their partners, children and families, and to invite them to change their beliefs, thoughts and actions towards respectful non-violent relationships.

Policy and procedures around the program

Policies and procedures have been developed as a framework for every aspect of the program and these policies adhere to the Department of Communities Practice Standards.

The program is conducted in the premises of Southport Community Corrections Office, and a security staff member is employed by Probation and Parole to be present on the premises for the two hour duration of the program. Security staff and facilitators are aware of the following:

- The location and availability of duress alarms.

- The physical location of facilitators in the group so they can be seen on camera.
- Procedures in response to an emergency.
- The automatic response of central security to a breach initiated by the duress alarm or by phone contact from security staff.
- Procedures for walk-by from local police beat officers during program break.
- Safety procedures at the conclusion of the program (walking to cars together and contact on arrival home).

Facilitators meet an hour before the program to plan the session. The women's (partner or ex-partner) reports are provided to the facilitators weekly by DVPC counsellors to consider when assessing risk levels and risk management and to inform practice in relation to the discrepancies between the men's stories and the experiences of victims.

After the men have left the building at the conclusion of the session, facilitators remain to complete risk assessments about each participant. This process can take up to an hour and a half depending on the number of men in the program and the risk management actions required. For example, if a person discloses a threat or admits recent violence, police are contacted to initiate an appropriate response which may be a request for a welfare check of the partner's address. Copies of the risk assessments are sent to the DVPC for inclusion on the files kept for all men and partners on the program, and to supervising probation and parole officers at each location. The assessments provide feedback to supervising probation and parole officers to discuss in reporting sessions with men who are on the program.

Participants

The program is an open group with a rolling enrolment format. The group is capped at 12. As people finish the group others are rolled in to start their 24 sessions, so at any time there may be men who have been in the group for 15 weeks and men who are just beginning the program. One of the advantages of this type of group is that not all the participants are at the same stage of denial, minimisation and blame. Often the men who have been in the program longer challenge and encourage the others to talk more honestly about their behaviours and attitudes. This positive peer influence works well to shorten the time some men spend in a denial stance. Obviously all the men are at different stages of change regardless of whether it is a closed or open group. New participants who see their peers being honest and trying to work on their problems engage earlier in the group process and are often less resentful and resistant to being in the program. Facilitators are reminded of this dynamic and the challenging nature of their work when several men with a positive influence in the group complete around the same time, and the group again becomes unsettled with new members colluding with the remaining men who may be at Week 5 or 6 but have not yet started to take responsibility. The task for facilitators is keeping the balance of holding men accountable while inviting change in the face of high and entrenched levels of denial and resistance, and doing this work in respectful, non-shaming ways.

There are cases where men who have been mandated to attend the program take their probation orders back to court with an appeal to the magistrate to remove the condition to attend the domestic violence program. Occasionally they are successful and no longer have to attend the program as a condition of their order.

In some ways, working with mandated clients who are under community based orders takes the pressure off facilitators, in that the men are held by the actual order and its conditions, and the facilitators are free to work with them towards change rather than constantly stressing compliance. Their reporting conditions and general compliance are monitored by their probation and parole officer. There are men who consistently attend the program to comply with the conditions of the order and who often do not realise that during this mandated period of attendance they may be slowly beginning to take responsibility for their domestic violence, and actually report positively about being in the group. They are men who, if it were not for the probation order, may not have volunteered for such a program.

Terminology used within the justice system may assist the men to minimise their behaviour. For example, being placed on a probation order for a breach of a DVO for locking the victim in her room or restraining her sends a different and less serious message than a charge of deprivation of liberty or assault. Or, it may be that the man has been charged with a breach of DVO for texting his partner. Often the context of the text appears irrelevant to the breach and in some cases contains direct or veiled threats to a woman's safety or life. Even the notion that he had been drinking at the time can imply absence of responsibility for domestic violence behaviours, and this is sometimes stated openly by solicitors in court, as part of the offender's defence and subsequently is sometimes considered by the magistrate as a mitigating factor when sentencing.

Facilitators consistently have to address minimisations with the participants, and because the control log, one of the main tools in the Duluth model, allows for a deconstruction of a domestic violence incident frame by frame, the men are able to see how they may be blaming others or minimising their behaviour. This process also allows them to identify their intents and beliefs, the effects of their control and violence, how a situation escalates, and clear decision points and alternative choices about behaviours. This type of "reviewing critical incidents remains a valuable method that advances men's thinking about their choices, shows them patterns of tension-building and encourages genuine efforts to change" (Wells 2003: 165).

Robertson (1992: 2) acknowledges that "changing the behaviour of batterers is difficult (and that) there are powerful cultural values which support men's privileged positions within their families and which condone their use of violence". One of the aims of the Duluth model is to deconstruct distorted belief systems about the roles of men and women where the belief supports men's needs being the most important. Men in the program often express beliefs that suggest that their needs are the priority. As Connell (2000: 3) puts it: "From a long history of gender relations, many men have a sense of entitlement to respect, deference, and service from women. If women fail to give it, some men will see this as bad conduct which ought to be punished". These kinds of beliefs are often expressed by men in the program and the challenging and changing of these beliefs is a core aim of the work in perpetrator programs.

Some men completely deny any occurrence of domestic violence at all, stating that the whole incident was conjured up by partners, police, neighbours etc. Others appear prepared to take some responsibility for some of their domestic violence behaviours but actively minimise with statements like "I didn't hit her – I just restrained her". The restraint behaviour may have involved pushing her to the ground and pinning her down. Facilitators spend time reframing the seriousness of this entitled behaviour over another person's body. If this behaviour were to be committed on a stranger the subsequent charge could be assault. It is quite normal to hear minimising statements during group discussion and they are occasionally challenged by other men who may have begun to take responsibility for their domestic violence and are no longer minimising. Blaming is often expressed by the classic statement, "she pushes my buttons". In addition some men in this population appear to be very dedicated to image management in the group setting and will go to amazing lengths, including complete denial of any form of domestic violence and telling their stories so that they appear to be the victims, in order to save face and to maintain a sense of control. Many express resentment that "she" did this to me, and are angry that it appears that their partners now have more control than they do (in effect she may have only some greater control over her own life), or that they cannot see their children. Sometimes it appears that the thought of their partners exerting control (by her calling the police) is more enraging to the men than not being able to see their children. McKendy (1992: 61) suggests that for men to take responsibility for their actions it requires them to "cut out of their accounts any references to the social relational contexts of their lives that might provide the grounds for excusing, justifying, denying or minimising their abuse". The work of facilitators is to challenge the men to see themselves as independent people, able to make decisions, and be fully responsible for their own behaviour.

The potential need for other or additional therapeutic interventions for some men participating in this group is evident. Many have experienced serious abuse in their past, including sexual and physical abuse, mental and emotional abuse, and neglect or abandonment. These issues are likely to come up during discussions about learned behaviour and attitudes towards domestic violence and responsible parenting. One man's memory was "I remember when I was young having to jump in front of my mum so she wouldn't get hit " and on seeing the rage expressed in a 10-year-old's painting, one man said "That's the way I felt when I saw my father push my mother down the stairs when I was 12". Another horrific incident that exemplifies the terror some boys have grown up in was recalled by one man who, in thinking of his childhood, wrapped himself into a ball on his chair and with his head down, in tears, said "We got used to the punches and the name calling but the worst was, one day my dad made all us kids go outside and he lined us up and made us watch while he shot the family dog".

While these kinds of disclosures are handled sensitively and respectfully by facilitators, most would agree the group setting is limited and inappropriate in any way to adequately process these kinds of experiences. Recommendations for further therapeutic interventions and counselling are made on the exit report and discussed with the participant by facilitators and their probation and parole officers.

Sessions

Each session begins with a check-in time where each man is asked about any incidents of abuse, control or violence in the past week, or a high risk time where they could have used abuse or violence but used respectful non-violent strategies. It is imperative that if high risk situations are disclosed that these scenarios be worked on in the main body of the session (through skills practice and role plays) so that this participant and others can see alternative decisions that can be made by them to ensure the immediate safety of their partners and children. Sometimes the content of a session can change because the imperative of dealing with the recent abuse or violence of a group member is paramount and their immediate incident may become the teaching tool for that session.

Often there are no admissions: however when a participant begins to take responsibility for his domestic violence this tends to correlate with more honest disclosure about current abuse. This may be confirmed or refuted by the content of partner reports. Conversely, men who are highly and currently dangerous may disclose serious violence during check-in. For example, one man admitted that the previous day he had punched his wife and dragged her through the house by her hair and was verbally abusive. Before the session started he had also disclosed this to his probation and parole officer. He made no attempt to remove himself from the situation or to employ any safety strategies during this incident. The police were not called to the incident. Facilitators were in a position of processing this incident in the group with the emphasis and concern on her safety, the seriousness of this abuse and what immediate actions would be taken due to this admission. The facilitators followed safety protocol, policy and procedures and called police to request a welfare visit to her address.

Observer role

The Men's Domestic Violence Education and Intervention Program uses accountability processes to ensure transparency of program content and enable partner agencies to observe group sessions. One of the ways this is achieved is by inviting observers to attend and review the process. Observers are screened by the coordinator of the men's program, and it is open to probation and parole officers, women's advocates, facilitators, student social workers, researchers or academics, members of the police service or judiciary (with the object of exposure and education). Observers read and sign a behaviour and confidentiality agreement. The feedback of observers is valuable and considered seriously by facilitators and the program coordinator. Feedback from women's advocates is especially important to ensure that the program remains accountable to victim experiences.

Exit reports – recommendations

The coordinator of the men's program completes an exit or exclusion report about each participant which is sent to the appropriate probation and parole officer. An exclusion report states the level of risk, details of attendance, participation and reason for exclusion (which may include non-attendance, drug and alcohol issues, consistent disruptive behaviour or continued stance of denial past 12 weeks) and a recommendation that the person receive appropriate intervention or begin the 24 week program again. The exit report includes level of risk at completion of the program, details of attendance and participation and a recommendation for further therapeutic intervention, counselling or group work. As stated above, in this client group many have issues with self-esteem, interpersonal skills, the results of childhood sexual, physical and mental abuse, or grief and loss. At times these issues arise for some men in the group setting and, though acknowledged at the time, may require appropriate individual intervention or counselling sessions at the conclusion of the program. These recommendations are clearly stated on the exit report with possible referral sources. The probation and parole officer reviews these exit reports with the offender during a regular reporting session.

Conclusion

The foundation of the Men's Domestic Violence Education and Intervention Program rests on the fact that a number of agencies take specific responsibilities in its operation. This integration allows for the safety of women and their children to be the primary concern in monitoring the men's participation in the program. Underpinning this are clear guidelines and procedures for managing all stages of participation in the program. An essential program element is the facilitation of opportunities for women to be engaged by advocates for support and feedback when their partner or former partner attends the program. As such the main strengths of the men's program as it operates within the integrated response are:

- It sends a clear message that violence is unacceptable in the community ;
- It holds men accountable for their violence;
- It holds men responsible for change;
- It keeps the safety of women and children central;
- It provides a practical opportunity and place for individual men to examine and challenge their own beliefs, attitudes and behaviours and to work towards respect, equality and non-violence;
- It is part of a broader cross-agency response to domestic violence.

There are many challenges in providing this type of program to offenders who are often reluctant and resistant to addressing their abusive and violent behaviour. Facilitators need to be sufficiently personally and professionally reflexive in their knowledge and skills in working in a gendered environment. Facilitators need to be professionally updated through reading widely on the subject, attending updated training, by critically analysing program aims, content and delivery and by receiving regular supervision and debriefing. Appropriate processes need to be in place to support facilitators with professional development, supervision and breaks to ensure sustainability. The key challenge for facilitators, however, is maintaining the balance between respectfully inviting the men to take responsibility and challenging entitled beliefs and attitudes towards the use of control and violence over women.

Chapter 8

Connecting Theory and Practice: Group Work

Tony Fletcher[1]

This chapter discusses some practices that I have found useful when working in a Men's Stopping Violence Group (MSVG) in South Australia. These practices encourage men to confront their sense of gendered entitlement. Male privilege is something that perpetrators of domestic violence take for granted when they join a group intervention program. The practice strategies described in this chapter aim to challenge and disrupt men's assumptions about their relationships and use of violence against women and children. The practices are informed by feminist assertions which promote the rights of women and children to live safely as the key priority in domestic violence interventions. The application of each practice is described in relation to its theoretical underpinnings. However, it is first important to say a little about how I became involved in this type of work.

A Brief History of Me in the World and in the Work

I was indirectly, and somewhat unexpectedly, introduced to working with men who use violence towards women and children in 1996 as a student at the then Department of Social Security. My memory is one of self-consciously trying to help a woman gain access to emergency payments so that she could escape further violence from her then "husband". I had an intellectual understanding of the potential impact of being subjected to violence, coupled with a personal belief in the right to safety. At the same time though, in retrospect, I had very little comprehension of the real

1 Although this paper appears under my name, many women and men have contributed over the years to the growth of the ideas contained within. In particular I would like to acknowledge the inspiration and contributions that I have received, and continue to receive, from Jussey Verco and Elaine Lloyd.

impact of domestic violence on women, children, and indeed on men. I decided to try to learn more about how men can hurt people they say that they care about, and this led me to examine the meaning of masculinity, and the process of becoming a man for both myself and for those who perpetrate violence against women.

Prior to going to university I had worked for five years on multi-storey building sites. I entered this job after five years of education at an all white, male private grammar school. The men I had been formally schooled with and the men I worked with manifested their masculinity in strikingly similar ways. What most struck me was how easily I had moved across the worlds of the lunch shed, old scholars club and then tutorial room. There was unmistakable and unavoidable, ridicule around perceived and/or actual transgressions of the dominant theme of heterosexual masculinity. Few of these men spoke of hurting women, yet statistically it is clear that a number of these men are likely to have been abusive to their partners at the time. I do remember one particular occasion when I overheard one man telling his work mates how he had told his partner to tell her parents that her black eye was a result of a suitcase falling off a cupboard. The men present were silent. At the time I did not understood this silence as supporting violence to women, but it is now clear to me how the collective silence of men perpetuates violence to women and children.

The sense of being able to offer little other then practical assistance to the woman in the Social Security office whose life had been so affected by a man's violence led me to take up an offer of a second practicum at the then Adelaide Central Mission Counselling Services team where my focus was working with men. It was through the work being done there and spending some time with the writings of Michael White (1989, 1991, 1995, 1997, 2000) and Alan Jenkins (1990) that I began to develop my practice and ideas in line with feminist theories regarding men's uses of violence. I then worked as a Regional Men's Domestic Violence Worker before moving to the Northern Violence Intervention Program (NVIP) where I currently work as a Senior Men's Worker, while also studying for a PhD.

The Northern Violence Intervention Project

The NVIP was set up in Adelaide in 1997 as part of an integrated program bringing together a criminal justice and therapeutic response to men's uses of violence to female partners and/or children. The work done at the program is underpinned by the principles of safety, responsibility, accountability and respect. Men are typically referred to the program as part of a community corrections order, although the program also works with "socially mandated" men - voluntary clients who experience informal pressure to change their behaviour, either from family and friends or other agencies. A man who is assessed as suitable for a MSVG has stated that he is willing to accept that he has used violence, and accepts some level of responsibility for his violence. He is then invited (or in the case of men who come via correctional services directed) to attend a 26 week MSVG. The project also offers services to women and children who have been affected by the man's violence.

Theoretical understandings of violence

Therapeutic work with individual perpetrators has developed from a diverse range of theories and practices (see Chung, Zanettino and O'Leary 2004; Holder 2001; Laing 2000, 2002). Sometimes practitioners feel that theories do little to inform their practice, and yet the theoretical position often determines how the ontology of the problem is constituted. The practices discussed in this chapter have their basis in feminist theories[2] and post-structural social theories of knowledge. Although this can be a contested partnership, the linking of post-structural and feminist theories to the practices of intervention is important for my work. Thus, language, and not assuming that what a word means is the same for all of us, is paramount (White 1997). The words we use to describe our lives have the capacity to perform what Foucault (1972) describes as an "enunciative function". That is, statements about violence contain descriptive words that determine how the problem is understood, and both constrain and enable any possibilities for change.

In my work the naming of violence and discussion around the term "responsibility" is an important part of the assessment sessions. The MSVG provides an important opportunity for men to reiterate their earlier acknowledgment of their violence and their commitment to change in front of other men, both individually and as a group. Therapeutic practices of unconditional believing are not helpful here. The worker has a responsibility to invite the man to face inconsistencies in his story, to confront the man about missing pieces that cover over important aspects of his decision making. It is important to be clear that the MSVG is a stopping violence group. The rest of this chapter deals with three different aspects of the way in which the issue of stopping violence is described.

Deciding

I align with feminist theories that men's uses of violence are *decisions* that men make in a socio-cultural context of gendered entitlement and male privilege. The aim is to encourage the man to connect the intention of his decision to act violently with the notion that violence is a strategy used to maintain power and control over his partner.

---

2 Margaret McLaren (1997: 119) comments that feminists are diverse in their epistemological positions whilst sharing a recognition of the oppression of women. [W]ithin contemporary feminist discourses on violence against women power is seen as understood as oppressive, coercive or subjugating force: a means of domination in which the dominant agent affects the subordinate agent in a negative manner via a host of hierarchical social relationships, social contexts and institutionalise structures and practices (Wartenburg 1990).

When inviting men to consider how they make the decision to use violence, I have found it important to consider the ways in which "culture constructs the scope of our identities" (Sinfield 1992: 204). Connell (2000: 18) further comments that "understanding gender requires more than an examination of men as a statistical category ... we must examine men's gender practices, and the ways that the gender order defines, positions, empowers and constrains men". This invites us to consider male identity as fluid rather than fixed or static, and our clients as men who have used or "do" violence, rather than as "violent men".

Responsibility

Men's attempts to externalise responsibility for their use of violence have been understood by researchers and practitioners as a means of escaping being held accountable (Jenkins 1990). Male privilege allows men to move through their communities with an exaggerated sense of their entitlement to exert power and authority over others. Many men when spoken to after having used violence will discuss a feeling of powerlessness at the time, a long history of abuse and disrespect at the hands of other men, and relationships with alcohol, other drugs, and life stressors on which they then choose to blame the violence. They place the responsibility for the actual violence outside of themselves and their conscious decision making. However, it is important that these stories of racial, class and economic injustice are not summarily dismissed - the material effects of injustice on individual men's lives are very real (Smith 1996).

Thin descriptions of men's lives can limit discussions to over-simplified ways of thinking about men which can offer further support to the very ideas that alienate practice, and men, from the context of gendered inequalities. However, it is essential that the primary focus of the intervention remains on the safety of women and children. Inquiring into experiences of injustice and disrespect may help clients to reconnect with anti-violence stances they have taken, yet inquiry must be applied strategically towards the overall aim of increasing the safety of women and children. From my own work with men, the "doxa[3] of male domination" (Bourdieu 2001) can have men looking for opportunities to discuss anything but their uses of violence. Sometimes this can be a slightly more comfortable place for workers too.

Feedback from men in the program is that the use of diagrams on whiteboards to demonstrate concepts is particularly useful to them. With this in mind much of my work has been an attempt to bring what can seem like complex ideas into easily understandable and retainable visual representations. The following diagram demonstrates a technique for highlighting the importance of taking full responsibility (see Figure 8.1).

---

3 Pervasiveness or lack of paradox.

Figure 8.1. Responsibility Facing Exercise

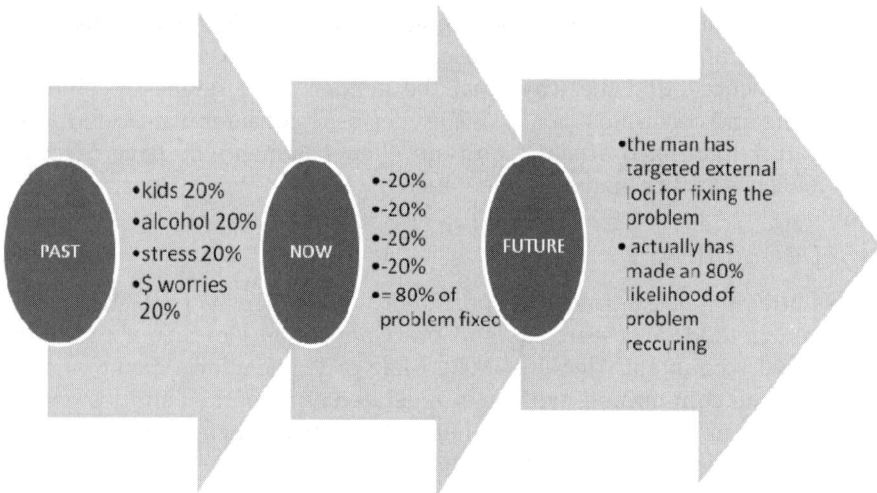

I explain that men can try to solve problems, sometimes with honourable intentions, in ways that actually contribute further to the problem. Jenkins (1990) refers to these as "misguided attempts". In this exercise I encourage men to look outside themselves. The discussion goes somewhat as follows:

> *[O]ften when we meet with men they indicate to us that a whole lot of "things" have contributed to their using violence. Men often discuss these events and things in their lives as the actual problem. They then set about thinking that each "thing" adds to the other "thing" to exert pressure on him and that this is the reason the violence occurred. Something like giving 20 per cent to alcohol, 20 per cent to noisy kids, 20 per cent to an abusive boss, 20 per cent to money worries, etc. A bloke can then set about "fixing" those problems. One man discussed moving to afternoon shift so he won't be able to drink after work, the kids are all in bed when he gets home and at school during the day, he is getting better money and gets along better with that afternoon shift boss. So he then tricks himself into thinking that 80 per cent of the problem is fixed. Our take on this is that he has given 80 per cent of the responsibility to things and/or situations meaning that he has actually created an 80 per cent likelihood of violence recurring. We also find that most men when we first meet with them want to blame their partner for at least 50 per cent of the reason the man has used the violence, by saying things like, "it takes two to tango", "you can't argue by yourself", etc. Some blame her more, some a bit less. My guess is that men here have at times got caught up in wanting to shift at least some of the responsibility to the person they scared and/or hurt. So if for this man we add his "mis-guided efforts" to the blaming of his partner he has potentially locked in a 130 per cent chance*

> *of future violence. Now many men might have one or two things that they give varying percentages of responsibility to. If it was 10 per cent or 130 per cent, how much percentage of a risk of future violence do you think your family should live with?(Answers are usually "none".) Which ideas about blame are more likely to support the intention to reintroduce a violence free life for you and your family?*

This straightforward approach clearly articulates a potential problem with continuing stories of full responsibility taking (not blaming other people or things). I would now like to spend some more time on this issue of connecting men to ways of thinking about taking responsibility.

I have begun to examine the use and meaning of the word "responsibility" when talking with men in practice. After long conversations with Jussey Verco[4] (social worker, colleague and friend) that were stimulated by thinking that men "just didn't get it", or "refused to", or "didn't have to", we spent some time questioning the way we and the men used and responded to the word "responsibility". It was a challenging conversation for both of us because our practice had been guided by the almost unquestionable assumption of "men taking total responsibility for their actions". Boldly expecting men to accept full responsibility for the acts of violence they had perpetrated underpins all our conversations with men and is considered optimal practice. However, in conversations with men the term "responsibility" seemed to lack directness. This "at times" made it easier for men to avoid facing the strategic application of violence and proved problematic in terms of inviting men to discuss future decision making. This led to an exercise at the MSVG where we invited men to respond to questions such as: *"What hopes do you have for your relationship with your partner and children?"*, *"What kind of father do you wish to be?"* and *"What words would you like your children to use to describe you?"*

We wanted to ask men about the ways in which they hoped their role in the family might be described by people affected by, and witness to, their efforts to be a partner, father and/or carer. What we hoped for were responses such as:

- The men stood by their word (so if they were going to take kids to sporting activities, they would make sure they were there to do so and they would do this willingly, not begrudgingly, so their children and partners could rely on them).
- The men did not wish to cause their children and partners distress (so if they had a hard day at work, they would find ways to address anger/ frustrations / disappointments that did not include taking their anger out on the family. Maybe they would go for a walk

4 I would really like to thank and acknowledge Jussey for her years of contribution to this work and her fantastic support in getting this particular idea into our practice and into this chapter.

before going home. Maybe they would just talk it calmly through with their partner, etc).

- The men would pay their fair share of the bills (and not put pressure on their partner to meet all the household costs while they kept money for their "personal expenses" – beer, cigarettes, hobbies, drugs, etc).

The questions were designed to encourage men to think about their actions and the impact of their actions on their partner and children. We were hoping that the men would be thinking about more loving, kind, respectful, inclusive ways of being with them. Ways of being a "man" which meant that they *did* have to think about their actions and *did* need to take into account what they said and why. We were hoping that men would be thinking about ways in which they are responsible, but in ways that expressed love, affection, tenderness, commitment and so on.

What the men spoke about were ways of being partners, fathers and carers that drew from the dominant discourses of heterosexual masculinity. There were clear stories about being "responsible" men, but these stories seemed more attached to the mechanistic type of man as breadwinner, disciplinarian, decision maker, authority figure, apex of the family, "king of the castle". Notwithstanding that these gendered positions may encompass important ethical positions on the part of the men in relation to their honourable intentions towards their families, our concerns are the potentially unhelpful consequences when these ideas are uncritically adopted by men and workers as "evidence of change", "what he really stands for", or "who he really is". Many examples that the men offered regarding "responsible acts" reflected and reinforced normative male gender roles and appeared to contribute to the man being able to exceptionalise his use of violence and present himself as the "responsible, yet sometimes violent man" (eg, *"I may not be perfect but at least I support my family, that's more than some blokes")*. The increased tension and fear that women and children experience when men build stories that they should be congratulated, thanked and/or exceptionalised for attending the MSVG has been fed back to facilitators. It has been important to invite men to rethink that any sense of alienation from their family is a result of their abuses, and not the family's lack of appreciation for his efforts to provide.

In short, the rhetoric of responsibility provided disengagement points for men that tended to undermine the intentions of therapy. A less ambiguous word was needed. Thus we began to invite men to think more about practices of "blaming" and "not blaming" when discussing their violence, and to promote intimate relationships that are more about partnership than ownership. Our experience so far is that these semantic shifts have made it harder for men to avoid these issues. Later in this chapter you will notice that the terms "blaming" and "not blaming" are used in conjunction with building an ethical platform from which men can speak about non-violence and take stances against violence.

Naming violence

Laing (2000: 1) has commented that "there is no uncontested terminology or definition of behaviours referred to as domestic and family violence". When it has come to issues of definition most men I have worked with have not struggled with naming physical acts as violence, and have often commented ontologically regarding psychological abuse and /or emotional abuse. In the initial stages of meeting with men it is important for the therapist[5] and the man to be clear as to the dimensions of the problem to be discussed. Responsibility models advocate inviting the man to name his own behaviours as violent in the initial stages of therapy, and/or the worker taking the responsibility to introduce the concept. I have found this practice politically and therapeutically important, and would further suggest that this naming of behaviours as acts of violence should be ongoing.

Laing (2000) has described how men's acknowledgment of their use of violence can be related to the continued revisiting of "problem definition". This means that it is potentially unhelpful to develop "fixed" stories and we should find a way to discuss the use of violence that allows us to move with the possibility, that as time goes on, the man may experience a desire, consciousness and/or commitment to change that offers him a space to also describe other acts as violence. Violence is thus configured within ideological, cultural and political moments of social formations. Within therapeutic responses the events containing violence are understood as having greater significance than the perpetration of an act alone but become where violence functions in the production of a masculinity that is a situational accomplishment of identity in a context of gendered entitlement and male privilege (Kaufman 1993; Butler 1995)

Traditionally, the process of "defining violence" entailed separating violence into distinct categories and then inviting the men at the group to fill in the categories. Categories such as "physical", "psychological", "emotional", "spiritual", "social" and "sexual" violence can be used for this purpose. Categorical naming is useful in encouraging men to identify an action and /or range of actions as a form of violence. However practices of categorisation can introduce problems as described in Table 8.1.

An important aim of intervention is to engage men in broadening their understanding of what violence they engage in. Men are asked to comment on their use of violence starting with thinking about the impact on their female partner and/or children. This shift starts with the practice of decentring male definitions of violence. Groups can be invited to clarify the sorts of things men do that hurt, frighten and intimidate women and children. Men can be invited to consider what it would mean to be *unwilling* to spend time examining what they do that has these effects on women and children.

5 Though the term "therapist" can be contentious. Given that situates the work that is being done with the man and how it constitutes the problem, I choose to refer to the person working with the man as the "therapist".

Table 8.1. Possible Problems Arising from Violence Categorisations

Hierarchalisation	Where a man may decide that these categories need to be ordered in terms of seriousness, thus directing him away from attending to actions he regards as "not so serious"
Minimisation	Where a man may decide that, as he has not named that he has used violence in certain categories, he is therefore "not as bad" as other men in the room and thus does not really need to address his use of violence
Impermeability	The density, or "doxa" of the term "violence" having been defined through a lens of physical violence seeming at times almost impenetrable for some men, ie, violence is just like this and thus not that. This can be reinforced by the responses of the criminal justice system
Dispersion	Broadening the term to include a wide range of acts which can have the unintended effect of men stepping away from the goal as unachievable
Dilution	Expanding the definition unintentionally which offers men space to make invisible important acknowledgments related to the severity of some acts, eg, a serious physical assault gets collapsed back into the range of actions and thus loses it's severity
Patriachalisation	Important questions of what might it mean for men who have used violence to engage in practices of generating what violence consists of, and thus a possible unhelpful binary of what it does not – men can reinvest in a masculinity of "expert" as a way of negotiating shame
Invisibilisation	Where women and children's voices of their experiences of men's uses of violence are invisible
Professionalisation	Reconstituting the discourse regarding violence through the lens of professional discourses can have the effect of separating men's use of violence from issues of broader structural gender inequality and reconfiguring it as a problem that resides within *men* as a collective, or individual men[6] – the psycholisation of context.
Decontextualising	Defining violence as categorised acts can have the effect of separating the actions from the intentions, invisibilising a socio-cultural context of male domination[7]
Exaggeration	Men being able to clearly engage with the naming of violence as an academic exercise, as an out there in the world phenomena, has led to some men then over exaggerating this naming in the overall goal of "stopping violence"

6 Bagshaw and Chung (2000: 12) comment that "to be relevant it must be theoretically based and take into account the social and cultural context and the diversity of people's experiences … by ignoring issues of power and gender as central to domestic violence, the issue of masculine violence is ignored, placing female victims of domestic violence in a more dangerous and more fearful position".

7 Stanko (1985: 18) has commented that "by separating women's experiences of physical and sexual assault from women's experiences of sexual and physical intimidation, as many are likely to do, we see each assault as an aberration or a random occurrence … a 'person problem' … if we link them together we can create new information on the overall treatment of women by men. What emerges is not random or isolated. What emerges is a flood of common experiences". This Stanko believes will foreground that "men's power is not an individual, but a collective one" (1985: 57).

The process engages men in commenting on:

> *[W]hat sorts of actions have you done, know about or guess could cause* physical injury *... have a partner or child feel* intimidated *... get that partner or child to feel* threatened *by you ... get them to be* frightened *that you might hurt them further ... and thus have them feel* restricted *about what they do or say around you?*

The men can be invited to discuss:

> *What sorts of things do men do that can have women and/or children feeling threatened?*
>
> *What sorts of activities do men engage in that can have women and children feeling frightened?*
>
> *What sorts of actions can men use in an effort to intimidate women and/or children?*
>
> *What actions can men engage in that physically harm?*

Before the conversation moves towards connecting the actions with an intention, it is important that the issue of sexual violence is named. Within MSVGs that are facilitated by a man and a woman, it has been the male facilitator's responsibility to introduce this.[8] I have attempted to do this by seeking to open the space for this conversation in the following way:

> *There are some really important ways in which men can relate to women that have not been clearly named or spoken about tonight ... ways that men are often very hesitant to discuss. Conversations with women who have been through this program have highlighted how important it is that men speak about how they relate to women regarding issues of physical intimacy. What we have come to understand is that sometimes when men are seeking physical intimacy with their female partners there is tension. Are there men here who reckon they have noticed those tensions?*

The term "tension" is used strategically to overcome men's general hesitance to begin to discuss sexual violence. At this point the conversation may be taken up with one or a number of men who have displayed a willingness to face this issue:

---

8 When I have co-facilitated MSVGs with other men, it has been important to engage appropriate gender accountability practices. The move has been to initiate a pre-MSVG discussion with female colleagues about the upcoming intention to name men's uses of sexual violence at the MSVG. These conversations regarding men's uses of sexual violence require particular attention to frank and honest discussion that is governed by respectful ways of describing women and children. This is the responsibility of the facilitators, but it is also important to consult with female colleagues. I would like to acknowledge the contributions of Natalie Marshall, who as a female colleague provided generous and considered conversation that contributed greatly to this way of dealing with the issue.

What sorts of tensions have you noticed?

How did you understand that at the time?

My guess is that there would have been times when you would have struggled to negotiate that tension. What sorts of things have you tried to do to get an outcome that was more about what you wanted to happen?

Talking about this now, has that affected how you think about those actions? In what ways?

I know that she is not here to ask, so we are really making a bit of a guess, but what do you think it might have been like for her when you treated her that way?

During this exercise the men's responses are transcribed onto a whiteboard amongst the "various forms of violence". Sometimes the board fills up quickly. Sometimes the men need prompting. Sometimes a facilitator has had to open the space with questions about the silence, and the implications of the men allowing the silence to continue. Men can then be invited to consider what it means if they let this sense of shame silence them. Once the board begins to fill up the men are invited to comment on what is written in front of them. Some comments that men have made include:

There are so many things that she could feel abused by.

I never thought there would be so many.

Some of those things I would have done, but I would never have realised that they could have affected her like that.

I don't realise that I do some of those things, but I reckon that I would have.

It is so much more than the physical stuff.

It's a lot more than the physical. I reckon that the non-physical things tend to happen more often too.

There would be lots of ongoing effects from this stuff wouldn't there?

All of this would have to affect their (women partners) self-esteem. Affect how they are around you ... lots of ongoing effects too.

It sort of shows you how you could be abusing her even when you aren't even angry.

A number of the statements above illustrate ways in which a man may get away from acknowledging that his uses of violence were decisions he made with a hoped for outcome. The next step is to invite the men to open a space to question the intention of their actions: "*How is it that these sorts of actions can have women and children feeling restricted by you?*"

If the men have not raised it, the concept of fear is introduced into the conversation. Rarely will men suggest that fear is a goal, a strategic manoeuvre that helps them to realign or invigorate hierarchies of gendered male authority. However one man chillingly reported *"You know if she's scared enough she will do anything for you ... it's all easy from there on"*. Previously, I noted the problematic nature of inviting men to define women's experiences, however we would now move the exercise into the area of men's assumptions about the impact of their actions. It is important to remind men that those affected by their violence are not there to comment, so we are making some predictions and/or guesses. Another is to issue an invitation to men to speak about the impact they have noticed their uses of violence have had on their partner and/or children. What is most useful is if individual men are first encouraged to speak about the manifestations of fear (tears, requests to stop, leaving, cowering, etc), then to build this conversation into one about the restrictions the threat and/or fear of future violence places upon women. At this point in the conversation I have used a visual representation of the impact. This is the trust graph (see Figure 8.2). The conversation begins by renaming the hopes men might have had for their relationships. What comes out of this are such things as happiness, love, trust, respect, honesty.

Figure 8.2. Exploring the Impact of Violence – The Trust Graph

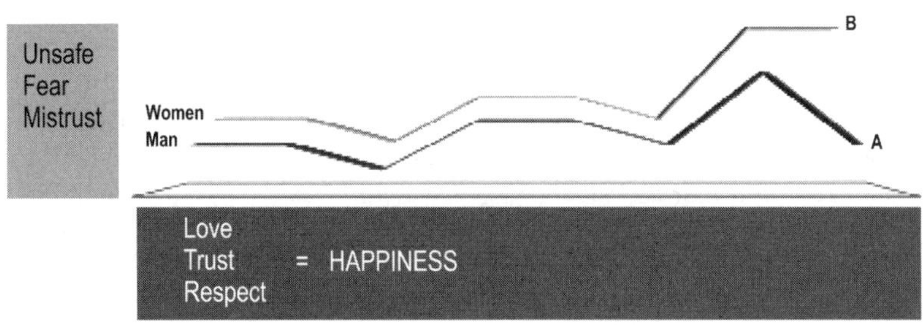

When I have facilitated this exercise I have opened it in the following way:

Men often say to us that they have some hopes about their lives. One hope has often been to meet a woman and have a satisfying relationship with her. This may have started with the man and the woman working towards goals of love, trust, respect, happiness (mark the y axis to show the start of the path for the man just underneath a path for the women). *Yet men here have all told us that there have been times when they have betrayed these goals and acted violently towards their female partner* (draw a line that heads towards the x axis, then stop and move diagonally upwards and away). *These uses of violence move the man and the woman away from the preferred type of relationship* (point to x axis and draw a line for the women that mirrors that of the man), *and introduce and/ or amplify fear and mistrust of you* (point to y axis). *What we have come to understand is that when we meet with men there has usually been a history of the man acting abusively accompanied by a history of trying to work back toward the preferred relationship* (repeat heading towards x axis and away again in a series of up and downs getting progressively further away from the x-axis). *What this can mean for the woman is that she has been abused and then encouraged and/or expected to move with the man back into trust, etc, then she is abused again and is again encouraged and/or expected to move back towards trust, etc. This can occur many times* (draw a series of lines heading to x then sharp inclines, then move back towards the x axis then sharp inclines – almost mirroring the way the line for the men goes up and down. It is important that with each move away from the x-axis the distance from x increases). *When we meet men they are often about here* (point to A), *desperate to get to* (point to x axis) *as fast as possible. The efforts of the man then can become caught up in how quickly he wants to feel like he is in a loving relationship and tend to cover over what it might have been like for the his partner and children. This can then be where a man might use denial, minimisation, justifications and/or put pressure on others to "forget the past" and join him back on working on, or just expecting, love and trust. If your partner has been through this what do you think it might be like for her to now feel pressured to go where you want to* (point to the x axis)? *What might it suggest to her if she felt any pressure from you to hurry up and forget, or to take you back, or even to stay with you, if she may not want that or if she wants time or space to think it through?*

At this point men often start to discuss their sense of what might be the women's experience of being encouraged and/or pressured to prematurely disengage with fear and mistrust (point B): *Scarey. She wouldn't want to trust you. It would just be like abusing her again. It would just be showing her that you haven't changed at all. It would tell her that things will be the same again later, same abuse and violence as you did to her before.*

It has then been useful to consider how it is that men can delude themselves regarding the experience of women and children who have been subjected to abuse. An exercise has been used that invites consideration of the role of gendered entitlement in men's efforts to construct a partial genealogy of the relationship (see Figure 3). This exercise invites the men to consider our experience that men prefer to construct their relationships through progressive narratives where acts of violence become displaced by "the good times".

Figure 8.3. Exercise on Gendered Entitlement

This exercise can proceed in the following way:

Our experiences of working with men and hearing the stories of women and children is that men can get themselves caught up in wanting to think about acts of violence as isolated incidents.

How men attempt to describe the current state of their relationship

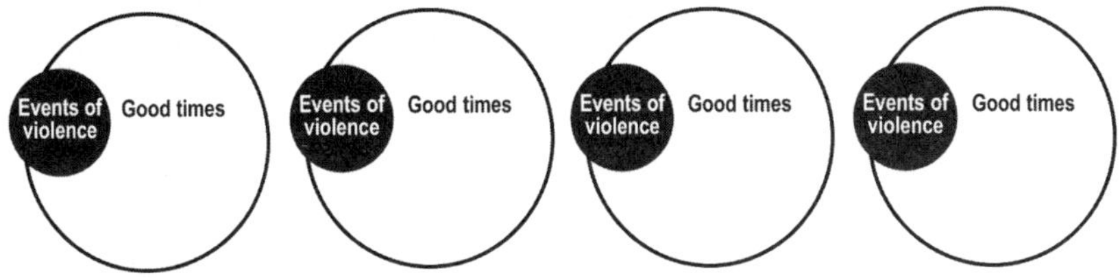

Acts of violence are described as slips in the relationship, setbacks and mistakes that are relegated to the history of the relationship. Men have also represented their relationships as being a mixture of times when they abused their partner and "lots of good times" as well. What we notice men tend to do with these two pieces of information is to subtract one from the other.

Ways men describe the relationship to themselves to avoid there being a problem

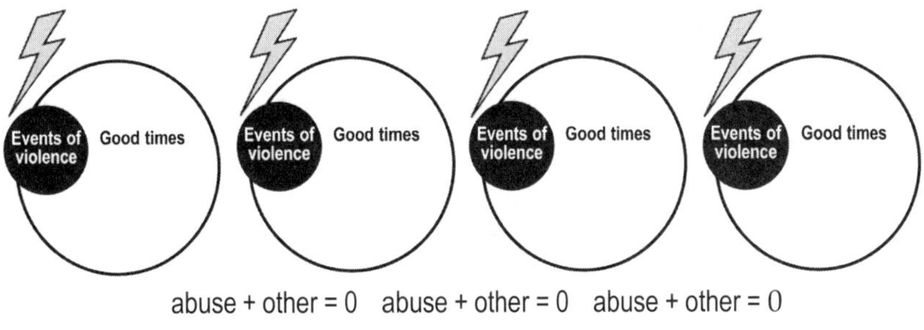

Cancelling out the violence with the "good times" shows how the man can attempt to describe the relationship as containing violence, but overall as being good. Our experience of talking with women and children is that for them it is often incremental. Each time they are hurt and frightened contributes to an over all story of fear and tension. Though the women and children may also value, and even enjoy, the good times, the relationship is one that occurs with a growing fear and mistrust of both the man and *the good times. This contributes to an experience that women and children often talk of as being like walking on eggshells.*

Women and children's experiences of a history of violence used against them

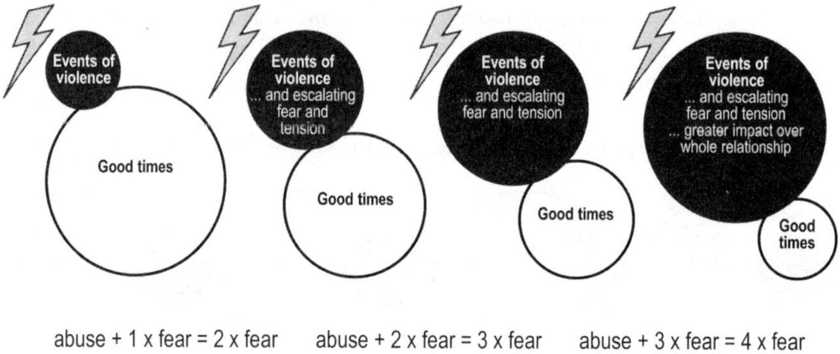

The connection that men can then be helped to make is how it is that they have allowed themselves to become caught up in such a one-sided view of the state of fear and mistrust in their family. This discussion is important for the man to realise that any emotional distance he may experience from his family, no matter how great the good times may be, may be attributed to their fear, distrust, anger and even dislike or loathing of him based on his having repeatedly hurt them, rather than to what he describes as their "ingratitude".

The next step is to invite men to interrogate the "Big 5" when it comes to their descriptions of relationships with female partners: love, trust, respect, honesty, happiness (see Figure 8.4).

It is helpful to discuss what men have told us they see as valuable in relationships: love, trust, respect, honesty and happiness ("*What men have told us they are working for*"), and then to discuss the fact that all the men in the group have told us that they have hurt people they care about by using a form or forms of violence, and that naming that was an important step they have all acknowledged they needed to take ("*The presenting problem*"). It is then possible to observe that many men come to join the group with a story that attributes blame to something external to themselves ("*What men describe as the problem*"). The men are then invited to consider that they arrived with a problem that they described as an inability to exert inner control and/or an inability to control the effects of external stimuli upon their behaviour. Each man has then been through an individual and collective process where he has been expected to face that his use of violence was a decision that he made. The men are asked what it has meant to be able to have this opportunity to open up what they may have allowed themselves to assume was "normal" or what they worked hard to be able to describe as "OK". I then ask the men: "*What would it mean if some other concepts that you had been working with were flawed? What if not just the ideas that you used to understand your uses of violence were a problem,*

Figure 8.4. Relationships Exercise

The men can be introduced to the exercise by talking through the diagram below:

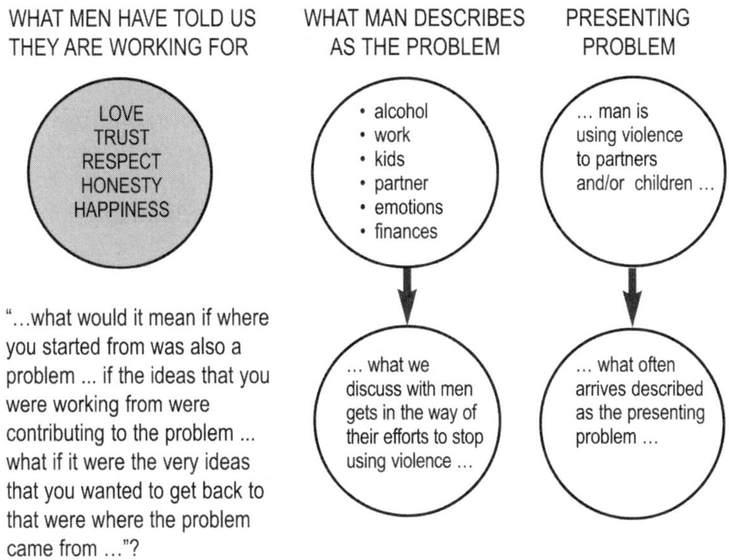

but the way you thought about relationships and what is important is a problem also? Would that be something you would want to know about?" The next step is to identify the issue of gendered entitlement in the man's ideas about what constitutes a successful relationship. This conversation is required to form a link with men's use of violence as tactical and strategic.

The intention in these exercises is to extend the practice of violence to the theory of gendered entitlement. At times, I have discussed with a man that when he sets out to achieve a particular outcome he works under a theory. A theory either about mechanics, electricity, loads and weights, what type of screw to use, etc. This type of mechanistic description of the relationship between the practices of violence and the theory of gendered entitlement has often made the link of a "theory to action" more available for men. These conversations help connect men to that their has been a rationale that has underpinned using violence to a woman partner. Similar to a tradesperson deciding to use a screw or a nail based on the outcome required, it is suggested to men that the types of violence chosen are also informed by a right 'tool for the job' relationship. The job being maintaining male privilege in their intimate relationship. It is often clear that the theories men carry about what underpins a "good relationship" are based on what is "good" for the man, rather than on the hopes and rights of women and children. Once again the intention is to invoke the binary. The men can be asked to consider what the use of violence has gained them. Men have in my experience had little trouble identifying such outcomes as: "*You can get your point across*", "*She will shut up and listen to you*", or "*Sometimes you just have had enough of the fight and you know that you can end it real easy if you break something or thump her*".

The men are then invited to comment on the role that respect for others plays in the use of violence to a female partner. In my experience this discussion has then moved into naming that it is a certain type of respect that supports the use of violence to women. This is worked through with all five relationship concepts (see Figure 8.5).

Figure 8.5. Invoking the Strategic Binary

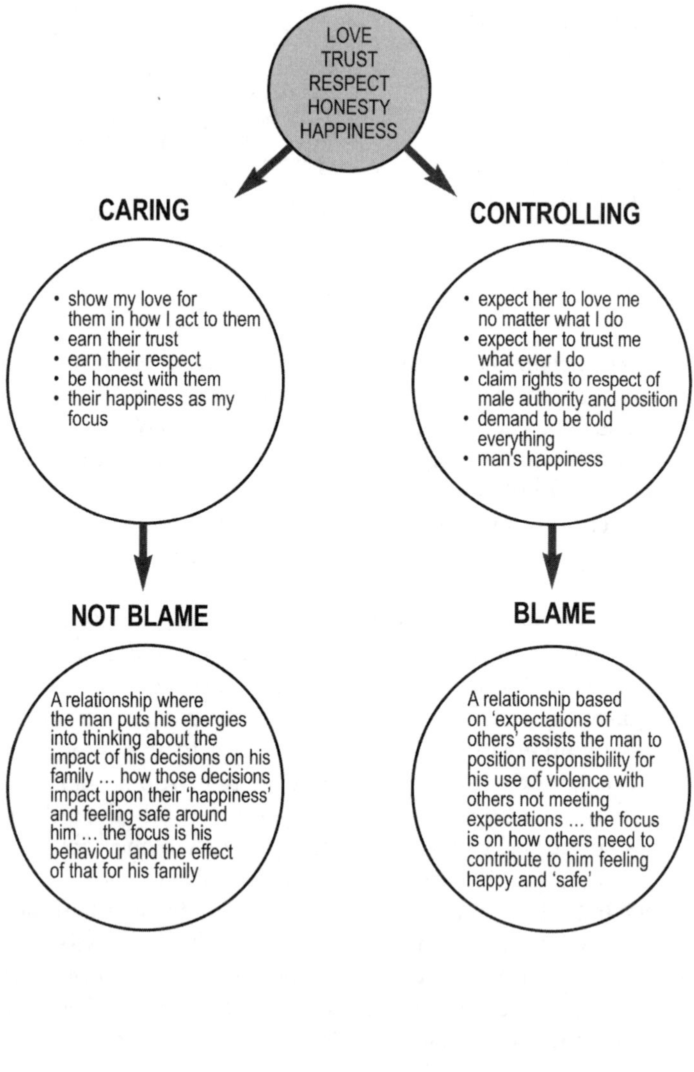

The implications for the man's family and for his self-respect if he were to continue to operate from a theory of controlling and practices of blaming are sought. I have often found it useful to invite men to consider at various points in these exercises what it means to have named these positions as caring vs controlling: "*What might it suggest about your priorities if, after having been offered this knowledge, you continue to argue for a lifestyle underpinned by what we named as controlling, and maintained your practices of blaming others for your abuse of them? How would that fit with how you would prefer to think about yourself? What would it mean for your partner and/or children? What would it take you to not care about to be able to continue to engage with controlling and ownership ways of being a man?*"

This exercise is often extended into conversations about how the men describe women in relation to the claims that they decide they are justified to make on women's lives. We do this through exploring how ideas of controlling and ownership frame the claims that men might make on women. We ask the men to consider taking a problem home and the different decisions made if they call in at a friend's house or go straight home. With the same levels of anger, frustration, upset, etc this exercise clearly demonstrates that the men make different *decisions* regarding behaviour based on how they frame what it is okay to subject a partner to, and appropriate behaviour to male friends. What is discussed is the man's focus on the woman's role in meeting his wants and desires, and his almost total overlooking of her as a mother, sister, friend, worker, someone's daughter, hoper, dreamer ... as a person. The first time we did this exercise we were overwhelmed about the effect on some men of considering their female partner as a person. This led to a man commenting "*I had never thought of her as a person before – she is just the missus*". Other men then joined in and one man contributed "*I had never even thought about her as a person with things she might want to do – or not. I never knew anything about her at all, yet she needed to know everything about me and even be able to predict what I wanted or risk getting a thump*".

What really helped in these exercises was maintaining a position of "not knowing" with the men. Our experience is that when worked through with "trouble and patience" (Jenkins 1990) men are willing to "educate" the facilitators.

What was highlighted for us was that if we are hoping to be successful in working with men so that they have more respectful and non-violent relationships with women, we need to make a serious effort to dismantle the men's doxa of gendered entitlement systematically, with clear deliberate attempts to expose and name patriarchal practices in an inquiring and experiential format.

Further conversations

To work effectively with men's violence, workers must be able to envisage male privilege while at the same time holding individual men accountable for their decisions. Workers must encourage men to think about their ideas about what it means to be a man. I hope that this chapter has highlighted the relationship of theory to practice, and has clarified that that theory is a form of practice. By talking about violence intervention, we are "doing" violence intervention. Therefore, it is so important that we take the time to question the presuppositions that inform how we put together concepts in the intervention.

Non-violence is not something that just occurs in the absence of violence. To fully acknowledge the density of practices of patriarchy and the claims these practices make on the lives of women (Pease 2001), practices of non-violence need to be engaged in. Such practices are unambiguously described to the men as distinctly different from ways in which they have come to understand their gendered power. To name men's uses of violence and not to connect this to a context of gendered entitlement, has been described as, at the best, unhelpful, but most probably as dangerous. Thinking about intervention practices and the lives of men we work with as not existing in a social vacuum helps us to avoid practices that are informed by "mechanistic" and/or simplistic theories of masculinities that are separated from culture. Feminist theories regarding discussions of power, knowledge, gender, identity and culture have offered my work with men a solid foundation for tackling individual men's uses of violence within a broader struggle for a gender equitable community.

As a practitioner I have placed great emphasis on spending time with theory. Developing a capacity to articulate the "the history of the whys, what do words *do* over what do they *mean*, and how words are connected together to produce things that are real but cannot be said to exist in essence, I see as an important way to display how I have put together knowledge and meaning in my work. The intention is to clarify how I have interrogated my privilege, understanding and political position in responding to men's use of violence towards women and children. This is an ongoing commitment that acknowledges that white men have a history of colonising knowledge and of using knowledge to colonise. In my practice I have found that the more attention I pay to these issues, the more competent I have become in engaging with the complexities of men as a group and each man as an individual. The challenge can be to avoid using theory too optimistically, pessimistically and/or uncritically. As Christopher McLean (1996: 12) succinctly puts it: "I am not interested in theory at all for its own sake … but I am interested in its role in facilitating change".

Chapter 9

Incubated in Terror,[1] Growing up to Terrorise: Implications for Domestic Violence Group Work Interventions

Maggie Woodhead

> [T]he victim was cooking a meal for the family. The accused became angry over the amount of hamburgers one of the six children present wanted … The victim has intervened and defended the child … The accused grabbed the victim by the shirt and punched the victim twice in the head with a closed right fist. The victim has then fallen to the ground. The accused then pulled out his genitals and said "I have the balls in this family, I'm the man". He then kicked the victim in the head with his right foot. The victim regained her feet and continued to cook the family meal. The accused … banged her head into the kitchen door three or four times. The accused sat back down on the couch and when the victim regained her composure she continued cooking. There were six children present during the incident. (*Extract from police statement of material facts*)

> [A]s she got out (of her car) the defendant grabbed her by the throat and dragged her into the house. The defendant dragged the complainant into the main bedroom of the house where he made her strip naked, punching her to the head and body. He dragged her into the bathroom by the hair and slammed her head into the edge of the toilet bowl several times before pushing her head into the toilet telling her he was going to kill her (he repeated this threat numerous times) … The defendant returned a few minutes later with a large kitchen knife and with a downward motion stabbed the complainant to the right hand side of the head, penetrating approximately 5 millimetres. He then made jabbing motions with the knife towards the complainant's stomach which she warded off with her arms (no wound caused). He repeatedly demanded the phone and laptop. She told him it was

1 This term was originally used by Perry (1997).

> in her car and he dragged her into the loungeroom again slamming her head into the walls and floor. He kicked her numerous times. He tied her hands with the belt from a dressing gown. (*Extract from police statement of material facts*)

> The accused and the complainant are in a defacto relationship and have been together for approximately 20 years. The accused is 40 years of age, 170 centimetres tall and medium build. The complainant is 45 years, 170 centimetres tall and slim build … the accused and the victim were at home watching television. The accused and the victim had been drinking earlier in the night. The accused started to accuse the victim of having an affair, a small verbal argument has developed. The accused went into the kitchen and smashed the spice rack on the kitchen floor. The accused called the victim into the kitchen and told her to clean the kitchen up. As the victim knelt down to pick up the spices and the broken rack, the accused kicked the victim to the right hand side of her chest that rendered her breathless and made her collapse to the floor. Whilst the victim lay motionless on the floor on her side, the accused stomped on her chest. While the victim was still on the floor the accused climbed on top of her and sat on her chest pinning her body to the floor. The accused took hold of both of the victim's arms and pinned them above her head. As the victim tried to get the accused off her, the accused headbutted the victim to the face causing the victim's nose to swell severely and start bleeding profusely. The accused released the victim's arms and punched the victim to the face, forehead and ear. This caused severe swelling to the forehead, swelling and bleeding to the ear, swelling and bleeding to her cheek. Upon police arrival the accused forced the victim into the bathroom and told her to clean her face and wash the blood off which the victim did as she was in fear that if she did not the accused would assault her again. The victim required medical attention and was conveyed to hospital by St John Ambulance. The accused was arrested and charged. (*Extract from police statement of material facts*)

These three brief descriptions illustrate vividly the behaviour that leads to referral to a perpetrators domestic violence program. This chapter proposes that the types of group work intervention for mandated domestically violent clients generally favoured by the criminal justice system (McGuire 1995) may not necessarily be the most effective form of intervention for a particular sub-group of domestically violent males who are mandated by the courts to attend domestic violence behaviour change programs. A model other than that of psycho-educational groups, most usually based on the Duluth model, is proposed.

It is widely acknowledged in the literature that domestic violence remains amongst the most common and the most under-reported of all crimes in Australia (Commonwealth Australia 2003) and different statistics regarding the prevalence and effects of domestic violence are reported in various parts of this book. Whilst the rate of females reporting incidents of physical assault by a male perpetrator has almost doubled over the last decade, from 19 per cent to 36 per cent (ABS 2006), these figures do not relate specifically or exclusively to the reporting of intimate partner violence. The Australian component of the International Violence Against Women Survey (Mouzos and Makkai 2004) identified that only 14 per cent of women reported the most recent incident of domestic violence to police. Western Australia police records show that over a 12 month period between 2007 and 2008 police attended 33,213 incidents of family and domestic violence in Western Australia. Between May 2007 and April 2008, 21 people lost their lives in Western Australia as a direct result of family and domestic violence. However, the drop-off rate between committing a domestic violence offence, through being charged, pleading or being found guilty and then on to becoming a court-mandated referral into a men's domestic violence perpetrator program is immense. In metropolitan Perth in October 2007 there were only 261 adult males on community based orders or parole who were either currently engaged in a domestic violence intervention program (155) or waitlisted to enter such a group (55). This suggests that any male who ends up in the judicial system with a domestic violence conviction and who is then mandated to participate in a domestic violence program is going to belong to a particular sub-set - more violent, more often and whose behaviour has greater negative consequences for adult and child victims.

Data collection

An electronic search of files on these 261 males revealed that their profile was similar to that of offenders generally, in regard to age (see Figure 9.1) and ethnicity (see Figure 9.2).

Figure 9.1. Age Distribution

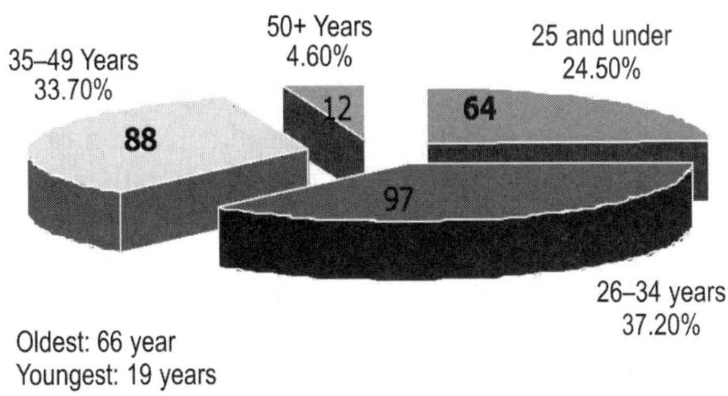

Figure 9.2. Ethnicity of Clients

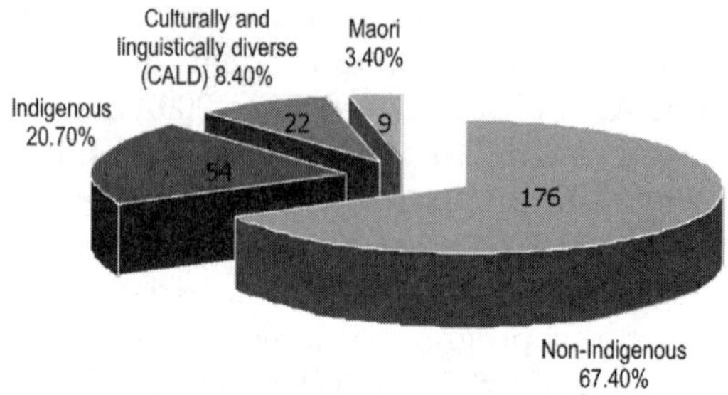

However, the percentage of these clients who had prior criminal histories (see Figure 3), most commonly drug and motor vehicle offences as well as, in almost half the cases, prior domestic violence related offences, was higher (82.8 per cent) than those on community based orders generally and, we might assume, very significantly higher than the vast majority of domestic violence perpetrators who never come within the ambit of the justice system.

Figure 9.3. Criminal with a Prior Criminal History

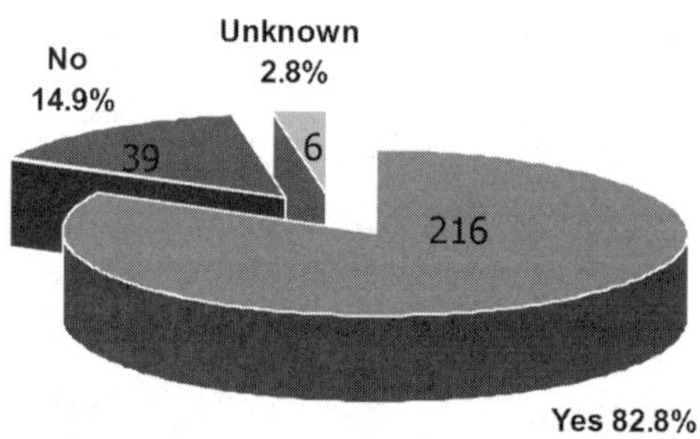

Every single one of these 261 clients had been convicted of actual physical violence against their (ex)partners, which is also not always the case across the spectrum of domestic violence perpetration.

Given the premise of this chapter that being "incubated in terror" (Perry 1997) is a major contributing pathway into growing up to perpetrate domestic violence as an adult, a key data area is that of delineating the childhood histories of these clients – particularly any known histories of being exposed to domestic violence as children. Dutton (2000) suggests that a combination for the child of: exposure to physical abuse (witnessing and/ or being directly targeted); insecure attachment due to the inability of both the victimising and victimised adult to proffer security and protection; and being shamed over a prolonged period during vulnerable developmental phases, constitutes a dramatic, powerful and long-lasting trauma source that moulds the personality of the vulnerable, traumatised child into that of the abusive adult.

Childhood histories are a part of the background information that is routinely gathered by Corrective Services staff. This information comes from several sources, primarily from the client himself as well as from family members and from departmental records. Community Corrections officers use this information to compile a pre-sentence report (PSR). This report is written post-conviction and pre-sentence and is designed to assist the magistrate or judge when deciding sentencing options. The majority of clients in the community justice setting will have had such a report compiled on them and, amongst the 261 clients in this study, a PSR was available electronically for 174 (67 per cent). Given that only 33 of the 174 reports accessed made no reference to the presence or absence of domestic violence in childhood it would appear questions about any exposure to violence as a child are routinely asked of clients with domestic violence offences when gathering information for a PSR.

Just over two thirds (67.2 per cent) of these reports noted that the client had been exposed to domestic violence as a child.

Figure 9.4. Childhood Violence

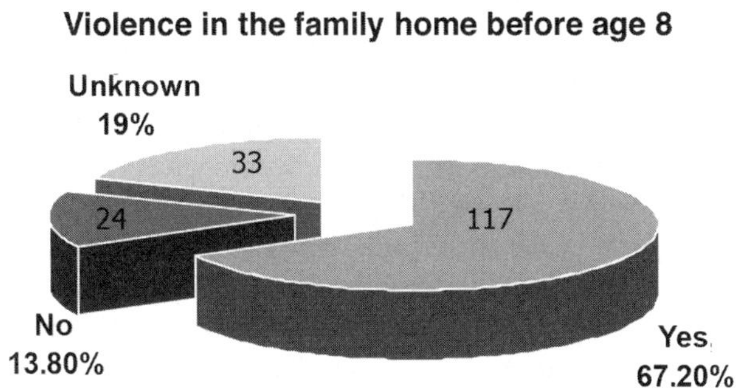

Most often this information appeared to come from the client himself; sometimes confirmed by other family members and sometimes reiterated as the "truth" by other family members, even when the client denied that this had been the case. In only 24 of these reports (14 per cent) was it clearly stated that there had been no family violence experienced by the client in childhood.

The violence experienced by the adult male when a child, as reported within the PSR was often extreme:

> Mr H can recall numerous events where he had attempted to protect his mother from the abuse (by his father). He recalls several occasions when he

> had to call the ambulance for her and one occasion when he had to resuscitate her himself. He considers that this may be the reason for the "indifferent" relationship he has with his father.

> Mr S mentioned in primary school intervening to protect his mother from his father who was hitting her with a crowbar. He discovered after that his father had four sets of large garbage bags and ties in his car; his mother believed that he had intended to kill her and the three children.

There are some who believe that offenders over-emphasise or confabulate their victim experiences as a way of attempting to take the focus off themselves as perpetrators. Whilst this is overwhelmingly true in regard to adult perpetrators of domestic violence portraying themselves as the real victim (rather than the female partners and any children they have victimised) this appears to be much less often the case when asked about their own childhood experiences. The large body of research on adult perpetrators of child sexual abuse (for example, Briggs 1995; Henry 2003; Salter 1995) generally concludes there is a significant under-reporting by this cohort - as children and as adults - of their own sexual abuse experiences as children.

In Western Australia it has only been in the last four years that the Child Protection Agency has put in standard practice measures that acknowledge that children living with domestic violence are legitimate victims, needing to be recognised, categorised, counted and serviced as such. Therefore it is likely that none of the adult males in this research (the youngest of whom was 19 years and the oldest 66 years) who stated that they had lived with domestic violence as a child, is likely to have had that reality officially confirmed for them unless, in addition, they had experienced direct physical harm as a consequence. When such childhood experiences are not acknowledged (because there is no one to say it to, because it feels too shameful, because you learn that it needs to be kept hidden, because it feels too potentially dangerous or disloyal to disclose, and so on), then it may be repressed. As a consequence, rather than over-reporting childhood trauma experiences there is a natural under-reporting or glossing over by adults of their childhood trauma experiences to self, partners and other family members, as well as to correctional staff.

> Mr C described himself as a "difficult" child who was always looking for and getting into trouble. For this reason Mr C stated that his stepfather was particularly hard upon him in terms of physical punishment. Mr C displayed no bitterness when recounting this punishment which always involved the use of a cat of nine tails and, on at least one occasion, having a gun put to his head. He stated that his stepfather always apologised afterwards and that the two would then discuss his behaviour. He was aware that his mother was too afraid to interfere. (*Extract from pre-sentence report*)

The impact of domestic violence on child development

It has been suggested that the need to repress overwhelming experiences from a young age leads to denial of child trauma and terror at the individual, familial and societal levels. Thus the intimate connection between being "incubated in terror" as a child and how that plays out in adult lives and relationships is lost. One of the most important things that my clients have taught me over several years of therapeutic work with adults who as children had experienced overwhelming abuse and violence, is that it is often preferable, and safer, to experience the self as bad than to see yourself as powerless. The need not to get in touch (again) with the reality of overwhelming powerlessness as a child, when you are physically, emotionally and intellectually incapable of preventing violence and abuse towards yourself, your siblings or your mother can be so imperative that almost any other feeling is preferable, including that of holding yourself culpable. Hence the usual answer of "*no more than I deserved*" when these clients are asked about the level of physical punishment meted out to them as children.

Where particular details of violence were specified in the files of the 117 males identified as having been exposed to violence within the home as children, information from a variety of sources contained stories of these children having: witnessed the murder and/or attempted murder of their mother by their (step)father; of experiencing physical abuse and violence from every adult male their mother was ever in a relationship with; of being ritualistically and repeatedly beaten up by fathers in order to "toughen them up"; of having guns held to their head by (step)fathers; of being left at home with no adults to care for them while mothers were in hospital recovering from physical assaults; of being removed from the home as infants due to ongoing violence and then having suffered further violence and abuse in out-of-home care arrangements. Several of these PSRs refer to an initial disclosure of merely being "treated fairly badly" or being "the black sheep of the family", further specific questioning being required to elicit many of the details mentioned above.

> Mr M spoke of his father "toughening him up" through a process of taking him into the backyard each birthday from the age of seven and asking him if he was a man yet – before fighting him. Because of the size difference this always ended up in him being badly beaten – sometimes requiring hospitalisation.
>
> (Stepfather) used to torture the household pets; including forcing Mr F as a six year old to tie up the pet dog and watch him starve, and eventually die over several weeks. Mr F was distressed recounting this.

The reality for the developing child who lives in the war zone of domestic violence can be characterised as constituting all of the following to a greater or lesser extent: experiencing the father (figure) as huge, overwhelming, capable of killing mother, unpredictable, fear-inducing, monstrous; experiencing the unavailability of the mother and her capacity to soothe – experiencing and internalising the mother's own fearful state; longing for safety in attachment relationships but fearing abandonment; developing a resultant insecure attachment style, most usually avoidant or disorganised (Ainsworth et al 1978; Bowlby 1979, 1988; Hazen and Shaver 1987); and being preoccupied with the unachievable task of trying to feel safe in an unsafe world that has no one they can rely on.

Whilst it is beyond the scope of this chapter to articulate in any depth the process of attachment style development and the detrimental impact of insecure attachments, it is now generally accepted that early attachment has major socio-biological significance and constitutes a powerful human survival motive (Bowlby 1969). Further, that the attachment style that was prevalent in the infant is, most usually, the style that carries through into adult life (Hazen and Shaver 1987). Likewise, whilst it is again beyond the scope of this chapter to discuss the long-term impact of trauma, it is again widely accepted that being exposed to ongoing trauma throughout childhood when key developmental tasks need to be achieved is likely to have severe long-term ramifications. For those males who grow up to commit repeated acts of domestic violence the most relevant of these sequelae would appear to be: lessening the capacity to understand and interpret human behaviour in terms of the mental states underpinning it; a lack of empathic connection with self and others; and, resorting to manifest displays of anger, "the primary function of which was to generate displays that would lead to the return of the absent mother" (Bowlby 1969: 17) in their attempts "to recapture the object that can soothe tension and anxiety" (Sonkin and Dutton 2003: 7).

The majority of the males who make up this cohort of serious domestic violence perpetrators within the criminal justice system can be understood, therefore, as people whose personalities as abusive adults have been moulded by their still unacknowledged, and often largely repressed, experiences as vulnerable, traumatised children. They are people who are unlikely to have rarely, if ever, had any deep feelings of personal power. They long for closeness and connection whilst never having been exposed (sufficiently) to an environment which can nurture the capacity to achieve this in respectful and honest ways. Their experience of themselves, and their adult and child victims, in any familial-type relationship remains largely predicated on those unacknowledged and repressed stories that deformed their developing personalities as children. Amongst other consequences this often translates to a view of themselves as the powerless, smaller, more vulnerable one who is always fearful that the person he needs to lean on, the one with the capacity to nurture and look after him (the adult victim/mother figure), will abandon him; an option that cannot be tolerated. Peter Fonagy (1997: 13-14) explains this as follows:

> The individual, when alone, feels unsafe because of a torturing representation from which he cannot escape because it is experienced from within the self. Unless the relationship permits externalisation, the individual feels at risk of disappearance ... violent men have to establish a relationship in which the partner acts as a vehicle for intolerable self states ... (the same process that all developing infants go through with the mother(figure)) ... they resort to violence at times when the independent mental existence of the other threatens this process of externalisation.

How the adult and child victims experience the war zone of domestic violence and the partner who subjects them to it is likely to be the antithesis of how the male experiences himself, his partner, the violence and the purpose behind it. So, while group work intervention for the victims of domestic violence based on the capacity to understand and empathise with the victim's experiences has proved beneficial for adult and child victims of domestic violence, it is the contention of this chapter that basing groups for perpetrators of violence on the same knowledge base is likely to result in the perpetrator feeling unheard, misunderstood and having his own reality disregarded. Just because the adult and child victims legitimately and understandably experience the domestic violence perpetrator as powerfully exerting his right to dominate, control and instil terror, it does not automatically follow that this is either the dominant force driving his behaviour or is necessarily how he experiences himself within the domestic violence encounter. This is particularly likely to be the case for that sub-set of convicted offenders; most of whom, as previously discussed, tend to operate from an internal "abandoned powerless child" psychological state. The primary goal of any intervention with those who have perpetrated acts of violence, domination, threat and control has to be to work towards reducing the likelihood of them perpetrating any more violence and causing any more harm. How we might get there has many possible paths; none of them quick or easy but with those operating from a base of being alongside the client likely to have more chance of solid, second-order change success than those which have been built primarily, or even solely, from the knowledge of how the violence has been experienced by the victim.

Implications for programs

It is the contention of this chapter that in order to assist the domestically violent male to decrease or cease his offending we have to come from the basis of exploring, sitting with and understanding his reality; and the why, how and when he experienced the need to create it. It is this dominant reality that needs to be explored and deconstructed in order to make room for the development of a non-offending lifestyle based on safety, trust and respect (White 1995). It is possible to provide a group program model that is driven by the needs and rights of adult and child domestic violence victims - past, present and future - to be safe, respected and valued and to do this from a basis of working with, and respectfully challenging, the skewed realities that have informed abusive behaviours. Importantly, such a focus is proposed not as a softer option, nor as an option that provides excuses for violence, but rather as an option that avoids committing the primary mistake of any therapeutic intervention – a lack of acknowledgment of the client's reality (Dutton and Corvo 2006: 459) – a mistake that actively works against good outcomes.

Over the 30 years since the first groups for domestic violence perpetrators were established in North America, approaches to understanding and responding to perpetrators of domestic violence have tended to be polarised, emphasising either a socio-political perspective or an individual/psychological perspective (Laing 2002). The latter approach is most often adopted by those therapists in private practice who come from a trauma perspective. Such practitioners might also have adopted aspects of the Compassion*Power* (Stosny 1995) model, based on the psychological perspective of the healing power of compassion as the antidote to emotional abuse, verbal abuse and domestic violence. In Australia, the Jenkins (1990) Theory of Restraint model, which has a narrative therapy base, incorporates aspects from both the socio-political and psychological perspectives in understanding and working to change violence. Individual and group work interventions can be informed by either or both of these approaches.

The Duluth model, first developed in Duluth, Minnesota in 1977, and grounded in the socio-political feminist, patriarchal, understandings of the causes and effects of interpersonal violence by males towards their female partners continues to form the primary base for group work intervention in Australia. This model was developed through hearing the experiences of women who had been on the receiving end of domestic violence describing what it had been like for them (Pence and Paymar 1993), and from this framework a group work program for domestic violence perpetrators was developed and trialled in the early 1980s. This model has been most consistently and widely used over the last 30 years in North America and for the last 20 of those years in Australia. Corrective Services in Western Australia currently funds a range of service providers who broadly follow either a Duluth or Stozny framework of intervention.

There is a growing body of literature (Bolen 2005; Dutton and Corvo 2006; Fonagy 1999; Sonkin and Dutton 2003) to support the development of groups for domestically violent males that have content and processes based on an understanding of the impact of insecure attachments and thus have a therapeutic, rather than a psycho-educational emphasis. The basic assumption behind this is that the successful exploration and completion of some key developmental tasks will lead to a reduction or cessation of domestically violent behaviours through an understanding and reconfiguring of the psychological processes that have been operating to drive these behaviours. Sonkin and Dutton (2003) summarise these tasks as: creating a safe and secure base; exploring current relationships with attachment figures; exploring the relationship between early childhood attachment experiences and current relationships; exploring relationships with (facilitators and group members) as attachment figures, and finding new ways of regulating attachment anxiety when the attachment behavioural system is activated. Inherent in such group models is a clear appreciation of the extent to which the therapist (or facilitator) personally contributes to the group outcomes. If the therapist fails to notice the client's strategies and their psychological function the therapist's responses will most probably confirm the client's inner working models of self and others and reinforce the attachment behavioural system as it currently manifests. However if the therapist is attuned they will look beyond the client's response set and, through helping the client feel understood, seen and cared for, can assist in helping the client alter their inner working models of self and others, to those which result in response sets that do not hinge on tactics of violence, threat and control.

The psycho-therapeutic group work community has a wealth of knowledge about the primacy of the role of facilitator, the importance of process over and above any "manualised content" (following a program manual[2]), the value of the here and now, and the processing of that to effect change (Corey and Corey 1997; Kaplan and Sadock 1993; Rogers 1970; Whitaker 1987; Yalom and Leszcz 2005). However this knowledge is largely absent from domestic violence group work interventions currently favoured for convicted offenders currently favoured in Australia. This appears to be surprising at best, and almost negligent at worst.

Overview of a framework for an alternative "taking responsibility for perpetrating and reducing violence" group

We envisage such a group would constitute a paradigm shift away from the Duluth-based psycho-educational, manualised groups currently favoured by correctional services in Australia. It would be process, rather than manualised content driven. It would actively seek to incorporate the lived realities of those adults and children on the receiving end of domestic violence as a key factor in any change process. It would also focus on the here and now and on accompanying questioning - *How were you feeling when she said that? What did you notice about your body then? Your hand has started shaking; do you know what that might be about? Look in this mirror - do you feel as old as you look or younger? What do you think that might be about? What can you do about that right now that does not involve violence?*- as a way

2 Set content based on elements of psycho-education problem solving training usually required to be rigorously adhered to by facilitators to ensure program integrity (sometimes to the detriment of attending to group process and modifying the content to suite the group).

of assisting clients to view their response set (their attachment behaviours) from a different perspective.

The aim behind the group work program would be to help participants move to a position where perpetrating further violence onto intimate others would become incompatible with the empathic understandings of what it feels like to be hurt and abused. A key foundational belief informing group content and processes is that the childhoods of these perpetrators cut off the opportunity for them to achieve the key psychological task of empathy for others from the natural progression pathway of developing empathy for self through secure attachments. Such a group would also focus on providing the environment in which exploration of the representational models of self and attachment figures arising from original traumas can be made known, reappraised and restructured, rather than the occasional achievement of this by skilled facilitators, in spite of the focus on delivering manualised content that can actively work against achieving this. The voices and experiences of child and adult victims of domestic violence will therefore form the cornerstone of the group.

The incorporation of "reflecting teamwork" (Perlesz et al 1994; White 1995; Young et al 1989) is one way through which these tasks may be achieved. The stories and presence of female survivors of domestic violence can be used as a key element of this reflecting team process. It is the experience of the author, and of many of those who work with adult survivors of domestic violence, that they long for the opportunity to share what they have learnt with others in ways that will contribute to the reduction of domestic violence and the harm it causes everyone - adult and child victims and perpetrators. We have had initial conversations with several such women about their preparedness to do what they have done before in recovery groups - to talk openly about what it was like for themselves and their children living through the reign of terror that their partner/perpetrator subjected them to, although this time to have an audience of domestic violence perpetrators in the same room respectfully listening to the women speak. We have been frankly astonished at the willingness, even eagerness, with which this idea has been embraced by the women we have proposed it to so far. They have spoken of seeing this as an opportunity for them to continue their personal healing process alongside contributing to a worthwhile endeavour to reduce the amount of domestic violence that other women and children continue to be exposed to. We have also been amazed at the degree of empathy that many of the women we have approached have expressed towards the males who would be hearing their stories and their real hope that they can contribute to the healing that they believe these men also are likely to be craving. The Sycamore Tree Project, a faith-based program that brings victims into prisons to meet with unrelated offenders to discuss together issues related to crime and its consequences, is already demonstrating the restorative power that such approaches can have for both victims and perpetrators of violent crimes.

The Envisioned Group Work Process

PRE-GROUP

Two to three assessment sessions are conducted individually with intended participants and also with survivors who have volunteered their services.

GROUP

Sessions 1-6

First 90 minutes

- Six carefully chosen and already "primed" survivors of domestic violence as children and/or adults share in a circle their experiences as children, partners and mothers of being subjected to domestic violence.
- Up to eight clients *(not related to visitors)* sit in another circle in the same room; listening and silently reflecting.
- Clients then share in a circle reflecting on what they have heard – visitors listen.
- Visitors then reflect on what they have heard from the clients.

Second 90 minutes – Client group and visitor group separately facilitated

- Process material from the first half of the group – participants reflect in a group and facilitators listen, followed by facilitators reflecting and participants listening.
- With client group – facilitator reflections will attempt to heighten awareness amongst participants regarding what drove their behaviour as adults, and the impact of that on their adult (and child) victims.
- At the end of each session – check with both groups regarding impact, coping strategies, support mechanisms. For any client or visitor (self) identified as requiring additional support ensure this is put in place.

Sessions 7-12 – Clients only

- Continuation of reflecting team processes. Facilitator reflections continuing to be directed at: heightening awareness amongst participants regarding what drove their behaviour as adults; the impact of that on their adult (and child) victims; increasing empathy for others via reflections that invite an ability to empathise with their own unmet needs as children. Can include inviting clients to "role reverse" and reflect as a team of adult survivors.

Session 13 – Both groups together

- Reflecting team process used to notice and remark on progress and changes.

Follow up

- Reflecting team sessions with the two groups, separately and jointly at three and six months interval

Partner work

- Establish contact with those partners who wished to remain in the relationship, and depending on their wishes would:
  - facilitate two to three reflecting team processes with them as a group
  - facilitate a final reflecting team process with the clients and their partners or ex-partners.

Even when we have explained further our vision of the degree of involvement we might be seeking from them - two or three individual sessions, followed by six or seven group sessions where, after they have spoken as a group about some of their own and their children's experiences of surviving domestic violence, they will be invited to swop places with the male participants and listen while the males reflect as a group on what it was like for them hearing the women's stories - they continue to be eager to participate.

Key influences on the success of any group work intervention

Several research inquiries have demonstrated that positive outcome is significantly correlated with expectations of the intervention being helpful: high expectations in this regard being related to positive outcomes (Yalom and Leszcz 2005). Most perpetrators who attend a domestic violence group do not come of their own volition and, depending on the degree of coercion they feel (from partners, other family members, child protection or Family Court agencies through to being mandated by the criminal justice system) are likely to have resentment, rather than hope, as their dominant feeling when entering a group intervention. Therefore, regardless of the model of intervention, if facilitators themselves believe in the validity of the approach of the model they use, and also believe in the capacity of the model to facilitate positive outcomes, they will be well placed to instil this sense of hope in participants, leading to the enhanced possibility of positive outcomes no matter what group work framework is used.

There are several other factors in group work processes that research consistently indicates support good outcomes, regardless of either the framework of intervention or the program content. Factors such as:

- the facilitator's ability to achieve a sense of cohesiveness;
- the perpetrator feeling safe enough to express disagreement with the facilitator (Pepitone and Reichling 1955);
- ensuring that such occasions are used to strengthen the group and that gains are made;
- being able to deal constructively with group conflict;
- creating a group culture that supports risk taking, empathic listening and feedback;
- engendering a feeling of acceptance from other group members;
- creating a therapeutic atmosphere "that removes the obstacles that block the progress of growth" (Yalom and Leszcz 2005);
- actively seeking out and facilitating the inclination towards growth and self-fulfilment that the facilitator believes is inherent in

everyone - a view that underpins any intervention coming from a strengths-based perspective.

These factors can be present or absent in any model of group work for domestic violence perpetrators and are likely to influence group work outcomes to a greater extent than adherence to any particular model. Whilst group work models that rely significantly on didactic instruction and advice-giving have tended to be evaluated more negatively (Yalom and Leszcz 2005), both didactic instruction and advice-giving will have a place in any group work with domestic violence perpetrators whose ways of understanding the world and their place in it is replete with cognitive distortions. Yalom (2005: 11) believes that "it is rare that a specific suggestion for some problem will directly benefit ... however *indirectly* advice-giving serves a purpose" with the process conveying mutual understanding and care.

The personal qualities of the facilitator are pivotal in these processes: his or her values, beliefs, attitudes, background, experience, views regarding offenders as well as their views regarding the role of facilitator, and so on, influence outcomes enormously. The really skilled and less respectful facilitator is going to help participants achieve better outcomes than the less skilled and less respectful facilitator, no matter which model of domestic violence group work intervention they use. Whilst most of these factors are more likely to be supported by the model of group work intervention presented in this chapter than perhaps some other models of group work with domestic violence perpetrators, this model is also more likely than other models to work against good outcomes for client and victims alike if the skill and knowledge level of the facilitators is not sufficient for the task.

Conclusion

The central argument of this chapter has been that the majority of males who find themselves within the justice system and ordered to undertake a domestic violence program are highly likely to be "repeat assaulters - the most dangerous" (Gondolf 2000: 191). This group tends to have the least successful outcomes through participation in the Duluth-type psycho-educational groups currently favoured throughout Australia. It is suggested that these clients are more likely to have been subjected to ongoing and extreme domestic violence as a child, and that, as adults, they perpetrate behaviours from this "stuck" position of feeling vulnerable, needy and insecure. They continue to be preoccupied, as they were as children, with trying to feel safe in an unsafe world that has no one they can rely on, including themselves. However, as a grown adult rather than a child, they can now use violence to keep the person they most need to lean on "close" to them. The growing body of attachment and trauma literature in the domestic violence field generally supports the belief that the avenue to a life of non-violence and respectful relationships has, of necessity, to include a pathway back to re-evaluating the impact of these experiences.

This chapter has further proposed a group work model of intervention for achieving the key tasks involved in understanding and reconfiguring the psychological processes that have been operating to drive these behaviours. It has been proposed that a key component towards achieving this would be through a team of survivors of domestic violence, a number of whom express enthusiasm for this task. This represents a fairly radical departure from the type of domestic violence programs for mandated clients most commonly used throughout the Australian justice system. Not only would the group work process actively use the participation of survivors, it would also involve a shift away from manualised content to a focus on using the here and now in a process-driven agenda by highly skilled therapists or group facilitators. Group work intervention that facilitates the possibility of healing, in the course of moving towards a choice of non-violence is most definitely not a soft option and is not therapy for therapy's sake. It is a pathway to a more respectful future and fewer adult and child victims of domestic violence.

Part IV

RESEARCH

Chapter 10

Integration in Practice: A Series of Case Studies

Donna Chung, Patrick O'Leary, Donna Justo and Di Lucas

A central feature of any integrated response to domestic violence is a system where the behaviour of men can be monitored closely through their attendance at programs and a responsive support and contact system is provided to women and children. All parties can then transit effectively through the different agencies. It is at this systemic level that information and strategies can be shared that support women and their children's safety. This provides a nexus between the criminal justice system and social intervention programs. The purpose of this chapter is to illustrate how the integrated response has responded to changes in risk and the progression of both men and women through the system. Whilst victims and offenders share similar circumstances, changes in social and family factors invariably influence the risk of further violence occurring. Monitoring and responding to risk is critical for integrated responses and key to this process is a formal and ongoing risk assessment. The chapter starts with explaining how risk is assessed for both men and women, highlighting integration strategies at various stages of progress and risk. Parallel to intervention with offenders is engagement with the men's partners or ex-partners who have been subjected to violence. These women are engaged by a woman-centred service which offers women support and women provide feedback on their experience of their partners' use of violence while the man attends the offender program. Five examples have been selected to represent a broad selection of cases encountered. This includes offenders who completed a 26 week program, as well as offenders who failed to complete or were excluded from the program. In each of the cases we provide a brief profile of the male offender and some details about their former or current woman partner. All details of cases have been anonymised and altered where appropriate to preserve confidentiality.

Risk assessment

As part of the process of risk assessment at the Gold Coast integrated response, information on risk is collected at every point of contact. This is

Table 10.1. Ratings of Risk

√	Risk Level	Definition
	Low	No violence or abusive incidents or threats reported while man is in program Partner reports feeling safe for a significant period of time Information from partner is consistent with facilitator's perceptions and other sources Man displays evidence of clear conceptual understanding Man takes clear position on non-violence articulated through group participation No evidence of denial, minimisation, blame or collusion Safety strategies developed, articulated and demonstrated
	Medium	No violent or abusive incidents or threats reported for a significant period of time Some inconsistencies between perception of facilitators and information supplied by partner and other sources Some evidence of man's conceptual understanding and position taking on non-violence articulated through group participation Some use of denial, minimisation, blame or collusion Some safety strategies developed, articulated and demonstrated
	Moderate	Violent and/or abusive incident reported while man is participating in program Clear inconsistencies between perception of facilitators and information supplied by partner or other sources Limited evidence of man's conceptual understanding and position taking on non-violence Man continues to use denial, minimisation, blame or collusion Some safety strategies articulated but limited demonstration
	High	Violence and/or abusive incident reported while man is participating in program Clear inconsistencies between perception of facilitators and information supplied by partner and other sources Man has disclosed suicidal or self-harm thoughts or plans No evidence of man's conceptual understanding, safety strategies No position taking on non-violence Man has continued high levels of denial, minimisation, blame or collusion No safety strategies developed, articulated or demonstrated.

because risk can change throughout involvement with the program. For example, a situation of low risk may quickly change if a Family Court ruling conflicts with offender expectations, or a high risk situation may change to medium risk if the woman has moved away and the offender no longer knows her whereabouts. Risk assessment relies on people from a variety of sources collecting as much information as possible from key informants and includes professionals working with the man, woman and her children. Offenders are also asked to assess their own risk, as a means of prompting them to consider their own risk of using violence. Moreover contact with women forms a central component of the risk assessment process - their insight into risk and safety inform the process undertaken with offenders participating in the program. In Table 10.1 some of the definitions of risk that are used in the program are presented.

Case examples

Case 1: Male Offender A - Age 45

Criminal history

Offender has a history of criminal charges as a juvenile mostly relating to drug offences. Over the last 15 years there have been domestic violence related offences including:

- assault occasioning bodily harm;
- wilful and unlawful damage;
- threaten life;
- five breaches of domestic violence orders.

Background information

The offender had been imprisoned for three months for breaches of a domestic violence order and released after 28 days and referred to the program. He was assessed as suitable for the program. While in prison his partner separated from him. He is the father of three children aged eight, five and four years of age. All children reside with their mother, supervised access is offered fortnightly. The offender is currently unemployed. After 14 sessions he was excluded from the program because of consistently disruptive behaviour in the group. He was warned several times about this behaviour and also failed a drug test on two occasions. The offender has a long history of drug and alcohol-related problems. He has been treated by psychiatric services for depression following his separation. Program facilitators consistently reported him as having poor insight into his use of violence and when challenged in the group setting he could become quickly agitated and aggressive towards other participants and facilitators. From assessment through to exclusion of the group he was assessed as high risk of using violence. Assessment on the dangerousness checklist revealed a high level of risk and denial.

Woman Partner A – Age 36

Background information

Part-time casual bar work and fulltime mother for children aged eight, five and four years. Woman has consented to be contacted by women's service while her former partner attends the program. Since separating from the offender her main concern is the safety of her children in supervised access visits. While attending the program the offender has text messaged her on several occasions. The woman regularly uses the women's worker as a central contact in her safety strategies. She has requested ongoing support since the offender has been excluded from the program and summoned to appear in court for breaches of order. The woman is suspicious that the offender may know her whereabouts and she has recently received some strange phone calls. However, the women's worker has assessed the level of risk as medium but this would quickly change should there be concrete evidence that the offender knows her whereabouts.

System integration

This case highlights how the referral of men to the domestic violence program also provides women with an important opportunity to connect with support services. In this case the woman when contacted by the women's service requested further ongoing assistance. Part of this work with the woman has included greater enhancement of her own assessments of risk and subsequent safety planning strategies. These developments have enabled a clear safety plan should the offender contact her. Participation in community development activities aimed to promote self-esteem after numerous difficulties related to the effects of domestic violence on her and the children. Intervention with the man was limited but the program assessment of risk in addition to the woman's reports of his behaviour ensured that correctional services and police have greater knowledge of his risk and consequently they have increased his reporting responsibilities while he is on bail to attend court.

Case 2: Male Offender B – Age 31

Criminal history

The offender has a history of domestic violence related offences in Australia since moving from overseas in 2004 with his former partner and children. His first offence in Queensland was in 2006 when he and his partner separated, at this time he was found guilty of illegally possessing his partner's property. This was followed by two charges of breaching a domestic violence order. At this time the man was referred to the offender program and attended for 11 sessions before breaching his domestic violence orders and assaulting his former partner and one of her family members. He was charged with four breaches of a domestic violence order and a series of physical assault charges - the most serious being occasioning actual bodily harm and wilful damage. He was sentenced to 12 months prison and released after six months. Upon release he was referred back to the offender program. His participation in the program was sometimes disruptive and on occasions it was noted that he conceptually understood program material but there was a disparity between this and his comments about his former partner. After arriving at the program affected by drugs three times in a row he was excluded from the program and sent back to court. At this time he was rated as very high risk.

Woman Partner B - *Age 31*

Background information

At the first point of contact after her partner was referred to the program the woman was reluctant to be involved. Partly this was because of her ongoing fear of the offender and her suspicion that the women's service might work with child protection authorities to remove her children. However, the woman agreed to phone contact to be updated about her partner's participation in the offenders program. It was during one of these routine phone calls that separation strategies and links to resources was first discussed and subsequently planned.

System integration

Throughout this case the assessment of risk from both program facilitators and women's support services has been high. Although the offender did not complete the program and his level of responsibility and potential to commit violence remained relatively unchanged, there was a period of time where his partner was able to implement some safety strategies to better prepare for separation. The woman and her children were able to relocate to a new house and the location was withheld from the offender. During one of the group program sessions the man disclosed that he had recently assaulted his former partner at her new address. He also made various statements that indicated continuing high risk of using violence. It was likely that this would result in an exclusion from the program and further court action. An immediate response from facilitators was needed so they could implement policy procedures in regard to the woman and her children's safety. This included immediate contact with police to carry out a welfare check at the woman's address as well as monitoring the offender's movements while they were waiting for a court order warrant for his arrest. Correctional services were contacted to ensure a breach of order was reported and acted upon. The relevant women's advocate worker was informed so that timely contact could be made with the woman and her children. This contact was also combined with a child protection assessment to ensure the role of the two agencies were separate but coordinated to honour the woman's attempts to keep her and the children safe. At the time of the man being excluded from the group, safety strategies were implemented to inform his former partner that he was being excluded and her address was marked for police communications to monitor. The relevant Community Corrections officer was informed and preparations were made for the offender to be breached and returned to court to face further charges. An added aspect to this case was the involvement of child protection and regular communication was made between the service working with the woman and the local child protection authority.

Six months later the criminal matter went to court and the man was sentenced to 15 months prison but only served six months before being released on probation and again referred to the program. Upon release the offender completed a six week drug and alcohol rehabilitation program before commencing in the domestic violence offender program. After nine weeks of attending the program the offender came to three successive sessions in an intoxicated state and was excluded. The man is now awaiting court. He remains listed at high risk but this is moderated by the fact that he does not know the location of his former partner and her children. Since the time of referral, the offender's former partner and children had to move on three occasions because the offender had found their new residences. Supervised access has been offered to the offender in order to have contact with his children. This is a major area of concern for the children's mother as she had a growing sense of the children's fear following contact.

This case example illustrates that the system response is paramount. The offender in this case committed further violence while attending the program, but this should not be viewed as a failure of an integrated response because if he had not been referred it is unlikely that the response to the woman would have involved the range of safety strategies it did – albeit that they were not always successful. It is also likely that violence would have been unreported. The response in this case enabled a system response for the woman and her children while also ensuring a direct communication path to the criminal justice system to maintain the man's accountability.

Case 3: Male Offender C – Age 27

Criminal history

This man has a juvenile criminal history of burglary, larceny and disorderly behaviour related offences. In the last four years there have been two violent assaults of other men in licensed premises. He has been imprisoned on one occasion for three months. In the last two years there have been three breaches of domestic violence orders following a relationship breakup. The man has also been convicted of two counts of wilful damage and one count of common assault of his former partner.

Background information

These breaches and offences were the justification for him to receive a suspended prison sentence and be referred to the offenders program. At the point of referral he was generally reluctant to attend the program and had a poor level of responsibility for any of his violent behaviour. At this time the man had commenced a new relationship and was no longer in contact with the woman he assaulted. This woman was contacted by the women's service and also reported no contact but was still highly fearful of the offender. The man attended all sessions and his progress was assessed at the mid-way point in the program. It was observed that there had been positive change in his participation in the program and he had finally supplied the correct contact details of his new partner. He had some general remorse for his past violent behaviour and although he did not fully take responsibility there was a significant shift from his initial blame of his victims. Insight into some of the patterns of his offending was also observed and the man had changed his alcohol usage and some of his social associates. At the time of program completion the man was assessed as low to medium risk.

Two women have been subjected to violence by this offender:

Woman Partner C1 – Age 23

Contact was initially made after the man's referral to the offenders program. This was some eight months since the offence and four months since the woman reported her last contact with the man. After two more contacts by the women's service the woman reported she was happy that she had been contacted but did not want any further contact as she had moved on and was not as fearful of any further contact. The woman agreed to contact the service again should there be any new contact or other needs arise. At this time the woman was assessed at low risk.

Woman Partner C2 – Age 29

The man reported having a new partner not related to his attendance at the offender program. It is part of men's contract agreements that while attending the program they release contact details of any new partners. The man initially was reluctant to do this and for several weeks gave phone numbers that appeared to be incorrect. In line with some conceptual developments in understanding his offending, along with a threat for a breach of contract meaning a return to court, the man gave his new partner's contact details. It became evident to the women's worker that the man had not been accurate in his recount of why he was attending the offender program. It was assessed that the woman was cautious in what she disclosed, perhaps because of fear and ongoing control from the man. However, the woman did report that there had been some positive changes in the man's attitude over recent weeks corresponding with observed positive changes in the man's participation in the program. The woman agreed to have phone contact and was able to be reached spasmodically. When the man completed the program the woman was assessed by her worker as at medium risk.

System integration

An integrated response to domestic violence offenders in this case has enabled contact with two women. It illustrates the transient nature of relationships along with the many factors that influence risk. Whilst the man had responded to aspects of the offender program positively, cautious assessment of effectiveness needs to be made in light of incomplete information from his former and current partners. It is also evident in this case that shared values about the importance of contact with potential victims of violence were pursed by the relevant agencies. This example also highlights the importance of information sharing between agencies and the need to ensure that information about new partners is passed on and that it is not within the offender's control to decide about this contact information. This, of course, does not cover situations where men do not reveal that they have a new partner. Intervention with men cannot be simply classified as a success or failure in terms of attitudinal or behaviour change at a single point, because of the entrenchment of abusive behaviour influenced by various personal and social factors in their environment.

Case 4: Male Offender D – Age 34

Criminal history

The offender had no prior criminal history until two breaches of domestic violence orders. He was ordered by the court to attend the offenders program as a result of the breaches.

Background information

This man was compliant in meeting requirements for the program, was always on time and attended all sessions. At the commencement of the program the man minimised his violence and considered his violence to be "less serious" compared with other men in the group. He was assessed as a moderate level of risk by facilitators and women's services. At the mid-way point in the program, facilitators reported positive change including greater honesty and insight into his violence. He continued to live with his partner and she consistently reported that the man showed positive changes and her reports were consistent with what he disclosed in the group. The most notable change being better self-control and respect for her and the children. At program completion the man requested further counselling support and was referred to a local counselling service.

Woman Partner D – Age 31

Background information

When the woman was first contacted by the women's service she was keen to engage in regular contact and attended counselling services. Prior to this she had not considered accessing a domestic violence service because she had not seen the violence as serious or abnormal. During this time she regularly engaged with her partner's progress in the group program. At first she was sceptical about his participation because he had blamed her and saw the violence as a "relationship issue". Later in the program she began to experience some positive changes in his level of responsibility and respect. Whilst cautious about future episodes of violence, there had been none since he had attended the program and she reported feeling much safer.

System integration

There is modest evidence from a number of sources that this man has made some positive change. The most crucial evidence is his partner's report of increased sense of safety and respect in her relationship with the man. Whilst the court order for the man has expired, system integration will enable contact with the woman for as long as she needs and the man has been referred for non-mandated counselling. Central to monitoring success in this case is whether sustainable change has been achieved by the man. Underpinning this case is the fact that both parties are engaged in the system and prevention activities. This highlights the dynamic nature of achieving change in domestic violence for both men and women.

Case 5: Male Offender E – Age 42

Criminal history

The offender has no history of violent offences, has convictions for drink driving and possession of prohibited substance. The man was sent to the offenders program after one breach of a domestic violence order.

Background information

On referral to the program there was strong resistance to attend and accept responsibility for his violence. His initial views were that he had been misjudged and he was the victim of violence. However, there was a strong level of compliance and fear of further legal action. He cited relationship difficulties after the death of his and his partner's five year old daughter in a road accident. Early in the process the man was able to identify ways in which he had been controlling and emotionally abusive. At this time he articulated how in the past he had deflated the tyres on his partner's car to prevent her from going out while he was at work. He was also able to identify a range of behaviours that were designed to monitor his partner in response to his jealousy. During his attendance at the program he continued to live with his partner. The man was on time for all sessions and completed the program to schedule. Because of ongoing control issues reported by the man and woman he was assessed as moderate risk.

Woman Partner E – Age 38

Background information

Initially the partner was reluctant to have regular contact with the women's service. As a result, irregular contact was maintained every four to six weeks. The woman took some of the responsibility for the man's violence and requested some counselling support. Issues of shame and stigma were also evident from the first contact. The woman reported positive change with regard to the man's physical violence and aggressive behaviour. However, the worker assessed there were still various issues of control. An important point of engagement for the women's service was ongoing sharing of the issues covered in the offenders program as well as an opportunity to better target the effects of controlling behaviour that was evident from the man's disclosures in the group sessions.

System integration

In this case engagement with the partner was challenging and required careful managing so not to enforce it on the woman but engage her in an empowering way that offered information about her partner's attendance at the offenders program. Information shared by the program facilitators with the women's service helped them to raise the woman's own awareness of controlling and non-physically violent forms of domestic violence. This helped the woman to be more aware of the broad spectrum of violence she had experienced while also allowing her to understand why she had blamed herself. Information from the women's service helped program facilitators to better use material on non-physical forms of domestic violence so that they could better confront this man's use of violence. This case is consistent with evidence that indicates intervention with men is more successful in reducing physical violence (Gondolf 2002). Whereas more insidious forms of domestic violence, such as control tactics, are often highly sophisticated and not only difficult to eradicate but also challenging to use as formal evidence of non-program compliance or reoffending, as physical evidence remains a key to credible evidence.

Discussion and conclusion

It is evident from these cases that any assessment of risk needs to be conducted in a comprehensive manner, relying on different sources of information collected from various parts of the system. Assessments based solely on the offender's involvement in programs can be misleading because positive change in the man needs to be verified with his partner and associated professionals. The integrated response where women partners are contracted to assess risk also offers the opportunity for her to receive support from victim services. These support services for the woman can be continued even if he leaves the program. An important aspect of promoting women's safety in this approach is that where couples continue to live together, the women's service can offer women realistic information about the likelihood and sustainability of men's changed behaviour. This enables women to have a more accurate understanding about men's changes and to understand that change cannot always be sustained and that support after the expiration of an order can be helpful to maintaining changes.

This chapter has highlighted a range of cases with different levels of offender risk, but the real focus has been on how the integrated response allows for a range of responses to be offered relative to risk and the situational variables. With regard to concern about whether such approaches are successful, the cases show this cannot be answered with a yes or no, rather there is a variability and range of outcomes that result from an integrated program for offenders which may or may not include the man's cessation of violence and abuse. The organisation of the integrated services may result in the opportunity for women to make longer term safety arrangements, such as leaving the home, as the man is being monitored in the offenders program. In this circumstance the engagement of the man may not have reduced the man's potential to use violence but his partner was able to leave - an outcome not likely if there had been solely a criminal justice response. Linking services and sharing information are key benefits of this response. A comprehensive assessment of program effectiveness needs to be based on the quality of services and the capacity for agencies to respond seamlessly in partnership to work towards the primary goal of promoting women's and children's safety, in what can be volatile and unstable situations amongst families where there is domestic violence. An integrated response offers opportunities for the observation of risk at all points of contact with the offender and the woman, reports of elevated risk can be assessed and where necessary immediate action maybe required. Whilst the reduction of men's violence and abusive behaviour is a most valuable outcome of an offender program, this is not always achieved. However, as the above cases show, other important outcomes which do indicate success are: the improved safety of women and children in various ways, women's greater safety awareness and planning skills, contact with relevant support services and greater knowledge amongst these women of the dynamics of men who use violence in intimate relationships.

In the next four chapters we turn our focus to men who participated in the research by examining their characteristics, readiness for intervention, change following the program completion and women's perspectives of the men's change as a result of the program.

Chapter 11

The Characteristics of Men who Participate in the Gold Coast Domestic Violence Program

Adam Gerace and Andrew Day

When considering what might be the most appropriate intervention responses for male perpetrators of domestic violence it is first necessary to consider the characteristics of the particular group of men who might be involved. Whilst domestic violence is pervasive, cutting across all sections of the community, it is also apparent that considerable heterogeneity exists amongst offenders. Individual differences may exist in relation to the nature, frequency and seriousness of offences, as well as in attitudes towards intervention. This is important information that can inform the planning of programs. The program described in Chapter 8 of this book is a good example of what is commonly referred to as an integrated program, where participants are legally required to attend, typically as part of a community corrections order. The consequences of non-attendance can be serious, and typically involve a return to court. As such the men who attend this program are likely to differ in important ways from groups of men who self-refer for intervention.

In this chapter we describe some of the characteristics of participants in the Gold Coast men's program. The data reported here was gathered by Community Corrections officers as part of their assessment and case management process, prior to referral to the program. It is based on a sub-sample of 27 participants who attended the program between 2006 and 2008.[1] We start by describing the demographic characteristics of the men and their legal status, before examining what is known about their relationships (past and present). We then describe data relating to their personal backgrounds, before finishing with some information on their perceived treatment needs and attitudes to intervention.

---

1 In some areas, however, data was missing and so frequencies do not always total 27.

Demographics

The mean age of the men was 35.44 years (SD=8.50; Range=19-53). The majority of participants were born in Australia and all spoke English as their first language. Twenty participants were employed, and reported a median weekly income of $775.00 (16 participants; Range=200-1500). There was some diversity in occupation of the men; a third of the sample reported a trade (for example, painter, plumber, electrician) and other jobs included those in landscaping, chef and food processing, and self-employment.

All of the participants were currently on parole and probation orders, with four participants also awaiting a legal outcome/sentencing for another offence (for example, breach of Domestic Violence Order DVO, breaking and entering/wilful damage). Participants were also asked if they had been previously convicted for a number of offences, with some records showing a history of robbery (two participants), assault/physical violence against another person (12 participants), assault with a weapon (three participants), drug-related offences (eight participants), and drink driving (13 participants). No participants reported a sexual assault. Eleven participants indicated that they had been jailed either as a minor or adult, the majority of these indicating one previous period of incarceration (although one participant indicated two convictions and 15 incarcerations). Four participants indicated that they had no previous convictions.

At the time of assessment, 13 of the 27 participants reported that they were currently in a relationship (with 10 participants living with this partner), while 14 were single or separated. Twenty-three were parents, with between one to five children (M=2.18; SD=0.94). All but two participants had children under the age of 18 years.

For those who had separated from a partner, the separation had typically been for less than a year (Median=6 months; Range=1-48),[2] and was, for the most part, a permanent arrangement (separation permanent, seven participants; temporary, two participants; unsure, four participants). In all cases, the separation was not the sole decision of the participant: in six cases, the partner had initiated the separation, whilst in five other cases the separation was initiated by both partner and participant (one participant indicated that the police had initiated the separation via a DVO).

Six participants indicated that they had had some negative contact with their ex-partner since separation (for example, making unwelcome phone calls or contact, verbal or emotional abuse, threatened physical abuse). Ten participants had a current domestic violence order or other restraining order served against them, and all but two of these participants had had a restraining order against them in the past (most of whom had

2 Of participants who had not separated from their partner at time of interview, six of these participants indicated that they had previously separated from this partner, although they were back together at the time of the assessment.

had one restraining order; in total, all 14 participants either currently or in the past had had a restraining order of some sort against them[3]). Seven of the participants with a restraining order against them said that their partner had initiated contact in spite of this (three participants said that they ignored or ended this contact), and seven participants indicated that they had knowingly breached a restraining order (with six charged for this).

Relationships

Current or most recent relationship

In describing their current or most recent relationship (in the case of those who were separated or single), participants reported a mean age for their partner of 34.92 years (SD=9.01; Range=18-53). Participants had been in this relationship for an average of 6.75 years (SD=5.08), and all but one participant indicated that they had cohabited with this partner and had done so for some time (M=5.31 years; SD=4.85; Range=0-20). Four participants reported that they were married to this present/most recent partner (M=7.75 years; SD=5.12).

When asked about the frequency of physical violence in the last year of this relationship, there was much variation (median=1.00 episodes; Range=0-182). Five participants reported no episodes in the last year, while 18 participants indicated between one (10 participants) and five episodes. Three participants seemed to be responsible for the large variation in incidents, recording 12,[4] 26 and 182 (this equates to abuse every two to three days) episodes, respectively. It should be remembered that this data comes from the men themselves at the point of referral to a program, and as such is likely to underestimate the true frequency of violence (see Chapter 3 describing the women's experiences).

Generally, participants believed that their violence, rated on a 1 ("not at all serious") to 10 ("very serious") Likert-type response, scale was of "moderate seriousness" (M=4.76; SD=2.89; Range=1-10). While nine participants believed that the violence was less frequent in the latter part of the relationship than it had been at earlier times in the relationship, five participants believed it was more frequent, and eight indicated that there was no discernible change at different times in the relationship. Likewise, 10 participants indicated that they believed that the violence was less severe than it had been at an earlier time in the relationship, five indicated greater severity, while seven indicated no change. The majority (19 participants) indicated that they and their partner did not have sexual

3 Twelve of 13 participants who were not currently separated had had a restraining order against them in the past (one participant's information missing), and nine of these participants had knowingly breached a restraining order in the past.

4 This participant also indicated a large number of abusive behaviours in previous relationships (see section below).

intercourse after an episode of violence. Finally, participants described a number of different issues which were argued over most with their partner, with recurring themes of children, family, financial matters, past relationships, and relationship commitment.

Although not all participants could pinpoint events related to the beginning of the abuse, they identified a number of triggering events, including moving-in together, infidelity, events involving the partner's previous relationships, pregnancy and childbirth, employment, and emotional issues.

Data was also collected on how safe the men perceived their partner to be from future violence and threats of violence on a scale of 1 ("Not safe at all") to 10 ("Very safe"), with the majority of participants (20 participants) indicating that they believed that their partner was "very safe" (a score of 10; M=8.89; SD=2.42). There was, however, some variation. For example, two participants indicated that their partner was "not safe at all" (a score of 1), or was "quite unsafe" (a score of 3), two participants indicated "moderate safety", and three indicated "greater safety" (8 or 9). This shows that there is a marked variation in how serious these men consider their violence to be.

While almost 75 per cent of participants indicated that their partner was "very safe" (from them), many believed that their partners would overestimate the risk of future violence (M=7.40; SD=2.83). In fact, 10 participants indicated a belief that their partner would suggest that they are "very safe" (a score of 10), with almost 50 per cent of participants indicating a score between 8 and 10. However, there were more participants in the moderate area (10 participants indicating 5-7), and two participants in the "not at all safe" area. Participant ratings of their perceptions of safety, and how they believed their partner would feel were not statistically correlated, $r(25)=.23$, $p>.05$, suggesting that participants had some awareness that their partner may feel differently from them.[5]

Participants were also administered an adaptation of the Abusive Behavior Inventory (ABI; Shepard and Campbell 1992), which consisted of 32 items measuring psychological (23 items – for example, "swore, called her a name or criticised her") and physical (nine items – "pushed grabbed or shoved her") abuse in the last six months of the relationship. Participants (where applicable) responded to the items for both their present/most recent partner, as well as previous relationships (thus they had two scores for each scale). Participants responded on a 1 (Never) to 4 (Very often) Likert-type response scale.

5 Examination of individual cases indicated that 12 participants matched their ratings, and two others did so within one point. The remaining 11 participants had a discrepancy between 2-9 points (M=4.73; SD=2.24) and all but two of these participants indicated lesser perceived safety by the partner.

Table 11.1. Descriptive Statistics for the Abusive Behavior Inventory (pre-program)

	N	Minimum	Maximum	Mean	Std Deviation
Present Partner - Psychological Abuse	21	23.00	46.00	31.10	6.21
Previous Partner - Psychological Abuse	24	23.00	48.26	29.31	7.14
Present Partner - Physical Abuse	21	9.00	14.00	10.95	1.91
Previous Partner - Physical Abuse	24	9.00	21.00	10.46	2.54

Twenty-one participants completed the inventory for their present/most recent partner, and 24 responded to previous partners (18 responded to both) (see Table 11.1). Mean scores indicated that participants tended to report some psychological and physical abuse in both their present and previous relationships. For psychological abuse, one indicated no psychological abuse to their present or previous partner, one indicated no abuse to their present partner (but to a previous partner), and four indicated abuse to their current partner but not previous partner. For physical abuse, three indicated no previous abuse to present or previous partners, nine indicated no abuse to previous partner (but did to present partner), and three indicated no abuse to present partner (but did to previous partner). One participant indicated no abuse of any type to any previous or present partner.

Past relationships

Not including their current or most recent relationship, participants reported that they had been in an average of 3.50 previous intimate relationships (SD=2.95), with eight participants indicating that at least one of these relationships was a marriage. Abusive behaviour in these relationships was also relatively common, with areas investigated including physical abuse, use of a weapon, sexual abuse/assault, property damage, threats, coercion, jealousy, and verbal aggression.

In all, participants reported a mean of 3.23 physically abusive behaviours in previous relationships (SD=3.54[6]), although eight participants reported that they had not engaged in any of these behaviours. The most commonly reported acts of physical aggression (of 14 possible behaviours) were "pushed" "grabbed" "slapped" and "held" (the majority of participants who indicated that these or other behaviours had occurred indicated that they had happened "once" or "twice"). No participant reported having engaged in sexual abuse/assault, and only one participant reported using a weapon (not specified) once in a prior relationship. For property damage (for example, breaking objects) (five items), participants recorded a mean of 3.07 behaviours (SD=4.757[7]). For threats, while the overall mean (for five types of threat) was rather low (M=2.11; SD=3.54), as was actual prevalence by type of threat (threatened to hit or abuse M=.78; SD=1.5 threatened to destroy property M=.67; SD=1.39 threatened to kill partner M=.44; SD=1.19 threatened to commit suicide M=.22; SD=0.80 threats to sexually abuse were not reported by any participant), examination of frequency of occurrence of these serious threats indicated at least four participants reported that they had engaged in different types of threat three or more times. For both jealousy (M=0.96; SD=1.40) and engaging in verbal aggression (M=1.85; SD=1.92) reports were somewhat low (although these were both one-item measures), as was coercion (for example, forced to do something against will) (two items) (26 participants; M=.88; SD=1.86).

When calculating a total frequency (that is, number of times of occurrence) score for each participant (based on all 35 acts), mindful that this may be a underrepresentation (given the tendency to possibly underreport sensitive information and, as mentioned, the use of 4 to indicate more than three times—see footnotes 6 and 7 below), much variation is demonstrated (26 participants; median 6.50; Range=0-63), with examination of frequency indicating that 50 per cent of the sample engaged in 0-5 acts (31 per cent of the total sample indicating 0 acts), and that the highest number of acts by one person was more than twice (63 acts) the next highest prevalence (two participants who committed 35 acts).[8]

---

6 This figure does not include one participant who indicated at least 23 occurrences of physically abusive acts. This is because the response scale used (0=Nil; 1=Once; 2=Twice; 3=Three times; 4=More than three times) did not allow for a more precise number to be calculated once more than three behaviours had occurred. Therefore, this figure of 23 occurrences refers to *at least* 23 occurrences (this participant indicated a 4 for four behavioural acts). No other participant indicated a 4 for any behaviour, and the range of physically abusive behaviour was 0-13.

7 Unlike the previous calculation for physical acts which excluded one participant, this and all subsequent calculations include participants who indicated a 4, in spite of this not allowing a pure measure of frequency (that is, 4 is treated as four acts of violence). This was done as the selection of 4 was more common and not limited to one participant in all other measures.

8 The participant who indicated 182 acts of violence in their most current relationship scored 28 for previous relationships, the fifth highest score of the sample.

Family background, childhood and adolescence

Information was also collected on the family backgrounds of this group of men. The majority of participants either reported that their parents were married (N=13[9]), or that their parents had divorced or separated (N=13). One participant indicated that his parents were not in a relationship. For those whose parents had divorced or separated, on average this had occurred when the participant was 8.65 years old (10 participants; SD=4.03).

The fathers' reported occupations of fathers tended to be related to a trade (for example, builder, bricklayer, carpenter, painter, plumber) or manufacturing (for example, machinist), with a small minority involved in business or government occupations (for example, public servant). For the mothers, a substantial proportion were described as being involved in home duties, although other occupations included cleaner, food services and nursing. All but one participant indicated that they had at least one sibling (M=2.30; SD=1.10).

In most cases, participants defined their relationship with their parents as "close" (18 participants for fathers, 22 for mothers), rather than "distant" (nine for fathers, four for mothers). When asked to elaborate on the relationship, participants discussed both their relationship with their fathers as children as well as presently. They described these relationships in ways that stressed this closeness (for example, "close when a child and still close now"), as well as friendship ("he is like a close friend"), and regular contact ("see him regularly, do activities together"). For those who designated the relationship as distant, this distance was reflected by ambivalence (for example, "didn't seem to handle children well", "disciplinary", "on and off relationship"), often resulting in limited contact of both a physical and emotional nature (for example, "don't have anything to do with him", "left when five", "father didn't talk to me much"). Similarly, for relationships with mothers, close relationships were reflected in descriptions of a positive, close relationship ("good relationship", "very close with mother and sisters"), and regular contact ("talk to each other every second day, only one that knows about offences", "tell mum everything"). For those relationships described as distant, once again ambivalence or conflict was stressed ("clashes"), and contact ("asked to leave home at the age of nine", "don't have anything to do with her").

In terms of discipline in the family, neither the father nor the mother tended to be named more often as primary disciplinarian (father=10, mother=eight, both=nine). With respect to punishment, the majority (18) of the participants indicated that they were physically punished. There were common types of punishment, such as the use of belts, straps and wooden spoons, and descriptions of the punishment often

9 Two of these participants indicated that a parent was widowed, with one of these participant's parents remarrying.

as being "smacked" (for example, "smack on the bottom"). However, participants differed in describing the perceived purpose, nature or frequency of this punishment. For some, the punishment was perceived as being in some way relevant to the child's behaviour or societal factors (for example, "smack when naughty", "on two occasions when it was warranted", "physical discipline in accordance with societal values of that time"), while for others the punishment was described as physical abuse ("frequent physical abuse by both mother and father", "beatings with closed fist to the head and usually when drunk"). Punishment also varied in frequency ("very occasionally", "once a week", "frequent").

Four participants reported that they had either observed or knew of their father abusing their mother (physically, sexually, psychologically)[10]. Five participants reported that they considered themselves to have been physically or psychologically abused as a child, and one of these participants also indicated that they were a victim of sexual assault (by a stepfather). For those with siblings, four participants indicated that their siblings were physically (three participants), psychologically (one participant), or sexually (one participant) abused, with all indicating that they were also a victim of one or more of these types of abuse.

Seven participants reported that they had problems with violent behaviour during childhood or adolescence.[11] Most of this reported behaviour related to school and peers (for example, "fights at school when young", "expelled from school for fighting"), although some participants referred to becoming aggressive in threatening situations, taking their anger out on "whoever was around", and "always intimidated peers". Three of these participants indicated that their siblings also had problems with violent behaviour.

Finally, participants referred to a number of reasons or events which were related to their moving out of the family home. Often participants mentioned that they had a job, and that they moved in with either a partner or a friend. Only a minority of participants indicated that some element of the family home or family was responsible for this (for example, being removed due to abuse, being asked to leave, running away). For participants (N=18) who indicated what age they had moved out of home (not included two participants who left home before the age of 10[12]), the mean age was 17.17 years (SD=1.71; Range=14-21).

---

10 For participants with children, 11 of these 23 participants indicated that their child had observed or overheard arguments and/or violent episodes between the participant and partner.

11 Only two of 19 participants indicated that one of their children had behavioural problems at home or school, and only one of these participants referred to these problems being anger or aggression-related.

12 For these two participants, one was removed due to allegations of abuse or abuse at age nine, and one was kicked out of home at seven years of age, subsequently living in foster homes (and also serving some time in detention centres).

Intervention needs

Goals

All of the men (only one participant had data missing) indicated that they did *not* feel that their use of violence was an acceptable way of solving conflict. In assessing responsibility for their violence, however, participants indicated (on a scale of 1 "Not at all responsible" to 10 "Totally responsible") that they believed that they were moderately-to-highly responsible (M=7.27; SD=2.92; Range=1-10) and that their partner was less responsible (M=5.19; SD=2.94; Range 1-10), although their ratings suggested that partners were given some degree of responsibility. Thirteen participants assigned more responsibility to themselves, (mean difference=5.54) six participants assigned equal responsibility, while seven participants assigned greater responsibility to their partners (mean difference=2.57).

In addition, participants named a range of other factors as contributing to their violence. In describing these other factors, recurring responses included substance use, and issues related to family, financial matters, and work and employment.

Participants listed a number of diverse goals for treatment. The most prevalent were those related to psychological and mental health functioning. These included modifying cognitions, emotions and behaviours (for example, "resolves issues around insecurity and jealousy", "control temper", "learn better ways of reacting", "to learn to deal with conflict in relationship without resorting to violence"), as well as personal understanding ("gain a better perspective on behaviour", "identify triggers", "more of an understanding of why I get angry and how to control it", "to learn about myself and to gain knowledge about why previous DV occurred", "to work out what is wrong with me and get on with life and be happy"). Other goals were related to this, but were more holistic and personal ("become a better person", "everything to be successful").

A majority of participants (16 of 25 participants) indicated that they had received some form of counselling or psychotherapy in the past from a counsellor (most prevalent), psychologist or psychiatrist. For participants who indicated the reasons or area of concern, these included domestic violence, relationships and substance use, as well as depression subsequent to the end of their relationship. Five of these participants were also currently seeing another counsellor, psychologist or psychiatrist. Four participants had previously been hospitalised for mental health reasons, two related to suicide (threatening suicide and attempting suicide, respectively), one related to physical exhaustion, and one after a drinking binge. Eight participants indicated that they had had a serious accident or illness in the past, the majority of which (five participants) related to a road accident.

In addition to identifying needs in the area of mental health, a number of participants also reported ongoing problems with substance use. Almost all (24 of 26 participants) indicated that they drank alcohol, with the majority indicating that they do so at least once a week (12 participants), although five participants indicated less regularity, and six participants indicated that they did so daily. Participants varied on the number of standard drinks they drank at any one time (eight participants indicated one to three standard drinks, eight participants indicated four to six standard drinks, and seven indicated more than six standard drinks). When asked how often they get drunk, participants once again varied (five said once a week or more, five said monthly, seven said occasionally). Eleven of 25 participants indicated that they had used drugs in the previous 12 months. For those who indicated which substances, the most used was marijuana, seven participants indicated that they had used this substance once a week or more (two of those more than once a day), one participant had used tranquilizers (prescription drugs, other than those on doctor's instructions), one had used heroin (they had also used marijuana) more than once a day, and one had used "other" (non-specified) once a day. In terms of alcohol or drug-related violence, 18 of 26 participants indicated that they had acted violently while under the influence.[13]

Goals in relation to improving relationships were also commonly cited. This was apparent when participants were asked to reflect on general goals for treatment, as well as to articulate goals specific to the relationship or a relationship. For example, goals here included "not to engage in DV in the future", "to be a better partner, father, better son, better brother", "to reduce the angst in the relationship" and "to have better relationships in the future". Similar themes emerged when the men were asked to reflect on the relationship specifically ("to be happily married, open communication, focus on children", "enjoy life and make each other very happy"), and the increased welfare of their partner ("to keep them happy", "to be a good partner", "to show partner that I love her and willing to do anything for the relationship"). New relationships (where applicable) were also referenced ("to find happiness in future relationships", "learn from mistakes, better relationships in the future", "better all-round relationships", "to give my next partner everything that I didn't give to my last").

There were also other goals, such as those related to legal issues ("don't want to get in trouble with the law again", "to be rid of offences", "to resolve Family Court matters"). Only a small minority (three participants) indicated that they had no goals, or felt they did not require help (for example, "I don't need help. I haven't done anything I need help for").

Finally, participants indicated a number of current sources of support or understanding or assistance. Family, parents and friends were listed most frequently as a source of support, with partners also listed. Others listed (though only by one or two participants) were a psychiatrist, parole officers and a church network. All participants, save for three,

---

13 Five of these participants (and five other participants) indicated that they had acted violently while not under the influence of a substance.

indicated that they had access to at least one source of support; for these others, one of these participants indicated that he "relies on himself", while the other two said that they had nobody in this role. Participants indicated that they saw at least one of these sources of support daily (10 participants) or weekly (13 participants).

Conclusions

The information presented in this chapter provides an insight into the types of men who commit acts of domestic violence. Although based on their self-report, the data is consistent with that presented in other parts of this book. For example, many of the men take less responsibility for their behaviour than might be hoped for (with some blaming their partners) (see Chapter 12), and have significant needs in the areas of mental health and substance use. It is perhaps unsurprising to discover that the personal and family histories of these men reveal a picture in which abusive experiences were not uncommon, although often families were relatively stable. These issues are explored further in Chapter 9 in terms of what this may mean for intervention. It also suggests that there may be a small subset of offenders who have multiple needs, commit frequent and serious acts of violence, and display little motivation to engage in behaviour change. This is important in relation to program evaluation (see Chapter 13), and in particular the use of quantitative research designs which examine group differences over time. It may be that there is a need for assessment and selection processes which identify those men with multiple needs and more serious offending histories for more intensive intervention. At the same time this chapter reminds us of the considerable differences that exist amongst men who are referred to perpetrator programs. It is almost impossible to describe in any detail the typical offender. Our conclusion, then, is that it is important for program facilitators to conduct an individual assessment of the circumstances and context in which the offences occurred, before identifying which parts of the program are likely to be of most relevance to participants. In this way, programs can be matched to meet the needs of individual offenders, and as a consequence engage more men in a process of behaviour change.

Chapter 12

Resistant or Ready? The Challenges of Male Readiness for Offender Programs

Patrick O'Leary, Andrew Day, Gary Foster and Donna Chung

There are considerable challenges facing those who are involved in the delivery of domestic violence services. Not only is there a limited appreciation by the criminal justice system and the wider community of the harm caused by domestic violence, but integrated domestic violence responses typically strive to achieve multiple outcomes, often with limited resources. For example, integrated services aim to improve early detection and intervention by the police, secure appropriate penalties through the legal process, improve community awareness of the problem, offer practical and psycho-social support services for victims, as well as to deliver effective rehabilitation programs for known perpetrators and those who may be at risk of offending.

The aim of this chapter is to investigate one aspect of this work that is widely acknowledged to be a key issue in effective program delivery – the challenge of engaging domestically violent men in a process of behaviour change. High attrition rates in court mandated domestic violence offender programs have been reported in the majority of evaluation studies, in some cases up to 75 per cent (Buttell and Carney 2008). Gondolf (2008), for example, recently reported a completion rate of approximately 55 per cent for a 16 week group based program. High rates of attrition are a serious concern for victim safety, because the available evidence suggests that those men who start but fail to complete programs will be at higher risk of offending than those who do not enter programs at all (see DeMaris and Jackson 1987; McMurran and Theodosi 2006).

Many factors potentially impact on attrition rates, including offender demographic characteristics (Gondolf 2001), the time that lapses between the offence and program attendance (Dobash and Dobash 2005), and the type of legal order issued by courts for mandatory attendance (Buttell and Carney 2008). It is also apparent in the literature that men's readiness and motivation to accept treatment is both fragile and non-static (Eden, Lalos, Högerberg and Dahlegren 2008; Goldner 1999). This is probably unsurprising given the adversarial court process and the tendency for offenders to plead innocence or mitigation. As a result there are often a range of individual and systemic barriers to achieving therapeutic engagement in domestic violence perpetrator programs, especially in relation to offenders understanding and being concerned about the nature, extent and seriousness of their violence.

Domestic violence differs from many other types of violent offending in so far as offending typically occurs behind closed doors, where the only witnesses are victims. As a result the facts of the offence are often difficult to establish. Male perpetrators often dispute the evidence that is presented to the police and/or the courts in relation to the frequency and intensity of their violence, the reliability of the victim statements, and on a basic level the extent to which they consider themselves personally responsible. Researchers have often reported that men's explanations of their use of violence have centred on emotional responses to feeling threatened in terms of control and power (Denzin 1984). Male perpetrators, for example, often cite themselves as victims of circumstances (Thomas 2003). Mandated referral to a treatment program can often be seen by offenders as further vindication that men are without control and have been treated unjustly.

Given the above, it is perhaps unsurprising that program facilitators commonly report encountering hostility, resistance and non-compliance from their offenders - especially in the early stages of intervention. However, the available theoretical and empirical literature on the topic of treatment engagement in domestic violence programs is relatively sparse. In this chapter, the experiences and views of men who had just started a group-delivered legally mandated intervention program in the Gold Coast are analysed in terms of what has been termed "treatment readiness" (Howells and Day 2003).

Treatment readiness is a construct which, in recent years, has largely replaced the term "responsivity", a term commonly used in the offender rehabilitation literature. Whereas responsivity emphasises the need to adjust treatment delivery in ways that maximise learning (Andrews and Bonta 2003), treatment readiness is an overarching term which encompasses both the internal components of responsivity (for example, individual motivation to change, problem awareness, emotional capacity to engage with intervention programs, personal goals), and external components that may be specific to the context in which offender programs are commonly offered. Given that a major contributing factor to low levels of engagement and program attrition may be inconsistencies in the criminal justice and referral pathways for mandated offenders (see Chapter 15), this emphasis on factors that are external to the individual appears particularly appropriate for understanding therapeutic engagement in this population. Murphy and Baxter (1997) have also pointed to the need to consider the influence of situational and contextual factors on readiness to change, including the interpersonal dynamics of the relationship in which the violence occurs and the impact of changes in living arrangements on the individuals involved (for example, separation, reunification).

Research on different aspects of treatment readiness has, however, tended to focus on identifying and responding to individual difference factors. Howells and Day (2003), for example, in their analysis of treatment readiness in clients referred to anger management programs identified seven potential impediments to therapeutic engagement, including: the complexity of the cases presenting with anger problems; the setting in which anger management is conducted; existing client inferences about their anger "problem"; the influence of coerced or mandatory treatment; inadequate analysis of the context of personal goals within which the anger problem occurs; and gender and cultural issues. Similar themes have been picked up in the domestic violence literature. For example, Gilchrist (in press) has recently identified 10 potential implicit theories held by domestically violent men, each of which potentially undermine the extent to which perpetrators see their behaviour as problematic (for example, "women are dangerous", "the need for control", "women are objects", "entitlement/respect", "sex drives are uncontrollable", "real man"). Others have applied the transtheoretical model of change to domestic violence programs, a model which places emphasis on problem awareness, self-efficacy and motivation to change (see Casey, Day and Howells 2005; Eckhardt, Babcock and Homack 2004; Levesque, Velicer, Castle and Green 2008). This work suggests that many men who are referred to programs could be classified as in the early stages of change.

In this chapter we analyse the readiness of a sample of men who have been legally mandated to attend a group based domestic violence intervention program offered in the Gold Coast. Such research can inform the understanding of how readiness in domestically violent men can best be conceptualised, and can also help to identify potential avenues for responding in ways that enhance therapeutic engagement, reduce rates of attrition, and thereby promote better therapeutic outcomes.

Methodology

Participants

Participants were 38 men resident in the community in Southern Queensland, Australia. All had been convicted of domestic violence offences and as a consequence were mandated (by a court or the Department of Corrective Services) to attend a 24 week group intervention program as a condition of their order.

Participants' ages ranged from 19 to 53 years (data were available for 27 participants M=35.44; SD=8.50). The majority of participants were born in Australia, and all spoke English as their first language. At the commencement of the program, 19 of the participants reported that they were currently in a relationship, with 14 living with a partner. Participants reported a mean length for their present relationship (or, in the case of those who were single, most recent) of 6.49 years (26 participants; SD=5.15). For those who had separated (15 participants), a mean separation time of 11.43 months (SD=12.06) was reported.

Participants reported an average of 9.73 episodes of violence in the previous year of the relationship (26 participants; SD = 35.33), although this average was mostly due to three participants: two participants who reported that an episode occurred every two to three days or weekly; and one who reported "arguments" once a month. Without these participants, a mean of 1.43 episodes (SD=1.27) episodes of violence was reported.

As part of the program assessment participants are asked "Have you ever been required to attend this program?" Seventeen of 23 participants who responded to this question indicated "Not required to attend", with six indicating that the "Magistrate's Court" had required them to attend. Only a minority of participants knew that they had been required to attend the program.

Procedure

Each participant was interviewed individually by a male researcher during their attendance at an information session prior to entering the program. Men were asked open-ended questions starting with "*Can you tell me about your understanding and experience of being ordered to attend this program?*" Follow-up questions sought clarification and allowed participants to expand on the men's situations, experiences and expectations of being referred to the program. The interviews lasted between 15 and 30 minutes, were audio-recorded and transcribed for analysis.

Analysis

A phenomenological approach was employed in data analysis, given that the focus was on the participants' subjective experience (Schwandt 1994). Analysis began with a general examination of all transcripts to achieve an overall depth of familiarisation. Individual interviews were coded into themes, by the first author, relating to the core research question: "*What are the factors that constrain and enable therapeutic engagement with a domestic violence intervention program?*" Relevant text in each interview was extracted and labelled with a thematic code (Strauss and Corbin 1990). The codes identified in single cases were then cross-checked across cases to allow for emerging themes to be identified and elaborated. Textual evidence across cases is used to add to an understanding of the identified themes, to register contrary cases and to make decisions regarding the appropriateness of the theme's label.

Results

Four recurring themes emerged from the data in relation to treatment readiness: disregard or denial of responsibility for any acts of violence or abuse; little or no articulated understanding of the mandated process of referral to the program; encumbrance; and ambivalence. As the key themes indicate, in this sample levels of treatment readiness were uniformly low.

Theme 1: Disregard or denial of responsibility for any acts of violence or abuse

Provocation

Many men expressed a sense of injustice because they believed, at the very least, that their partners were equally responsible for the circumstances that led to their order to attend the program. Violence was often constructed as reciprocal or part of broader relationship problems. In other cases men felt that most, if not all, of the responsibility for the situation lay with their partner or other family members:" *I think it's dependent on the situation … you can say that most of the time it's 90 per cent her, other times I would say that you know it could be 70 per cent, but … I am never the instigator.*"

Men's claims of innocence were not a complete self-absolution of any wrong doing, rather (with one exception) men did acknowledge that they had acted wrongly in some way. It was not uncommon for men while recounting the reasons for their referral to give a discursive account of events and reflexively point out issues of injustice, while at the same time noting specific acts of their own that they could not condone. In essence, men rarely saw themselves as solely responsible for the violence, whilst acknowledging that the violence committed was not an acceptable way of behaving.

Men regularly cited provocation that led to their violence, and their belief that the response from courts to refer them to the program was an over-reaction (or injustice) because their partner was not ordered to also attend a program or penalised in some other way. This theme and its underlying sentiments are summed up in the following quote from one participant in response to a question about the circumstances of their referral:

> Under duress (willingness to attend the program) to be perfectly frank, um I'm unfortunately in the situation where I don't think I'm suitable for the course. I'm not innocent in relation to the few areas where I've crossed the line but what I am completely shocked at is the system where the other party is not brought to account because when she rings up the police because it's just a figment of her imagination that everything is going to get better

> because she's going to ring the police. The crux of the matter is we're having or have had a bad relationship every time her daughter comes back into the house.

This man believes that "duress" in some way makes him unsuitable for the program that he refers to as a "course". There is some admission of guilt, however, but the primary problem or "crux" is a bad relationship and the presence of his partner's daughter. Other Australian research asking men about their experiences of domestic violence programs similarly found that men described their reasons for attendance as due to having "relationship problems" (Bagshaw et al 1999). There is also a strong rebuttal of the need for police involvement. This same man goes on to talk about his sense of dissatisfaction with police, courts and Corrective Services "believing" his partner while at the same time "ignoring" his partner's actions against him. He recounts his breach of a domestic violence protection order (DVO) and a subsequent allegation of threatening to kill his partner:

> On a second occasion I went around to the house knocked on the door and the girlfriend answered the door again, she said "Oh you've breached the DVO". Anyway the accusation and apparently I accused and threatened to kill her and when I mentioned it to my ex partner she said, "You never threatened me at all what are you talking about?" and I said, "Well that's what the police said". So basically they can fabricate stories you know and then, "Oh I'm sorry it was just at the spur of the moment".

Here the inference is that police always believe victims stories, even in cases where allegations are fabricated. Similarly, another man stated that a DVO had been placed on him in what was described as dubious circumstances because his partner "*was apparently scared of me*".

Commonly men construct their situations as a jointly owned "relationship problem" where his use of violence is an individual reaction to "their" relationship problems for which they are both responsible. This is an appeal to a narrative of justice for which he expects her to take equal responsibility. An attempt to describe a context in which they refrained from using violence in the face of provocation also featured in a number of men's descriptions of the offences that led to the order to attend the program. Claims of assault from their partners were not uncommon. This was seen as part of the justification of their response, but importantly there was a clear position taken by the men that their use of violence was either minor, defensive, or restrained and controlled. The following quote highlights this position:

> She pushed me first, I pushed her back, it wasn't very hard like I didn't wind up and then push her as hard as I could, just enough to let her know I was there and then that was it, as soon as I pushed her she ran straight to the phone, rung the police and they came over and then yeah ... and (I was) charged with assault.

In a similar explanation another man describes the events leading up to his arrest:

> I've never hit a woman in my life. And in the end I got up to walk away and then she threw an ashtray in the back of my head, so I just turned around and said, "Look I've had enough of this", and pushed her out the way and she went down on the floor and next minute my son phoned the police or stepson phoned the police and that was it. That's when she had me carted away and then they took the DVO out on me.

In these accounts of provocation the men covertly show a high level of control in terms of restraint and minimisation of their violence. This was evident with numerous statements such as "*She said I punched her but all I did was push her, if I really punched her she would have ended up unconscious*". In contrast, statements from some other men were characterised by their reporting little or no memory of the acts of violence. Alcohol featured strongly in these statements as an explanation for being out of control and not recalling incidents.

Alcohol

It was noteworthy that alcohol or substance abuse was in some way implicated in 34 of 38 of the men's descriptions of their situations. Most often it was their own use of alcohol or other substances that was part of the rationalisation for their offending behaviour. In a few other cases alcohol used by the men's partner was cited as a cause of the men's violence. Men were often unclear in their memory of the acts of violence that had resulted in their referral to the program, men for example cited the effects of alcohol or in some cases simply said they had blanked out and "*Suddenly I was being handcuffed and taken away by the cops*". Difficulties in recalling events were often attributed to alcohol, but there was also recognition that such events are not usual:

> It all started one Friday night. We had been drinking quite heavily and from what I can understand I got a bit out of control because I was drunk. And the next minute I know the police were involved and I was getting arrested. Yeah so it was a bit of a blank, sort of fill in the gaps the next day sort of thing um we normally get on pretty well apart from that yeah.

The following quote is another example of alcohol being cited as an impediment to memory and ownership of their acts:

> We got drunk. I cannot remember, apparently I threw an empty coke bottle and it wasn't empty because it went all up the wall, I don't even know if she was in the room. I was angry with her whinging. I slammed the door and it came off the hinge and … what else did I do, there was something else um. I cannot think for the life of me.

In the above quote the man reveals details that might indicate greater recall of events than is intended (such as whether the bottle was empty or not). At the same time there is a disclosure that he does not dispute that these events were possible, even though he cannot be sure of his recollection.

Upon further analysis some men revealed some sense of difficulty in facing the reality of their actions, and in doing so revealed that they could recall details of their actions despite their state of intoxication or loss of control. Most often this was not so much about their own actions but the actions of others immediately prior to or after their use of violence. For example, a man who said he was intoxicated at the time of the offence and could not recall the type of charge, and thus the reason for his subsequent order by the court to attend the program, later recalled the events leading up to the arrest:

> It was Christmas Eve, drinking heavily and then both of us arguing and she punched me, so I thought well I'm not letting her get away with that. And she rung the police and they said basically I must have went off. There wasn't any physical contact but she was obviously worried enough that she rung the police and I sort of come to in the cells.

When this man was asked about how he "went off" he reflects that his behaviour was not acceptable and warranted some consequence:

> I got a bit abusive, locked her and the kids out of the house. And yeah she was obviously concerned enough to get the police involved which was fair enough. I can't behave like that and then get away with it so. Yeah yelling, apparently I threw a pot. Yeah wasn't any physical contact on her or the children but it wasn't called for basically.

In this last quote we can see the man struggling to come to terms with the memories of his actions and the impact of his behaviour. Such features may indicate some fragility in relation to his readiness for therapeutic engagement, but there are potential areas to focus on, such as his recognition that he should not behave in that way. Another man recounts an incident where he was arrested for assaulting his partner. First, he describes a situation of intoxication and provocation where he believes he has been dealt with badly, however he also describes his actions as at odds with his own principles:

> I had too much to drink and she started busting my stuff up, I was just trying to stop her doing what I am unhappy with, we were arguing … I didn't know what to do … I called the police when she threw a glass at me and cut my leg, I just sort of grabbed her by the throat … I've never ever hit a woman … never … don't have those principles behind me … like you know I admit I reacted appallingly … but I am the one who got taken away and I think that it involves two people in relationships yeah, she really needs to be here too.

There is some acknowledgment in this quote about his discomfort with his actions, but his primary attention is on justifying his actions along with a strong sense of dissatisfaction and injustice with the fact he was arrested and subsequently ordered to do the program.

Injustice

As we can see from the previous quote even in the light of some admission of wrongdoing there was often an overarching sense of injustice in their current order to attend the program. Men frequently expressed concerns about the "fairness" of their situation. Primarily men felt an injustice in how they were treated in comparison to their partners. Commonly they felt that police and other services had ignored or failed to act on their concerns. The following quote is fairly indicative of this sentiment:

> I've been having problems with my wife and the only way she could get me out was to take out a DVO. I didn't do anything but she said she was scared of me and that was enough for the police. Then, don't know what I was supposed to have done, they (police) charged me for breaching the order and that ... they didn't ask me nothing about it, they just believed her.

Entwined in their experience of this was a sense of injustice about having to attend. This is explored later in the theme of attendance as an encumbrance. The pervasive sense of injustice which is common in men's accounts is central to their beliefs about responsibility. As they see it, the violence is at best a joint problem and at worst her responsibility. The notion of fairness is invoked, whereby if both are responsible for the violence they should receive the same consequences. A related theme is that many men consider they are not given a fair hearing.

Theme 2: Little or no understanding of the mandated process of referral to the program

When men were asked about the court or correctional services ordering them to attend the program it was not uncommon for men to be unclear about this process. At one extreme some men claimed no understanding of the process, as illustrated by this quote:

> I didn't really understand it, I didn't understand any of it and I still don't understand any of it now to be honest with you. Didn't understand a thing, none of it was explained to me yeah. Even when I was in the police station they said they arrested me for a breach of an order and they didn't tell me what it was or anything like that. Section 81 or something or other and I didn't have a clue what it was all about, just didn't have a clue. It was supposed to be if I committed threatening behaviour towards her or her friends, well there's no friends around, all I was doing it was basically to the vehicle. So I understand that she's going to feel threatened by my actions at the time. So yeah I suppose that's my breach of that order yeah so, but it's very vague to me it was very vague the way it was all done.

The above quote reveals some contradiction, on one hand the man recounts being uninformed, but at the same time begins to answer some of the confusion by talking about the breach that he committed. For other men the lapse of time since offending and entry into the group program was important. Some men spoke of significant time lapses between the offence occurring and their attendance at the program, in some cases this was up to two or three years. Related to this was a poor understanding of why they had been referred to the program and the purpose of their attendance. In this context a majority of men stated that they had primarily resolved the issues that led to their referral to the program. This resolution was most strongly linked to the passage of time and the ending or reconciliation of the relationship with the victim, with statements such as *"I haven't seen her in over a year so there's no problem"* and *"We've sorted it out now, she knows me better now"*.

Some men felt that the referring court had not adequately informed them about the process or content of the program. Many men commented that they felt the length of the program was excessive, with one man commenting that he had been put on bonds that had not lasted as long as the program. There was some apprehension from men about content and the fact that they will be in a group with other men. The following quotes highlights one man's confusion about the referral process and program:

> Just a bit confused I suppose, no one told me what it's all about, I've waited about six months and then I find out it is 24 weeks I have to come or something, but I am curious as well yeah more than anything else yeah. Yeah I haven't got that I shouldn't be here attitude ... Just don't know what to expect.

Theme 3: Encumbrance

Generally, attendance was seen as a hindrance or imposition on their lives and not really part of the court procedure. Some men thought that the court penalty was adequate or that their attendance caused too much disruption to social or financial situations. For example some men commented on the cost of attending as a *"waste of money"* or *"stopped me earning money"*. The following quote highlights that attending the group has been disruptive to one man's work commitments:

> Well I mean it's not something I don't want to do it's um I mean I guess I don't really want to be here at this time of night. I start work at 5 in the morning you know I've been up since 4 and so this time of night I'm getting tired.

Other men commented that they were giving up their social life *"Thursdays are normally darts night"*. For many of the other men the encumbrance of attending was caught up with their own perceptions of innocence and injustice, this led to statements such as *"it's a waste of everyone's time"*. As a result numerous men were pessimistic of any therapeutic benefits that the -

group may offer. Sometimes this was based on past experiences of counselling that they found unhelpful. While others simply saw themselves as innocent and complying with the court: *"I don't think I should really be in the program to be honest but I have to come so that's basically it"*.

Part of the reluctance to attend was also attributed to the need to talk about *"personal matters in front of men they did not know"*. The group format of the program was a clear area of anxiety and trepidation in their motivation to attend. This is highlighted by one man who asks the question: *"Being in the room with the other men yeah that's often the challenge but it can take a bit of time to get used to it?"*

Another concern about participating in a group was the significant passage of time that had passed since the offence that led to their order to attend the program. For some they felt that they had moved on and were reluctant to revisit the issues associated with their order. One man in response to the question whether he thought it could be useful to attend the program stated: *"No because I've just shut Pandora's box and I don't really want to have to open it for people that I don't know about"*.

Theme 4: Ambivalence

Most men did not completely dismiss the potential for benefits to arise from their attendance at the group, sometimes even in the face of claims of innocence and the unfairness of the mandatory order. These motivations were not unrelated to their claims of innocence or injustice. There was a recurring theme of ambivalence towards any benefits from the program and this was indicated by a general resignation to the fact that they had to attend the program. Four men implied that they were reticent about attending in the future, one claiming employment responsibilities and three citing transport problems. Three subthemes were identified in relation to potential factors for therapeutic engagement:

- May as well give it a go;
- Systemic and social pressures;
- Reconciliation.

May as well give it a go

Within the general acquiescence that attendance was unavoidable, numerous men took the attitude that they would give the program a chance. For example, one man complained about the length of the program but added:

> [B]ut it's only two hours a night so hopefully it will fly by. Might learn something, so might learn to communicate a bit better, or that's what I'm hoping for anyway. But pity she can't come along for a few sessions but never mind.

The above quote shows the man's perceptions of where he believes some of the responsibility lies by suggesting his partner should also attend, while also hoping he may engage in learning. Other men were already looking towards the completion of the group with the hope that there might be some benefit gained that was not self-evident at the time of interview.

> Yeah I've been a bit anxious maybe or can't think of the word but um I think it's the once it's over I think its going to help, I'm pretty sure it will, otherwise I would hate to be sitting here and not getting anything out of 24 weeks.

Some men viewed the opportunity to talk about their experiences as potentially valuable, even though this would be done within a group context.

> I'm glad there is something out there sort of you know to talk about and stuff. I'm not real keen on the group therapy thing you know with strangers and stuff. Um got a strong opinion if it's my problem I'll deal with it myself and I don't really want them taking my shit on and I don't want to take their shit on but that's just the way I think about things I suppose and if I don't want to take their stuff on I don't have to.

Systemic and social pressures

In the face of possible imprisonment or the termination of relations with partner and/or children if they did not attend the program, men regarded attendance as a better option as highlighted by the following quote:

> Um better than jail, um I grew up with it and I think it's about time something was done. Really I mean sticking someone in jail and then letting them come out is not going to help them. If anything it's going to make them withdraw in more and become other, um that's what happened in my experience.

It was not consistently clear whether men's prime motivation was to be seen to be doing the program in order to satisfy partners or other authorities (for example, child protection) or to engage in a change process because they accepted they were culpable for their own violent behaviour. There was a general perception that attendance at the program may change their image to authorities, in some cases lawyers had encouraged compliance with the order. This was especially evident where men wanted to maintain or gain access to children –"*If I can get the visitation sorted out it will be fine, but as I said I don't want nothing to do with her at all*".

Reconciliation

Other men saw their attendance at the program as providing some opportunity for reconciliation with their partners. Often these motivations seemed to be associated with a desire to control their partner, or to prove a point:

> [H]ey I'm happy because when I got in there (court) I even told them I said look I went down to (city) I breached a DVO. Probably shouldn't have ... I said look I'm quite happy to do whatever I can to get this sorted. Because I have been begging (ex-partner) to sit down and deal with this with me for fucking two years and she won't do it. I said we made appointments to go and see a counsellor and she didn't go and we had organised every Sunday. I wouldn't talk to her for a week not a fucking word and Sunday afternoon or Sunday night from 8 to 10 we would sit down and talk about our shit, organising anything that had to be organised for the kids' day care whatever. She wouldn't do it, so I would beg and plead with her for like five or six hours to sit down and talk with me and try and discuss things.

Discussion

As is consistent with the experiences of those who deliver programs for domestically violent men, the results of this study confirmed that low readiness may be an important therapeutic issue for many men who are referred to domestic violence programs. Four themes were identified relating to denial of responsibility for behaviour: disregard or denial of responsibility for any acts of violence or abuse; ignorance or feeling uninformed about the legal process and referral into the group; encumbrance; and ambivalence about attending the program. These themes can be meaningfully grouped into individual and systemic factors, with the implication that low readiness can be understood and thus addressed across multiple levels.

Applying the transtheoretical model of change to these accounts suggests that most of the men could be regarded as in the pre-contemplation stage of change. According to this model, transition through each of the stages of change can be optimised with the appropriate focus on the processes of change aligned to each of the stages (Murphy and Baxter 1997). In the pre-contemplation stage, for example, this is achieved through consciousness-raising strategies (for example, educating perpetrators about the physical and mental consequences of violence on their victims), dramatic relief (for example, facilitating group discussions to encourage disclosure), and both environmental and self re-evaluation (for example, social comparison, self-monitoring exercises, group feedback regarding the impact of aggressive behaviour). Eckhardt et al (2004) noted that this model can be easily integrated into most domestic violence programs, including the use of methods such as motivational interviewing prior to entry into group programs.

Others such as Novaco, Ramm and Black (2001) provide accounts of how programs might be modified to meet the needs of those with low levels of readiness, including for example by introducing a more extended pre-intervention assessment, and a preparatory phase to develop necessary skills, and an extended, more intensive program. In addition, the Babcock, Green and Robie (2004) meta-analysis found that the most effective programs incorporated retention techniques within group therapy programs (such as reminder phone calls and follow-ups) to reduce attrition rates, and incorporate what they referred to as "emotion-focussed" interventions to improve emotional awareness and expression, empathy and communication skills.

Less direct attention has been paid to the impact of external or systemic factors on treatment readiness. This study suggests that a major contributing factor to low levels of readiness are inconsistencies and delays in the criminal justice and referral pathways for mandated domestic violence offenders. Although the service in which this research was conducted is in many ways a model of integrated service provision (Chung, O'Leary, and Zannettino 2004), systemic issues still appear to have a great influence on treatment readiness. For example, referral to an intervention program took place after a significant time delay, sometimes years after the offence. There is clearly a need for the criminal justice system to reinforce the link between the charges and attendance at a behaviour change program, and prior to program entry for Community Corrections officers to reinforce and clarify the legally mandated nature of the referral. Men's reports of ignorance and confusion regarding the referral process and purpose of the program can be attributed to a range of factors such as claims of innocence and injustice. However, the consistency with which men claimed poor comprehension of the program content and process at the very least suggests some mystification.

While there were numerous indicators of low treatment readiness, many of the men did reveal some areas for therapeutic engagement to improve readiness. Critically these areas are not unrelated to men's claims of innocence and injustice, but they are indicative of motivation for potential change. As such these areas of motivation and partial acknowledgment of responsibilities are likely to be areas where engagement can be achieved in the early stages of referral and program attendance. In some cases the opportunity to engage in a non-adversarial context may offer an opportunity for greater personal reflection and less defensiveness. Motivation may change over time and, as Gondolf (2001) has reported, timely intensive treatment is associated with higher levels of completion and lower levels of reoffending.

The construct of treatment readiness in this analysis would appear to be particularly appropriate for understanding low levels of engagement in domestically violent men. It is apparent that low readiness can reside either in the individual or the setting, or, indeed, in both (see Ward, Day, Howells, and Birgden 2004). In our view the primary responsibility for modifying low levels of readiness lies with the practitioner and the service in which she or he works. In other words, it is the program facilitator's duty to develop systems and find ways to deliver interventions that address low levels of readiness – the tendency to blame clients for low levels of problem awareness or to label them as resistant should be discouraged as to do so is clearly anti-therapeutic and unlikely to lead to improved levels of safety for women and children. Furthermore, methods of formally assessing levels of treatment readiness have been developed for use with violent offender populations and should form a key component of any pre-program assessment (see Day et al 2009; Levesque, Gelles and Velicer 2000). In conclusion then, this chapter clearly illustrates some of the challenges that practitioners face in engaging domestically violent men in a process of change, highlighting some of the areas that require attention if they are to engage in programs, and actively work on reducing the risk of perpetrating further violence.

Chapter 13

Have Male Offenders Changed? Men's Perspectives and Experiences at the End of the Program

Andrew Day, Patrick O'Leary, Gary Foster, Laura Bahnisch and Adam Gerace

The Gold Coast men's intervention program and the model upon which it is based (see Chapter 7) is focused on improving women's safety. Although the Duluth model upon which the program is based is much broader than intervention with offenders (see Chapter 2), the primary aim of the men's program is to assist participants to become more accountable for their actions. In Chapter 8, Tony Fletcher argues that a central position from feminist theorising is that men's uses of violence are decisions the man makes in a socio-cultural context of gendered entitlement and male privilege. He argues that the language of "decision" and "deciding" encourages the man to face issues of intentionality, and that any attempt to externalise responsibility can be perceived as an effort to escape being held accountable. The interviews with program participants at the start of the Gold Coast program (see Chapter 12) illustrate vividly how unable or unwilling many perpetrators are, at the beginning of a program, to accept full responsibility for their actions. Program participants typically see themselves as victims of circumstance, with mandated referral to a treatment program often regarded as further evidence that they have been treated unfairly.

There are substantial barriers and challenges involved in evaluating integrated responses, not least of which are differing views about how to operationalise success. In Chapter 2, for example, it was suggested that a key characteristic of an integrated response is accountability to women. Developing the means to assess whether a service is accountable (or not) is by no means straightforward, although the Duluth Safety Audit provides one approach to this type of evaluation. The most common type of evaluation, however, involves an assessment of the changes that occur in men over the course of attending the program. It is this data that is reported in this chapter, although clearly these are not the only outcomes that are important. A number of different data sources are used. First, data from interviews conducted with men upon completing the program offer an account of how they understood the program and the ways in which they felt it had affected them. Data on some questionnaires completed before starting and after completing the program is also reported, along with the session-by-session ratings of progress made by the facilitators.

Despite the need for the development of effective community responses to domestic violence, support for the delivery of perpetrator programs is neither consistent nor universal. To date, there has been a lack of research in Australia that examines the effectiveness of male perpetrator intervention programs (O'Leary, Chung, and Zannetino 2004), with Australian research on male perpetrator intervention programs largely confined to policy, procedural and organisational analysis. International research on program outcomes has been rather disappointing (see Babcock, Green and Robie 2004; Feder and Wilson 2005), with studies typically reporting very small effect sizes, especially when victim reports are used as the dependent variable, or when the study examines changes in men who are mandated to attend a program. Indeed, the research evidence supporting the effectiveness of compulsory or legally coerced treatment for many types of offender is probably best regarded as both inadequate and inconclusive (ANDC 2007). The present chapter thus aims to investigate the impact of a community based domestic violence program delivered to offenders who had been mandated as part of their community corrections order to attend the program. Given that the program under consideration is widely considered to represent good practice in an Australian context (see Chapter 2), an important aim of the study is to establish whether there is any evidence that male program participants are changing in ways that might be considered to indicate a reduction in risk.

The data reported here is drawn from 38 men resident in the community in the Gold Coast region of Queensland, Australia and attending the men's program, although data were not available on all measures for every person. All of the men had been convicted of domestic violence offences and, as a consequence, were mandated (by a court or by a Community Corrections officer) to attend a 24 week group intervention program as a condition of their order. Participants' ages ranged from 19 to 53 years (data were available for 27 participants; M=35.44; SD=8.50). The majority of participants were born in Australia, and all spoke English as their first language.

The interviews

A phenomenological approach was employed to analyse the experiences of men who were interviewed shortly after completing the program. As such the focus of the initial analysis was on the participants' subjective experience (Schwandt 1994). Analysis began with a general examination of all transcripts, and relevant text in each interview was then extracted and labelled with a thematic code (Strauss and Corbin 1990). The codes identified in single cases were then cross-checked across cases to allow for emerging themes to be identified and elaborated.

Analysis

Some men spoke explicitly about their legal status and how this had influenced their participation in the program. When asked about whether they had changed, a range of views were voiced, although most men clearly regarded themselves as of low risk of reoffending. What was apparent, however, particularly when the interviews are set alongside those conducted before the program started (described in Chapter 12), was that participants left the program with higher levels of problem awareness than when they began. When they were asked about what had helped, most participants described the development of communication skills, particularly in relation to other men in the group.

Program attendance as part of punishment

The first theme identified related to the perception that attendance at the program was primarily intended as a penalty or punishment for the offence. There was a variety of views on how important the mandated aspect of the program had been for them. For some, the court order was instrumental in getting them to address their behaviour:

> Would I have done it without a court order? Probably not ... I wouldn't have said no to doing something probably together with my partner but having gone down the path of being issued with a DVO (domestic violence order) and then breaching the DVO and being put in this course.

For another, the threat of further punishment (imprisonment) was at the forefront of his thinking, although this participant still did not make a clear association between the punishment and his behaviour:

> *Question*: So it sounds as though for you knowing that you have prison hanging over you was a real big factor?
>
> *Answer*: Oh sure most definitely right, because like in the past she used to hit me and torment me and now I don't react I just walk away which is a big thing. When alcohol was involved that was a different thing as well, a total different thing. I mean look what I'm here for is because it's with a different woman completely different woman.

One participant talked in terms of "paying for" his behaviour as follows, suggesting that his approach to the program was more about serving a punishment than seeking to change his behaviour:

> Oh it's been alright, it's pretty much just common sense, like I already pretty much knew everything that we do in the group, I just know that I made a stupid mistake before and now I'm paying for it so.

Changes since starting the program

A number of the men described how they had changed in positive ways since attending the program.

> It's been very helpful, very helpful. I guess, you know, from what I've heard from as guys have started the program we all come in here with the thought of this is a pain in the arse and you know every Thursday night for the next six months I'm going to have to be here and I'm not going to get anything out of this but I've got to be really honest, it's exactly the opposite. I've got a tremendous amount out of it and I've said over a period of time that the last few months or so that friends of mine not having seen for a while have actually said to me what an improvement there is in me not knowing that I'm doing this course.

> Well it just opened my eyes to see that you know what I mean. Like it is a big problem that and it's not just like I was saying, it's not just physical. There is verbal is a form of domestic violence you know what I mean. And I just couldn't get my head around that. I refused to fucking, when I first come here it's just oh you know, it's only a fucking argument you know, the neighbours should keep their fucking big ears out of it you know what I mean, they just should fucking mind their own business. But obviously they shouldn't really because if I look at now if that was me I would ring the police if I heard that.

For another man, the changes only seemed to occur after he had repeated the program:

> I mean I did the course one other time so this is my second time, and yeah the first time I was just blaming. I was blaming her for pushing, so called pushing my buttons, so forth and like yeah. I did listen but I wasn't able to stand back and have a good look at myself you know and focus on just my part ... I'm here because I didn't get it right the first time so I've got to change something with what I did last time, so that's what I've done.

For other participants, it was difficult to judge whether change had occurred. This participant begins by suggesting that he has not really grasped the material on gender imbalance, but then goes on to describe some positive changes in his relationship:

> I know it goes both ways – some women are just as violent as some men ... but men are stronger and muscle wise and it can cause more damage to a woman by the way they assault and they punch or push or anything along those lines and um yeah it's pretty much it ... Through the course I highlighted things in our relationship and I've also seen things that you know she needed to work on as well, but I'm just focussed on myself. That's all I can do and that's all I've sort of been doing is just looking and identifying things (in

> me). I know there are issues that in the past would escalate now I've taken a tack to making sure I don't use intimidation or isolation which is what I used to do if I didn't agree with something ... Probably the last two months we've sat down and talked about what's happened – the violence and everything and how it's affected her which is something I've never done before till now. I think through the course I picked up enough I suppose ownership and enough courage within myself to see how she truly felt about everything, because it wasn't there before it.

For some others, however, there was little in their accounts to suggest that they had changed in any meaningful way. Even though they professed to have changed, it seemed that they had only gained a limited appreciation of the program material:

> *Question*: Have the ways that you've viewed women changed in any way?
>
> *Answer*: No that's the first and last time I've ever done any violence with women when I pushed her, so yeah that's the only time.
>
> The course for me has basically taught me to be non-aggressive right um and as I said I've always respected (partner's name) and I've never treated her wrongly you know I never abused her physically or whatever just a few minor altercations, you know being more calm and you know and respectful.

Problem awareness

Most participants appeared to leave the program with a greater awareness of the nature of their problems, and an increased commitment to developing non-violent relationships:

> But when I first I sort of couldn't get my head around to begin with that, well it was only a fucking argument big deal you know, I couldn't even get my head around that. But since then well an argument is the stepping stone you know what I mean, and last thing I wanted to have with (partner's name) in this relationship is to graduate to full on violence if you know what I mean. And I'm just sort of you know glad that I've been made aware that it is. And when I look back on my last relationship that's what happened, we started arguing and it got worse and louder and eventually push come to shove.

For some, this awareness focussed on the role that substance use played in their aggression:

> It's just the fact of what's happened to me over the last 10 years is I hit the grog a lot right and because in the last five years I was going out with two women and you asked me why do I go out with two women, quite simple I was in love with both of them and I couldn't let go and it was very hard for me to let go. So I would spend three or four days as I said before with the other one and then on the Friday night I think how can I be with the other one so I used to have a few to drink as an excuse right and she might say something about something so then I would react for her to leave and that

> was it. I don't do that any more because she's not here and quite frankly when she does go I miss her.

What helped?

When asked what specifically had helped the men to change, they consistently identified two things – social support from other men in the program, and the development of communication skills in their intimate relationships:

> When I first come here I was a blubbering mess and didn't want to be here so although there was a lot of getting things off my chest and knowing I'm not the only one out there going through the same thing so it's been good.
>
> Well you know I suppose it's the group atmosphere you know because you think before you walk into the place you see your situation in isolation and you don't know what other people are going through. So therefore you know you don't know you're just I suppose you're in your own little cocoon then you hear the stories of other people who have you know their own stories to tell and I suppose you realise you share similar problems with other people um or your situation in life is similar to other people. You have the same frustrations and you know, dare I say it, you've all got something in common.
>
> I suppose talking the issues through with other people who have similar problems I suppose and then you know under the guidance of our counsellors, group coordinators you know, they keep you on track which is important because it's quite easy to get off the track and to you know talking over the issues and how to tackle problems from a different angle you know.
>
> It's talking and listening to the other boys.
>
> The group has done a lot for me sort of learning how to communicate with people and communicate my feelings and not bottle stuff up and just respect what other people are saying instead of being caught up in my own world you know.

For one person, these skills acquired in group may have influenced his communication at home:

> Yeah I listen a lot more. I understand um I try and protect her obviously that's what it's all about, is making her safe. Um whether who's in the right or in the wrong it doesn't matter it's the fact of what the end result is right, and believe it or not I am a harmonious person.

The questionnaires

The **Revised Conflict Tactics Scales** (CTS2; Straus, Hamby, Boney-McCoy and Sugarman 1996) is a 78-item measure consisting of four scales (each with two subscales), which measures the extent to which an individual engages in various behaviours when involved in conflict, and the extent to which their partner engages in these behaviours (as reported by the individual, not the partner). As such, there are 39 items which measures the acts of the individual (for example, "I insulted or swore at my partner"), and 39 which are the same items, but refer to the partner (for example, "My partner did this to me").

The negotiation scale purports to measure the use of constructive approaches to conflict resolution, of both an emotional (three items; for example, "I showed respect for my partner's feelings about an issue"), and cognitive tone (three items; for example, "I explained my side of a disagreement to my partner"). The psychological aggression scale measures psychologically aggressive behaviours engaged in when in conflict with a partner, and includes behaviours involving insults and verbal taunts, threats, or non-verbal behaviours, of both a minor (four items; for example, "I stomped out of the room or house or yard during a disagreement") and more severe (four items; for example, "I threatened to hit or throw something at my partner") nature. The physical assault scale measures acts of physical aggression directed toward a partner and includes items differing in severity, from comparatively lesser severity (five items; for example, "I grabbed my partner"), to those of greater severity (seven items; for example, "I beat up my partner"). The sexual coercion scale measures behaviours of a sexually aggressive nature, involving psychological pressure (for example, "I used threats to make my partner have sex"), as well as physical acts (for example, "I used force (like hitting, holding down, or using a weapon) to make my partner have sex"), which also differ in extent of severity (four items of severe coercion, and three items of lesser coercion). The injury scale measures injuries sustained during arguments, with two items of lesser severity (for example, "I had a sprain, bruise or small cut because of a fight with my partner"), and four items of a more severe nature (for example, "I went to a doctor because of a fight with my partner").

Participants indicate how often a behaviour occurred in the specified time period (once; twice; three to five times; six to 10 times; 11-20 times; more than 20 times; not in the time period but has occurred; has never happened). At pre-program, 21 participants reported incidents over the past year, while 16 participants reported for the previous six months. At post-program, participants reported for the previous six months.

Two types of main scores were calculated: a prevalence score for each scale/subscale, which indicates whether the participant engaged in any behaviour in that scale/subscale (Yes/No) in the time period; and a frequency score, which measures the frequency of occurrence of behaviours measured by each scale/subscale (a score of 3-5 is recoded to 4, 6-10 is recoded to 8, 11-20 is recoded to 15, and more than 20 is recoded to 25).

While Straus et al (1996) reported validational work where chronicity is calculated (where frequency for each scale/subscale only includes participants who indicated at least one act from that scale), in the present analysis scores from all participants were included. This was because it was important to know the range of reported behaviours (whether low or high) at the time of entry into the program, and not only the range using those participants who had committed at least one type of the acts being assessed. Of course, a score of 0 is, perhaps, even more meaningful at Time 2, where change in this direction is actually desired (for the four maladaptive behaviour scales). Assessing the differences by removing such scores from chronicity calculations resulted in predicted but small changes in means and standard deviations.

At program commencement, the responses of 37 participants were available for analysis, 21 of whom reported prevalence/frequency based on the previous year, and 16 participants who reported on these in the previous six months. At program completion, data was available for 11 participants, all of whom, as mentioned, responded with a six-month period in mind at Time 2. At Time 1, eight of these responded to a year period. Appendix 1 displays prevalence/frequency results for the total sample, as well as by time period for Time 1 (program commencement) and Time 2 (program completion).

Almost all participants (except two different participants at Time 1 and Time 2) indicated that they had engaged in at least one type of act measured by the entire scale at both time periods (one other participant at Time 1 indicated that the only behaviour they engaged in was negotiation, while at Time 2 this participant and two others indicated that these were their sole behaviours). At Time 1, both reports of prevalence (whether participants had engaged in at least one instance of a type of behaviour, examined for each scale) and frequency (how many times different conflict tactics had been engaged in, again examined for each scale) were somewhat similar regardless of time period sampled. While there was somewhat more variation in frequency scores in the six-month group at Time 1 (mostly owing to two participants who endorsed no acts at Time 1), there was still a high level of concordance. This may suggest that the frequency of aggressive acts may be less time-bound or vary little from six months to one year.

Overall, the prevalence statistics at program commencement suggest that, prior to commencement, each participant reported that he had engaged in at least one of four types of abusive behaviours, with almost all participants reporting the use of negotiation tactics. The ratings indicated that negotiation and psychologically aggressive tactics were committed the most often.

Self-reports of prevalence/frequency at post-program tended to suggest moderate declines over time, although the lack of data on more program participants (and the large number of participants who reported above 0 for particular types of acts), and lack of comparable time periods limited the strength and conclusive nature of these findings. It appeared that two participants exhibited significant problems at post-test in their use of physically/psychologically/sexually violent acts which may have skewed the responses. These participants exhibited only increases in negotiation at Time 2, and no other acts (one of these had no other acts at Time 1, and the other had a number of psychologically, physically, and self-injurious behaviours reported at Time 1). Other participants generally reported changes in the desired direction. Appendix 1 examines these changes in more depth.

The **Michigan Alcoholism Screening Test (MAST)** a 22-item version of the instrument developed by Selzer (1971), provides a measure of problem alcohol consumption, examining areas such as behaviours related to alcohol use (for example, "Have you ever gotten into physical fights when drinking?"), relationships (for example, "Has drinking ever created problems between you and a near relative or close friend?"), consequences (for example, "Have you ever lost a job because of drinking") and seeking help (for example, "Have you ever gone to anyone for help about your drinking?"). Participants respond on a dichotomous scale (Yes/No), and scores can range between 0 and 22. Scores of 0-2 are classified as "no apparent problem", 3-5 as "early or middle problem drinker", and a score of 6 or higher as "problem drinker".

Participant responses to the MAST at both Time 1 (35 participants; M=5.23; SD=4.97; Range=0-17) and Time 2 (seven participants; M=6.00; SD=6.66; Range=0-16) indicate that, at both points, most participants tended to fall within the category of "early or middle problem drinker", indicating some potential problems with alcohol use.

Since many of the items of the MAST are not amenable to change over time (for example, "Have you ever attended a meeting of Alcoholics Anonymous?"), total scores may be potentially misleading as to change over time. As such, participant responses to five questions which could change over time ("Do you feel you are a normal drinker?", "Does any near relative or close friend every worry or complain about your drinking?", "Can you stop drinking without difficulty after one or two drinks?", "Do you ever feel guilty about your drinking?", "Do you drink before noon fairly often?") were summed. In order to allow some comparison to a total scale score (particularly since total scale scores are used to classify the respondent), the totals were prorated (divided by five and multiplied by 22), such that at both Time 1 and Time 2 there could be some comparison to the MAST classification system (see Table 13.1[1]). As with the total scores,

1 When participants are compared according to whether they answered questions in relation to no specified time period (20 participants; M=.95; SD=1.15; or prorated M=4.18; SD=5.04), or six months (13 participants; M=1.31; SD=1.55; or prorated M=5.75; SD=6.81), there were some minor differences at Time 1. At Time 2, participants with no specified time period (three participants, M=.33; SD=.58; or prorated M=1.47; SD=2.54) seemed to differ somewhat from those with a six-month period (eight participants; M=1.25; SD=1.28; or prorated M=5.50; SD=5.64), with this due to the high scores of two participants.

Table 13.1. Descriptive Statistics for the MAST (five items) at Time 1 and Time 2

	Prorated		Total	
Scale	M (SD)	Range	M (SD)	Range
MAST - Time 1 (N=33)	4.80 (5.75)	0-22	1.09 (1.31)	0-5
MAST - Time 2 (N=11)	4.40 (5.21)	0-13.2	1.00 (1.18)	0-3

these scores suggested some potential problems with alcohol use, although there was variation between participants.

A paired-samples t-test (with participants for whom data was available) at both pre-program and post-program (11 participants) indicated a non-significant change from Time 1 (M=.64; SD=.81; or pro-rated M=2.80; SD=3.56) to Time 2 (M=1.00; SD=1.18; or pro-rated M=4.40; SD=5.21)[2], t(10)=-.94, p>.05 (one-tailed), r=.08.

The **Inventory of Beliefs about Wife Beating (IBWB)** an 11-item version of the instrument developed by Saunders, Lynch, Grayson and Linz (1987), measured attitudes toward physical abuse by husbands toward wives and consists of two subscales. The Wife Beating Is Justified subscale (nine items) measures attitudes regarding the acceptability of the use of such violence (for example, "A husband has no right to beat his wife even if she breaks agreements she has made with him"), and a higher score (after reverse-coding relevant items) indicates greater acceptance of justifications for abuse. The Help Should Be Given subscale (three items) measures beliefs that government or social agencies should address or provide help to victims of abuse (for example, "Wife beating should be given a high priority as a social problem by government agencies"), and higher scores on this subscale indicate agreement with such notions. Participants indicated their agreement on a seven point response scale, from "Strongly Agree" to "Strongly Disagree".

Participant scores on the IBVB were generally quite low for justification of wife beating (indicating lesser beliefs regarding the acceptability of this), and generally quite high for beliefs that help should be available. Participant mean responses to the IBVB subscales are presented in Table 13.2.

2 The relatively larger score at Time 2 is mostly due to one participant, whose scores ranged from 0 at Time 1 to 13.20 at Time 2. As can be expected, when this participant is excluded, the means at Time 1 (M=.70; SD=.82; or prorated M=3.08; SD=3.62) and Time 2 (M=.80; SD=1.03; or prorated M=3.52; SD=4.54) are even closer, t(9)=-.32, p>.05.

Table 13.2. Means and Standard Deviations of the IBWB Scale

Scale	M (SD)	Range
Wife Beating Is Justified - Time 1 (N=35)	18.82 (7.61)	8-32
Help Should Be Given - Time 1 (N=35)	17.11 (5.07)	3-21
Wife Beating Is Justified - Time 2 (N=12)	13.08 (6.39)	8-26
Help Should Be Given - Time 2 (N=12)	19.74 (1.66)	16-21

Two paired samples t-tests were conducted for participants where information was available at Time 1 and Time 2 (11 participants) to test the hypotheses that, subsequent to treatment, men would decrease their tendency to hold beliefs indicative of justifying wife beating, and would increase their beliefs that help and assistance should be provided to women who have been abused. In comparison with measures at the commencement of treatment (M=16.45; SD=6.52), participants did, indeed, endorse fewer statements justifying abuse at Time 2 (M=12.82; SD=6.63), with this difference approaching statistical significance, $t(10)=1.67$, $p = .06$ (one-tailed), $r = .22$. Similarly, participants did increase their perceptions that help should be given to victims of violence at Time 2 (M=17.91; SD=3.42), in comparison with prior to treatment (M=19.62; SD=1.69), $t(10)=-1.88$, $p=.05$ (one-tailed) $r=.26$.

There were only two participants for whom scores were available at Time 1, Time 2 and Time 3 (six months follow-up). One of these participants evidenced some change in the desired direction in their beliefs regarding justification (Time 1=18, Time 2=20, Time 3=14), with no change in beliefs regarding help (at all time points, they received the maximum score of 21), while the other participant indicated some increase for justification between Time 1 and Time 2 (a score of 8), and Time 3 (a score of 14), and minimal change for help (Time 1=21, Time 2=18, Time 3=20).

The facilitator ratings

These statistics were compiled from weekly reports made by the program facilitators. Reports were written by facilitators and the participants themselves from February 2006 to September 2007, and provide a general record of the progress of those men who completed the course. The data here compares the ratings of the first session of the program with those made in Session 10 (a mid-point), and then again at Session 20 (close to completion).

Reports of violence

Self-reports

Reports of the use of physical violence during the program were rare, with only three participants indicating that they had acted violently (two participants reported one act, one participant reported three acts) in the weeks previous to Session 5, Session 6 and Session 7, respectively. Reports of the use of verbal and emotional abuse were higher in the earlier part of the program, with at least one participant indicating the presence of such abuse (usually one act) in the weeks prior to Sessions 3-9. However, after this time, no further reports of verbal and emotional abuse were reported.

Information was also collected on whether participants reported physical violence/threats/stalking/other criminal behaviour (a more inclusive category than physical violence), as well as whether they reported any manipulative/controlling/verbally abusive behaviour. Participants reported minimal use of physically, violent behaviour and related acts as well as reductions in emotionally violent and manipulative behaviour.

Partner reports

In contrast, 13 partners reported that their partners had used physical violence/threats/stalking/other acts at Session 1, with reports of this reducing mid-way through the program (for example, seven reports at Session 10), but with nine of the 12 partners reporting such behaviour at Session 20. Reports of manipulative/controlling/verbally abusive behaviour showed a similar pattern, with 13 partners reporting this at Time 1, and reductions mid-way through the program (Session 10=7), but increasing towards the end (nine of 12 participants at Session 20).

Further charges

A follow up of program participants revealed that of the 20 men who completed the program, only seven men had further charges recorded against them. Of these four men had breached their domestic violence order (with other offences included those relating to substance use and driving). Of the 18 men who did not complete the program, 16 had further charges recorded, although this was sometimes the reason for the program non-completion. This data underscores the need for men to complete all sessions of the program if they are to be successful in their attempts at behaviour change.

Risk of future abuse

During each session, participants were asked to rate the likelihood of them acting in a violent/abusive way toward their partner in the next week (1=None, 2=Low, 3=Moderate, 4=Medium, 5=High). Generally these ratings were low across the entire program. For example, at Session 1, all but three of the participants indicated that there was no likelihood of abuse (the three others indicated a low likelihood). While this did vary over the sessions, at half way through the program (Session 10), and towards the end (at Session 20), no participants (for whom data was available) indicated that they believed that they were at risk of perpetrating future acts of violence (see Figure 13.1).

Figure 13.1. Perceptions of Risk of Future Violence

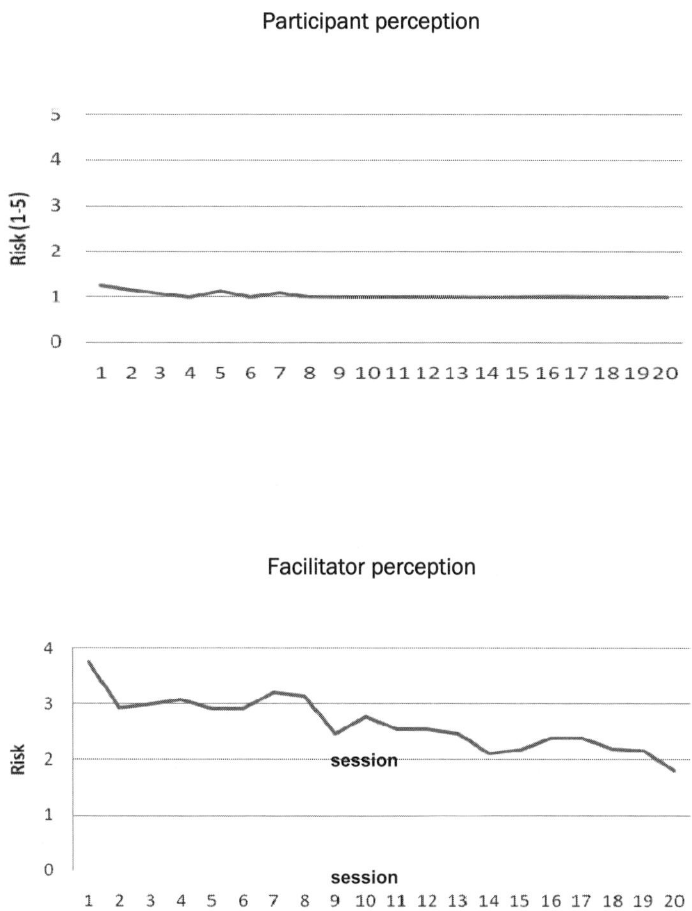

At the end of each session, facilitators also rated risk of violence/abuse occurring over the next week (1=Low, 2=Moderate, 3=Medium, 4=High). Changes in perceptions of risk are plotted in Figure 1 (above) and reveal some modest declines in perceptions of risk.

At Session 1, nine of the participants who completed the program were rated as high risk, and three as medium risk. By Session 10 there was some reduction, with six participants rated as low or moderate risk, and seven participants as medium (two participants) or high (five participants) risk.

At Session 20, two participants were assessed as being of low risk, six of moderate risk, and one of medium risk, with no reports of high risk.

Concepts learnt from the course

During each session, facilitators also rated participants on acceptance of responsibility for their abuse, addressing their use of minimisation, denial, blame, as well as their level of manipulation/collusion (ratings were made on a scale of Low 1-High 10) (see Figure 13.2 below).

For minimisation, ratings decreased from Session 1 (12 participants; M=7.83; SD=2.86) to Session 20 (10 participants; M=3.60; SD=2.55). Likewise, denial linearly decreased from Session 1 (14 participants; M=8.07; SD=2.70) to Session 20 (12 participants; M=3.17; SD=2.21). For blame, there was a similar decrease from Session 1 (14 participants; M=8.07; SD=2.70) to Session 20 (12 participants; M=3.58; SD=2.43). Finally, for manipulation which participants were relatively low on to begin with (Session 1: 10 participants; M=5.80; SD=3.77), ratings also decreased by Session 20 (12 participants; M=1.75; SD=1.77).

Similarly, facilitators indicated that participants showed an improved understanding of the main concepts covered in the sessions (Session 1: 13 participants; M=1.85; SD=1.34; Session 20: 10 participants; M=5.90; SD=1.73), and their use of examples to demonstrate understanding (Session 1: seven participants; M=2.00; SD=1.63; Session 20: nine participants; M=6.33; SD=2.35). Once again ratings were made on a scale from 1 None/Nil to 10 Excellent.

Ratings increased in relation to the item asking about how well each participant had demonstrated a position on non-violence (Session 1: nine participants; M=1.33; SD=1.32; Session 20: 10 participants; M=6.60; SD=1.96), and use of self-disclosure in sessions (Session 1: 14 participants; M=4.14; SD=1.99; Session 20: nine participants; M=6.44; SD=2.13) (see Figure 13.3).

Figure 13.2. Acceptance of Responsibility for Abuse over Time (facilitator ratings)

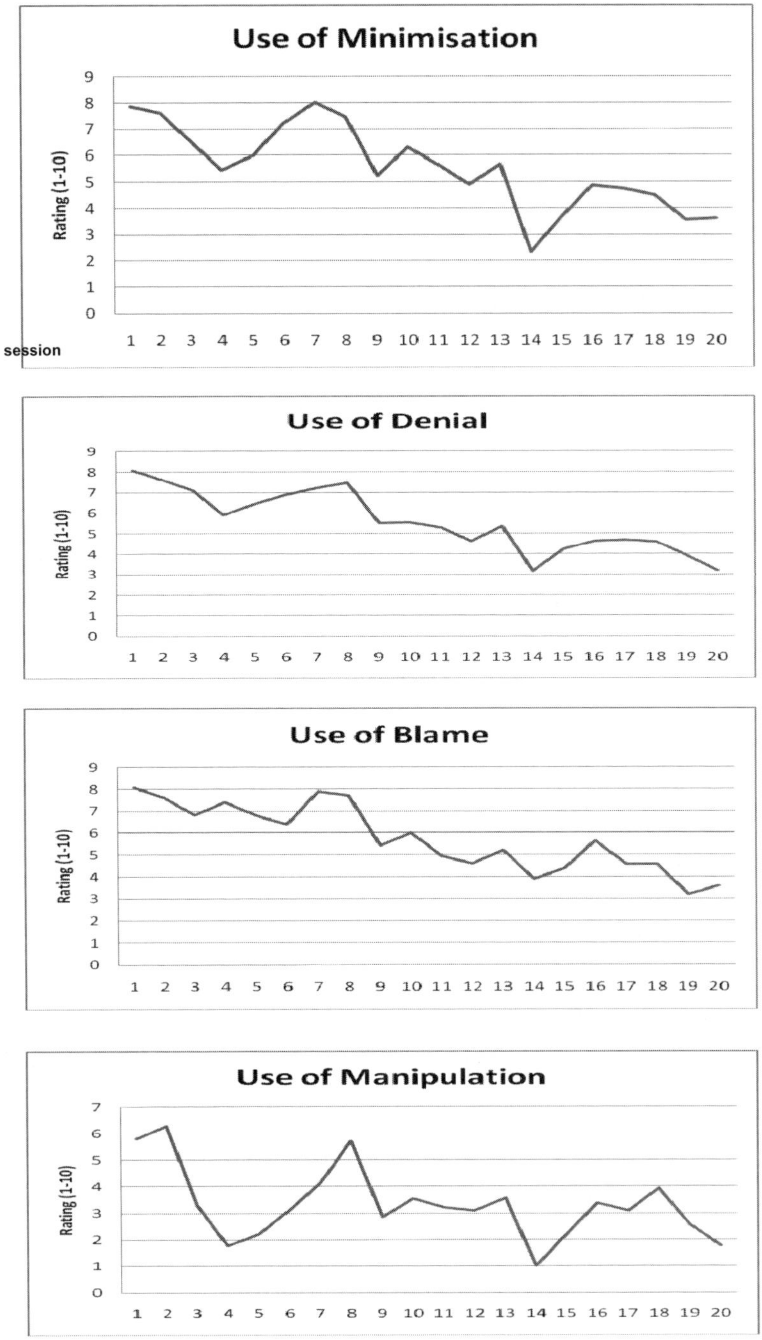

Figure 13.3. Understanding of Main Concepts (facilitator ratings)

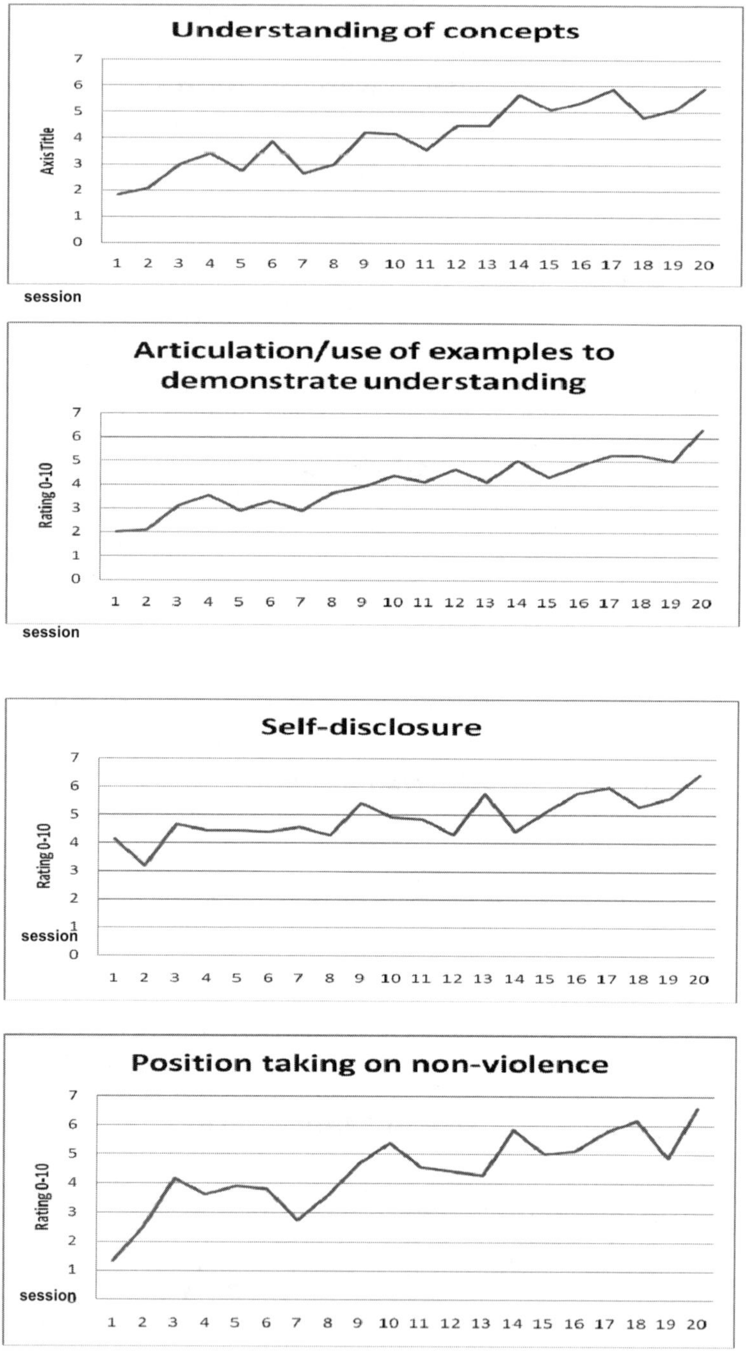

The extent to which participants had understood some of the concepts of the program were also rated after each session. Ratings were made on a 10 point scale with a rating of 1 indicating a low level of learning, and 10 as high. By measuring the means of the participants who finished the course, it is possible to track changes over time. This showed changes in understanding in the desired direction (see Figure 13.2 and Table 13.3).

Table 13.3. Ratings of Minimisation, Denial, Blame and Manipulation over Time

Concept	Number of men	Mean at Session 1	Mean at Session 10	Mean at Session 20
Minimisation	S1=12; S10=10; S20=10	3.17	4.70	7.40
Denial	S1=14; S10=11; S20=12	2.93	5.45	7.83
Blame	S1=14; S10=13; S20=12	2.93	5.00	7.42
Manipulation	S1=10; S10=13; S20=12	5.20	7.46	9.25

Note: S= session number
Lower scores indicate less acceptance of responsibility

A similar pattern of results was found for ratings of understanding, attitudes to violence, and self-disclosure (see Figure 13.3 and Table 13.4,). Again these ratings suggested improvement over time.

Table 13.4. Ratings of Understanding, Attitudes to Violence and Self-disclosure

Concept	Number of men	Mean at Session 1	Mean at Session 10	Mean at Session 20
Use of examples	S1=7; S10=11; S20=9	2.00	4.36	6.33
Demonstrated position on non-violence	S1=9; S10=10; S20=10	1.33	5.40	6.60
Level of self-disclosure	S1=14; S10=13; S20=9	4.14	4.92	6.44

Note: S= session number

Discussion

This chapter describes some of the changes in men who attended, and completed, the men's program. Collectively the pattern of findings reflects some improvements in the targets of intervention. For example, many of the men reported leaving the program with a greater awareness of the problematic nature of their behaviour than when they started. They expressed confidence in their ability not to act violently again in the future. They also showed some changes on the self-report measures which may indicate that they hold less supportive attitudes towards domestic violence, and their understanding of some of the key concepts in the program, as assessed by facilitators, appeared to improve over time.

These are all positive findings. However, there are a number of issues relating to this type of data which are critical to interpreting the significance of these changes. First, it is unclear whether the magnitude of the changes is sufficient to bring about real changes in behaviour. The changes, although in the desired direction, are mostly modest, and recent evidence suggests that changes on psychological measures may have limited or no association with behaviour change in domestically violent men (Bowen, Gilchrist and Beech 2008). A second issue relates to the nature of the information described here, which is largely self-report. Clearly men have a vested interest in reporting that they have made positive changes, or in other ways responding to the questions in a socially desirable manner. We are unable to assess the likely effects of invalid responding on this data as no check of social desirability was administered. However, it is concerning that the men's reports of their own behaviour was largely unsupported by the reports of their partners. Even more problematic is the lack of a comparison or control group. Research with other offender groups has shown that changes on these types of measure can occur naturally over time (see Howells et al 2005). In other words, participants in offender programs may have a tendency to show improvements on self-report measures, either because they understand the issues more, or because they understand better what is expected of them. The real question of effectiveness is whether this group of men changed more than a similar group who did not attend a program. It is only by making this comparison that an assessment of the value of the program can be made. Finally, there are problems in choosing measures that are likely to be responsive to change. It is clear that for an evaluation measure to be useful, change has to be possible, ratings need to be made over a comparable time period, and factors such as opportunity to offend need to be controlled for. For example, a man who has separated from his partner and is living alone will have significantly less opportunity to reoffend than a man who is still cohabiting.

Each of these issues limits the strength with which any conclusions about program effectiveness based on this data can be drawn. As noted above, there is also no means by which to assess the extent to which the different agencies involved in program delivery were successful in providing an integrated service, or the effectiveness of the criminal justice response alone. There was, for example, relatively little evidence that program content relating to gender role and gender inequity had had a profound influence on their thinking, or indeed of their awareness of the need for broader systemic responses to the problems presented by domestic violence. Nevertheless, the changes observed here do suggest that risk may have been reduced, albeit modestly. For many, if not most, the way in which the men spoke about their behaviour at the end of the program had changed. There was a clear tendency for participants to take more responsibility for behaviour, to hold themselves as accountable for past transgressions, and to be motivated to avoid further incidents of aggressive and violent behaviour. It is informative to see how the men had come to understand the legal requirement to attend the program, to value the process of joining a group and working with other men, and to focus their attention upon the development of relationship skills. The ways in which different men spoke of their experiences and their understanding of the program suggested that whilst some appeared to have made positive changes, for others the changes were likely to be relatively superficial. However, higher levels of problem awareness, although likely to be a necessary condition for behaviour change to occur (see Day et al 2006), may not be sufficient.

Chapter 14

Have Male Offenders Changed? Women's Experiences of Safety and Accountability at the End of the Program

Donna Chung, Di Lucas and Donna Justo

The introduction of perpetrator programs raised political and practical issues for feminist services, a number of which were introduced in Chapter 3. In the controversies and debates surrounding the use of domestic violence perpetrator programs, feminist-oriented services have always called for the inclusion of women's experiences both to promote their safety and to enable some form of accountability for men's use of violence. This is based on the knowledge that men who use violence against their partners have a tendency to report the violence as a joint problem for which both partners are responsible, and that they frequently minimise the types and level of violence perpetrated and the impacts it has on those who are the victims (Bagshaw et al 1999). In this chapter women partner contact[1] is discussed and some women's experiences of the process are outlined. The discussion about women partner contact is drawn from three sources: professional experience of undertaking women partner contact at the Gold Coast Domestic Violence Prevention Centre; Australian research experience of reviewing domestic violence programs; and other published literature.

Historically, the purpose of contacting women whose partners or ex-partners are in a domestic violence program was to gauge whether the man's self-reports were accurate and to offer her opportunities for support and safety planning. It was considered important that facilitators of

1 The term "women partner contact" is used to refer to all forms of contact with a female partner or ex-partner to describe the range of involvement while men are in the domestic violence program.

perpetrator programs have some insight into what happens to women and children in situations of domestic violence and understand the range and seriousness of effects and the types of attitudes, values, behaviours and dynamics that are the focus for change in men's programs.

Although much literature has been produced on women's and children's exposure to domestic violence, its effects and service responses, a relatively small amount of literature has been published about women's safety contact in perpetrator programs (Gondolf and White 2000, Gondolf and Heckert 2003). Whilst research on domestic violence perpetrators and perpetrator programs has included women's perspectives (Buzawa and Buzawa 2002; Gondolf 2002; Hague 2005), they are generally about how women's assessments of their partners or ex-partners' dangerousness compares with the information they have from the man and other agencies involved in the situation. This chapter aims to add to the existing knowledge about the women partners' experiences and perceptions of men's domestic violence perpetrator programs.

Purposes of women partner contact

Women partner contact has a number of purposes:

- To assess the safety of the woman partner or ex-partner and her children and provide access to support and/or safety planning as required.

To gather information about the man's use of violence in the overall assessment of the situation and his ongoing risk, in addition to his self-reports, police and other reports and facilitators' assessments.

- To provide women with information about the perpetrator program so that they understand what is involved and the program's purposes. This also involves opportunities to gain independent support for themselves and their children.
- To offer women some realistic expectations about what changes may occur during and after the program, including the likelihood of violent behaviour changing, tactics of violence and abuse changing and the sustainability of change.

Programs across Australia have focussed on some or all of these forms of women partner contact using written correspondence and/or telephone or mobile phone contact. Depending on the program, women's contact details are most often obtained from the man in the program as part of his contractual obligation to attend. In other programs the details may be provided by the courts or Department of Justice or Corrective Services.

Providers of women partner contact

Decisions about which agency and/or which service provider should undertake the role of women partner contact have varied across agencies in Australia. Often the decision is driven by differing philosophical attitudes about who should do the work, the types of services available and the integrated model in the local area. This has been a point of contention in some locations. In these instances women's services have argued that they should not undertake partner contact as that is doing the work of the perpetrator's program and their resources should not be used in that way (Chung et al 2003), whereas other women's services see it as their role to provide independent contact and a pathway for women to receive support who may not otherwise have contact. In other locations, particularly rural areas, the limited range of services often dictates which agency will be responsible. In summary there are various arrangements which have emerged over time. The workers and agencies undertaking safety contact include:

- A women's domestic violence service, independent of the men's perpetrator program.
- The female co-facilitator of the men's perpetrator program.
- A women's worker who is member of the agency or team which runs the men's perpetrator program.

In our experience, it is not the particular provider that is critical; rather we suggest that the process of undertaking partner contact in a comprehensive manner is the priority. In this regard we argue for a model of practice which is comprehensive in providing support and safety planning.

Ethical aspects and challenges in undertaking women partner contact

A key aspect of domestic violence practice with women has traditionally been to ensure they feel supported and able to make their own decisions, as they have often come from relationship experiences which have left them feeling isolated, unconfident and powerless. In relation to women partner contact practice, this means that women's refusal to participate in such arrangements is respected. The refusal may be for a number of reasons including: she sees her partner or ex-partner as solely responsible for his use of violence and that his changing should not involve her; where they have separated[2] she may not see herself as in danger and she does not wish to know about him as part of the separation process and she may not see

2 In some instances, there is a considerable time lag between the man's arrest at a domestic violence incident or breach of his order and the time he begins attending the group, for example 12 months. During this time women have separated and re-established their lives so find the thought of revisiting these issues and consideration of him unhelpful.

herself as in danger or that support services are of use to her. Whilst this decision is respected, it can pose an ethical dilemma where workers may consider the woman's safety to be at risk given their knowledge of the perpetrator and his behaviour. In these instances workers encourage women to have some form of contact and provide information in the hope that should she see the need for such support she knows how to access it. However, the file analysis indicated that women did provide relevant information about what has happening and in some cases the volatility of the situation is highlighted demonstrating the potential importance of having contact with the woman.

In situations where women are escaping domestic violence they are often in emergency and transitory accommodation, with the upheaval in their lives making it difficult to plan and maintain routines over any period of time. The changes that are often required to re-establish lives in conjunction with keeping her and her children safe can be a relatively demanding experience. Consequently, when workers are trying to contact women for partner contact they are often difficult to reach as they have changed their mobile numbers so that they cannot be contacted by their former partners[3] and can have competing priorities which make it difficult for women to regularly attend scheduled appointments. This often makes women's partner contact challenging and at times frustrating as it can be difficult to establish and maintain regular contact and safety planning for women whose partners are in programs when they are not in contact with any other services.

As part of the University of South Australia's research evaluating the effectiveness of perpetrator programs, the partner contact summaries were reviewed. About 20 per cent of women were never able to be contacted. Of the remaining women, attempts were made to contact them on average two or three times before contact was established, and then frequently contact was intermittent given the nature of these women's lives. It requires considerable persistence by workers to contact partners and this should be taken into account when the women's partner contact funding component is being costed in service agreements.

Brief overview of the Gold Coast Domestic Violence Prevention Centre approach to women partner contact

In summary the process for women partner contact which operates as part of the Gold Coast integrated response is as follows:

3 This can make it difficult when partner contact services rely on the man to provide the woman's contact details. Alternatively at other times, men may provide incorrect information to the facilitator which can prevent or delay contact.

- As part of the conditions of men attending the program they must provide current contact details for their partner or ex-partner. At various times men have provided incorrect information or outdated information. Where this is the case men are asked if they have other contact details, or other agencies which are part of the integrated response may be contacted for details as women may have new contact details as part of their safety arrangements.
- The contact details are given to the women's service of the Gold Coast Domestic Violence Prevention Centre as they provide the women partner contact. The centre may already have the woman's details if she has had previous contact with the police and had consented to her details being provided. In any case in this instance the woman is contacted generally by telephone initially in relation to partner contact. If telephone contact cannot be established after several attempts, a letter may be sent.
- Once partner contact is established the centre encourages women to attend for a face-to-face session so that, among other things, they can ensure that they are speaking to the woman without her partner or ex-partner being present (as this cannot always be established in an initial phone contact). Most women agree to attend, although it may take some time to set up the meeting. At the meeting, the program is explained to the women and their support and safety planning needs are discussed. Women are asked to complete forms about the types and frequencies of domestic violence (using the Abusive Behaviour Inventory) and to assess the level of risk. This information is shared with the men's program facilitators to compare the accounts and to consider when working with the man. Risk information is sought on a fortnightly basis from women for the duration of the program to provide a safety check and to advise facilitators of the man's risk. Future contacts with the woman may be on the telephone or face-to-face depending on what is possible and suitable for the woman.
- The women's advocate workers meet weekly with the facilitators of the men's program to advise about the women's safety contact information as it relates to the men and any relevant circumstances such as the woman moving out of the house. Obviously if during the process of women's contact a situation of high risk is identified or disclosed relevant staff and agencies are advised immediately. This could include program facilitators, the Department of Corrective Services or the police.

Did it make any difference? Women's experiences of the impact of the men's program

Case files of women whose partners had attended the men's program were examined and a sample of these women were interviewed (n=5) about their experiences. The sample group is small, however their experiences varied in terms of their ages, how long they had been in the relationship, whether they had children with the violent partner, the extent and duration of domestic violence, and whether or not they were currently living with their partner post-program. All women were interviewed after their partners or ex-partners had completed the program.

In relation to the women's partner contact process all those interviewed suggested that it was an important and welcome process. This is unsurprising given that these women were all willing to be contacted and motivated to participate in the post-program research interviews. The women appreciated being contacted for support options, getting further information about the men's domestic violence program and providing women's advocates with their perspectives about the violence and what was happening in their lives. Two women in particular commented that they thought it was important their views were being represented to the men's program facilitators.

Experiences prior to men's entry into the domestic violence program

All of the women had experiences of the police being called out to domestic violence incidents. Amongst the women interviewed three had partners who had received custodial sentences following a breach of their order or an assault charge. These men all commenced the domestic violence perpetrator program after release from prison. The women all perceived that the custodial sentence was the most important influence on behaviour change. One woman whose partner was in the program as a result of breaching the intervention order commented that *"It doesn't happen though the first time they breach it is again and again before anything happens"*. A related comment women made was that men needed to get information and intervention much more quickly than happened with the current system where there could be considerable time between when the offence was committed and the commencement of intervention. One woman compared it to her experience with the women's fax-back program run by the Gold Cost integrated project, whereby women receive information about domestic violence at the time of police callout and, with consent, are contacted by the women's service within a couple of days. As a minimum she thought men should receive written information at time of arrest.

Once a man was in a program the women felt that they could access the women's service as needed. One woman commented that she would have liked to have known more about the men's program.

Partner contact

Women all spoke very positively about the partner contact experience. A key observation was that the independence and non-judgmental attitude of women's advocates was very helpful. This was important particularly as women had found that their partners' families tended to deny their son's violence and attribute blame to them and when women did not leave violent partners that could also lead to being isolated from their own families who did not understand and lost patience. One woman said *"My father would not speak to me for two months after I took him back after violence"*. All this further isolated the women. The other point that women made was they were able to tell their story from beginning to end whereas in the legal processes associated with domestic violence they only told authorities the sections of the experience which they sought information about.

All women reported that the women's workers were supportive and very helpful in dealing with domestic violence. In relation to the men's progress during and following the domestic violence program women reported that they provided them with realistic information about the high likelihood of men returning to the use of violent and abusive behaviours which may have ceased or reduced during program attendance. One woman commented that partner contact had helped her to recognise what was healthy and unhealthy in a relationship and that she actively used this in making decisions about whether to remain with or leave her partner.

The impact of the men's domestic violence program

Two women believed that the domestic violence program had improved their partners' behaviour, two did not think it had made any difference, and one was unsure. One of the women who perceived positive change said that her partner was also using drugs at the time and that the ceasing of drug use and the program in combination had improved his behaviour. Another two women whose partners had been using drugs also commented on the importance of receiving drug treatment in order to maximise the positive impact of the perpetrator program.

One of the women whose partner had made no real change and who was still very fearful of him said that prior to and after prison he was still very angry and that he did not at any point perceive that he was responsible for changing. A woman who perceived her partner had changed described the difference as follows: *"What is most important to me is not that he stopped physically being violent but how he now speaks to me and treats me"*.

Another woman commented that there were four main changes she saw: "He leaves the situation rather than getting angry and violent, incidents of road rage have stopped and he seeks my views and does things in the house".

Even where women had experienced some positive change they were uncertain about the motivations: *"I knew he had to change but it was because he had to and not that he wanted to but he knew it would fall in on him otherwise".*

Women made the point that it was about being treated with a level of respect by their partner as much as not being physically abused. One woman who thought her partner had changed described it as successful as they now communicated and she had in fact separated within the last week and that it had not been acrimonious and she felt safe. All women felt that the main motivation for men's attendance and change was the risk of incarceration if change did not occur.

Trust and fear

None of the women felt completely safe after their partners completed the program: *"I am hopeful but don't have the full trust back. J (women's advocate) warned me that he might fall back into old behaviours. We have talked about this together and he knows six months won't completely change him".*

Another woman who had separated from her partner but still had contact with him when he picked up the children for contact visits commented: *"I don't feel 100 per cent safe – I still think possibly it can happen again. But I have the order extended and can easily go the police. I have support and I know where to get help".*

Unlike this woman, another woman whose children were a concern for Child Safety raised the issue that she would hesitate to call the police if he turned up and was violent because she worried that her children could be taken by the authorities if the police were called too frequently. This is an important concern for women which can seriously compromise the woman's and her children's safety.

Importantly whilst women felt less fearful and reported some changes, they were neither without fear nor felt completely safe. This indicates that the secondary goal of the program about men not using violence and abuse was not achieved according to these women's perspectives.

Changes and further opportunities to improve the situation

All women commented that domestic violence and its effects needs to be taken more seriously by authorities. They suggested the following changes:

- Longer prison sentences to reflect the seriousness of the offence.
- Responding to the first breach of an intervention order and not waiting for numerous breaches.
- Reducing the time between the offence and program attendance so that the men are very aware of the effects of their recent behaviour.
- Increasing the length of the program to 12 months as the entrenched behaviour could not be easily changed with one session

per week for 26 weeks. A 12 month program would demonstrate the seriousness of violence and give more time to change long term behaviour.

- Increase the length of orders so longer term changes could be monitored.

These suggestions do not vary from what many reports have previously advocated. Interestingly the women commented that there was a service gap for couples who remain together after the program. Two women suggested that couple counselling then be available so they can address how the relationship has changed and how conflict can be healthily addressed in the future to prevent violence and abuse.

Conclusions

Women partner contact is often a difficult task, particularly in establishing and maintaining regular contact with women. Some women understandably make a decision not to engage with partner contact as they are no longer in contact with their violent former partner and/or they see it as his responsibility to address his violence and that they should not have to contribute to this aspect. Other women are willing to participate but the process of escaping domestic violence and re-establishing their lives sometimes makes maintaining routines and appointments difficult. These challenges should not negate the importance of women partner contact and the role of agencies to proactively pursue contact.

The small number of women's voices that have been included in this chapter demonstrate that whilst for some men there are some changes, the women report being less fearful, but not living without fear, nor are they confident that such changes are sustainable in the long term. Those women whose partners or ex-partners had prison sentences reported they believed these were more effective than the program. Others stated that whilst their partners had found the program useful there would be no motivation to attend if they were not compelled by the courts. Unsurprisingly, women suggested that increasing the length of the program would be beneficial given the length of time the behaviour had existed and the serious effects of domestic violence. Women all had a realistic view about men's capacity to change and the likelihood of violent and abusive behaviour recurring.

The partner contact process enables women to gain information and a realistic perception of change, and knowledge that they have a source of support if and when it is required in the future. In considering the purposes of men's domestic violence programs, it would appear that the goal of promoting women's and children's safety is somewhat achieved, whereas that of men's behaviour change is far more tenuous.

Part V

COMMENTARY

Chapter 15

Debates, Dilemmas and Intentions in the Ongoing Development of Integrated Responses to Domestic Violence

Andrew Day, Donna Chung,
Patrick O'Leary and Ed Carson

So far, this book has voiced a range of different perspectives from those involved with the development and delivery of integrated responses to domestic violence. It is evident that much of the thinking behind these responses is derived from a primary and overarching concern with the safety of victims, both women and children. It is also apparent that these services have a much broader remit than simply providing programs for perpetrators of domestic violence. There is considerable debate on how integrated responses to perpetrators are best designed. In this context much of the development of current programs thus far has required substantial political lobbying at local levels. This has resulted in fragmented approaches with no consistent formula as to content, referral pathways, specific or related intervention needs, or legislation that provides a template for establishing an appropriately resourced integrated response to domestic violence offenders. In this chapter, our aim is to discuss how programs for male perpetrators might be conceptualised and what this means in practical terms for program content, program delivery, and research.

A starting point for this discussion is to acknowledge a number of things. First, many specialist domestic violence services have their origins in advocacy and volunteer based services for women. These services typically (and understandably) ascribe to a gendered explanation of domestic violence, and as such the development of perpetrator programs has occurred relatively independently from those which have been developed for use with other types of offenders, including violent offenders (see Day et al 2009). It is clear that approaches that are more psychologically focussed are typically regarded as lacking sufficient psycho-educational content on gendered power and stereotyped gender socialisation, and indeed this has been the source of considerable debate within the sector (Dutton and Corvo 2007). Second, perpetrator programs vary considerably in terms of their relationship with the criminal justice system and this will inevitably influence what is possible within programs. Around the world there is currently a range of responses, from programs run by community based agencies where men attend voluntarily and not by an order of the court, through to programs for men who have been found guilty of a criminal offence related to domestic violence and are mandated to attend. It is clear that the level of legal coercion to attend a program will have a profound impact on the types of men who arrive in programs, their level of motivation to attend, and how they might be best managed by program staff (see Chapter 16).

The dilemmas of developing effective intervention programs are heightened by the practicalities of service delivery in the corrections and community services arenas. Reviews of intervention programs in the United States (Jackson et al 2003) and Australia (Chung, O'Leary and Zannittino 2003) have observed variance in modes of intervention, and inconsistent operationalisation of principles even where services are nominally based on a common program. Program integrity issues are sometimes a matter of low levels of facilitator skill or knowledge in some programs but, more fundamentally, implementation gaps point to limitations in the prevalence of good practice, quality assurance, monitoring and evaluation. This is a continuing and central dilemma for all social policy analysis and can limit service delivery from inception, even though over time the variability may be exacerbated by problems associated with what Hollin (1995) has referred to as "program drift".

In short, domestic violence programs vary considerably in terms of their stated purpose, disciplinary emphases and core understandings of the nature of domestic violence, as well as the practical problems of delivery. The challenge is to deliver programs that are well informed by an understanding of the particular nature and context in which domestically violent and abusive acts occur, and are also psychologically meaningful and likely to be effective in bringing about behaviour change and/or promoting victim safety. The issue of behaviour change is of particular importance given the lack of empirical evidence supporting the proposition that perpetrator programs do actually lead to improvements in women's safety. While some studies have produced promising results (Gondolf 2007), evidence relating to the overall effectiveness of programs remains unconvincing. A meta-analysis by Babcock, Green and Robie (2004) concluded that the effect sizes associated with different types of approach to domestic violence intervention were typically small (d=0.35 for Duluth programs; d=0.29 for cognitive-behavioural programs), with the base rates of reoffending across studies reported to be 21 per cent based on police reports, and 35 per cent based on partner reports. However, when only those studies employing experimental designs were reviewed, these effect sizes reduced to d=.09 using victim reports as the outcome measure, and d=0.12 based on police reports. This was interpreted by the authors to mean that "a woman is 5 per cent less likely to be reassaulted by a man who was arrested, sanctioned and went to a batterers' program than by a man who was simply arrested and sanctioned" (Babcock et al 2004: 1032). Another meta-analysis on program outcomes with mandated clients concluded that "the mean effect for victim reported outcomes was zero" (Feder and Wilson 2005: 239).

In a previous Australian review of domestic violence perpetrator programs (O'Leary et al 2004) it was evident that some facilitators' styles often drew on Rogerian and humanist counselling techniques, which appeared to be at odds with program content that required a consideration of the impact on the victim, responsibility and individual agency, and which often require facilitators to convey very clear judgments about unacceptable attitudes and behaviours. On the other hand, highly structured and psycho-educational programs may limit the opportunities for facilitators to respond to the individual needs of participants - a factor which has been clearly demonstrated to be associated with positive behaviour change in offender programs (Andrews and Bonta 2003). There would, then, appear to be two issues that warrant some further consideration in the delivery of perpetrator programs: that of appropriate program content and method; and of how individualised program content should be.

Program content and method

Serin and Preston (2001a) have suggested that the following are important treatment targets in any program designed to reduce the risk of violent offending: hostility, impulsivity, substance abuse, major mental disorders - acute symptoms, antisocial or psychopathic personality, and social information-processing deficits. Persistently violent offenders have been shown to have greater needs than non-persistent violent offenders and non-violent offenders in these areas, particularly in the areas of employment, marital/family relationships, associations, substance abuse, community functioning, personal/emotional stability and criminal attitudes (Serin and Preston 2001b). These are all areas of need that should clearly be addressed within perpetrator programs or as part of a broader package of intervention of which the perpetrator program is one element.

Additionally, other priority areas of intervention appear to be more specific to the gendered nature of violence. Beesley and McGuire (2009) have, for example, recently suggested that there is now sufficient evidence to look seriously at interventions for violent offenders that target masculinity. This is particularly relevant given the gendered power dynamic of domestic violence and the gender differences in the experiences and meanings attributed to the violence. Jacobson, Gottman, Waltz, Rushe, Babcock and Holtzworth-Munroe (1994) found that partners of violent men were fearful during violent arguments, observing that once violence was instigated there was nothing that could be done to stop it, and that even withdrawing would not help. The wives expressed sadness and fear, while the men showed belligerence, contempt and a desire to control. Anderson and Umbertson (2001) further found that batterers excused, justified, rationalised and minimised violence, and constructed it as a rational response to extreme provocation. The participants explained their violence as a loss of control or a minor incident that was blown out of proportion. Traditional notions of masculinity and dominance are heavily implicated in the perpetration of domestic violence where there is a tendency to minimise responsibility for their use of violence and attribute blame to their female partner. This growing focus on masculinity is used by Gilchrist (2009) in recent work which identifies 10 potential implicit theories held by domestically violent men, each of which would form a treatment target in its own right. Importantly many of these (for example, "women are dangerous", "the need for control", "women are objects", "entitlement/ respect", "sex drives are uncontrollable", "real man") relate closely to the type of area in which programs typically aim to intervene. This body of research identifies a number of specific treatment targets that can usefully and directly inform program content to improve outcomes.

Wormwith, Simpson, Reitzel, Fagan and Morgan (2007) in their summary of extensive literature on the outcomes of offender rehabilitation programs concluded that, on average, specific types of treatment, notably cognitive-behavioural interventions, are likely to be the most effective in bringing about behaviour change. The content of cognitive-behavioural therapeutic interventions for anger and aggression has been described in a substantial number of clinical accounts, research reports and reviews, with Day, Howells, Mohr, Schall and Gerace (2008: 302) describing the approach in the following way:

> The cognitive behavioural method is based upon a careful and collaborative assessment of the problem behaviour, and the associated antecedents, and consequences, be they environmental, cognitive, physiological or behavioural. The approach to intervention typically centres around teaching the client to both recognise and dispute those beliefs and interpretations that lead to problematic behaviour. The client is then taught to both recognise and dispute those beliefs and interpretations. Whilst there are many different approaches to therapy, most adopt a Socratic method, involving the use of both open and closed questions to challenge or dispute unhelpful inferences and evaluations. The client's beliefs concerning the intentions and motives (attributions and appraisals) of other people involved would be become the focus of intervention, especially when these beliefs appear unrealistic or unhelpful. The client is then encouraged to examine these beliefs carefully and conduct experiments to establish the extent to which they are justified. Typically clients will be set homework tasks in which they are asked to practice disputation across a range of different situations. The final part of therapy typically involves generating alternative beliefs, and practising using these in the situations in which problems arise, often in conjunction with methods such as relaxation training to help control physiological arousal. In

addition, clients are often asked to complete homework tasks in which they are asked to practice disputation across a range of different situations.

It is unclear just how much of this type of approach is evident in many perpetrator programs, but given the observations of O'Leary et al (2004), it would seem likely that few programs in Australia would adopt this level of specificity in their approach to intervention. Interestingly, Gondolf (2007) has argued that Duluth programs do incorporate cognitive behavioural methods, although this view has been challenged by others (Dutton and Corvo 2007).

A second important aspect of cognitive-behavioural treatment is the emphasis on working collaboratively with offenders on motivational problems in order to engage them in treatment (Day 2003). This highlights the critical role of the therapeutic alliance in effective program delivery, a term which refers to three different aspects of the relationship between the client and therapist: the collaborative nature of the relationship; the affective bond between client and therapist; and the client's and therapist's ability to agree on treatment goals and tasks (Bordin 1994). The alliance has been shown to be a moderate but significant and consistent predictor of treatment outcome across a variety of therapeutic modalities and client groups (Bambling and King 2001; Horvath and Symonds 1991). In the broader literature on the rehabilitation of violent offenders Renwick, Black, Ramm and Novaco (1997) have pointed to the therapeutic pessimism felt by both clients and therapists to enduring problems of low motivation, treatment resistance and avoidance. These authors note the resentful, distrustful and even combative style of some offender participants in therapeutic groups. The approach advocated in some perpetrator programs is to adopt a strategy of consistent, direct and often intense confrontation of defences (see Murphy and Baxter 1997) to jolt the client into active behaviour change and overcome any claims that their behaviour was not serious, or that victims provoked or deserved the violence (Dutton 1986; Pence and Paymar 1983). This approach is based on the view that abusive behaviour is not simply poor impulse control but rather a result of premeditated decisions to assert power and control. It is largely inconsistent with the cognitive-behavioural method at any one point in time, although differing theoretical explanations are not necessarily dichotomous and may not necessarily be incompatible in a sequence of multiple strategies and interventions.

Individualised program content

It is perhaps a truism to suggest that interventions that are matched to the particular needs of the individual offender will be more effective than those which are not. A person whose sole serious problem is domestic violence requires a quite different treatment response than for a person who has, for example, an antisocial personality disorder, severe substance abuse problems, limited verbal skills, and the absence of family support. The issue of individual differences amongst domestically violent offenders has been approached by researchers in relation to different typologies. Perhaps the best known of these is that proposed by Holtzworth-Munroe and Stuart (1994). They identified three core intrapersonal elements that are associated with male violence towards their partners: (1) severity of violence; (2) generality of violence; and (3) psychopathy/personality disorder. They argue that developmental factors such as childhood abuse, exposure to violence, and involvement with deviant peers, and proximal factors such as impulsivity, social skill deficits, attitudes supportive of violence, hostility to women, and maladaptive attachment styles, combine to determine the severity and type of violence in each group (see Dempsey 2009). Although such analyses point to the importance of individualised assessment of each client's treatment needs (such that interventions can be matched to the particular needs of the individual offender), they appear to have had relatively little impact upon the practice of program delivery.

One of the most enduring and important distinctions has been between hostile and instrumental forms of aggression (McEllistrem 2004). Hostile aggression comprises a triggering event, typically in the form of a frustration and an internal state of negative emotional arousal and an impulse to hurt or harm the provoking agent. Instrumental aggression, on the other hand, is intended to secure an environmental reward and negative emotional arousal is less likely to be present as an antecedent (Howells 2008). It would seem that whilst many in the domestic violence field understand acts of aggression as instrumental in nature, psychologically informed interventions tend to focus on addressing hostile aggression. Indeed it is this dichotomising of the nature of violence that underpins many of the disagreements about how programs should be delivered. Day and Howells (2008) have argued that there are a number of problematic features of the angry versus instrumental distinction (see also Bushman and Anderson 2001: 18) as follows:

> The first is that the distinction is most appropriately applied to acts than to actors. A violent individual may engage in both forms of violence, though a particular type of offence may still predominate in his history. Secondly, the distinction between the two forms is often difficult to make in practice (Barratt and Slaughter 1998; Bushman and Anderson 2001). Thirdly, hostile aggression appears to be wrongly confounded with impulsive aggression and instrumental with planned violence. Many crimes of violence indicate that angry reactions to a provocation can be carefully rehearsed and nurtured over time until a planned retaliation, delayed revenge, is enacted.

These false dichotomies can also overlook or minimise the seriousness of various forms of non-physical abuse and coercive control. Stark (2007) has documented the extent of coercive control in domestic violence. He highlights how intimidation, isolation and the deprivation of women's liberty have often been overlooked by legal and social responses despite the significant negative effects on female victims. Whilst this is recognised by those working in domestic violence, it is often less thoroughly addressed in perpetrator programs and difficult to change. Change in non-physical forms of abuse and coercive control are also difficult to evaluate without some degree of qualitative feedback from victims or new intimate partners that have an awareness of less overt forms of abuse. Therefore comprehensive conclusions about change remain limited to physical forms of abuse.

In relation to matching participants with different program content, Day et al (2009) have proposed that the Transtheoretical Model of Change has value in understanding the individual needs of domestically violent men. According to this model, problem resolution involves a progression through a sequence of change stages (Prochaska and DiClemente 1992), each of which is characterised by different attitudes, thoughts, beliefs and values. A number of different stages of change have been described, including: *precontemplation* (no wish to change/no recognition of a problem), *contemplation* (intention to change problem behaviour within the next six months), *preparation* (intention to take immediate action, usually measured as within the next month), *action* (characterised by specific, overt modifications within the past six months), *maintenance* (relapse prevention), and *termination* (change process is complete/ no further need to prevent relapse) (Velicer, Prochaska, Fava, Norman and Redding 1998). Individuals in the pre-contemplative stage, for example, are those who are unwilling to acknowledge they have a problem and who minimise and/or deny the abusive behaviour and its consequences (Pence and Paymar 1993). They exhibit a tendency to provide excuses and justifications for their aggressive behaviour (Dutton 1986). Murphy and Baxter (1997) have argued that given many perpetrators arrive in treatment in the early stages of change (see Chapter 12), the stages of change construct provides a useful framework within which to motivate these individuals to change their behaviour (see also Levesque, Gelles and Velicer 2000). Day et al further suggest that in order to achieve the treatment goals of this stage (that is, increased awareness of the negative aspects of the problem, acknowledgment of the problem, and the accurate evaluation of self-regulation capacities), motivational discussions are considered most appropriate.

Most, if not all, practitioners working in this area can readily identify motivational problems on the part of participants as a major factor determining progress in program sessions, and yet motivational issues have been curiously neglected in the domestic violence literature. This is despite some studies reporting exceptionally high rates of attrition in domestic violence programs (up to half of all men who begin a program do not complete it: see Feazell, Mayers and Deschner 1984). Gondolf (2008) has recently reported a completion rate of approximately 55 per cent for a 16 week group program. These statistics are of major concern given recent evidence that those who start but who do not complete rehabilitation programs are left at higher risk of reoffending than those who do not enter programs at all. Such findings appear to be robust across a broad range of treatments and offense types (see McMurran and Theodosi 2006), have been supported by studies in domestic violence (DeMaris and Jackson 1987), and generally point to the potentially iatrogenic effects of interventions with domestically violent men.

A contributing factor, of course, may be inconsistencies in the criminal justice and referral pathways for mandated domestic violence offenders. Integrated responses often aim to develop systemic responses, but in some jurisdictions criminal justice referral to intervention programs can often take place after a significant time delay (sometimes up to a year or more) since the offence. Furthermore, the power to legally enforce an offender's program attendance can be inconsistent, and in many cases non-attendance has had no or lenient statutory consequences (Chung et al 2003).These matters collectively point to the importance of resourcing programs well enough to enable processing in a timely fashion (for example, to get offenders completing programs before court orders lapse) as well as the need for consistent consequences for non-attendance and reoffending. Whilst this is to some extent outside the remit of intervention programs, these system aspects are key to any effort to engage participants in a behaviour change process and compound the dilemmas of programs being able to generate demonstrable benefits for offenders who participate or for the safety of women.

Conclusion

The primary issue raised in this chapter is the viability and limitations of running homogeneous domestic violence programs for a diversity of male offenders. This issue is ideologically contentious, and has profound implications for how perpetrator programs are conceptualised and delivered. Conclusions from evaluating programs for male offenders will remain contentious while there remains a high level of variance in referral pathways, design and structure. Equally, evaluation needs to take place with programs that are resourced to a level to deliver consistent program and practice logic at multiple sites. Such programs need the support and structure of a criminal justice system that delivers a timely response to different offender needs at the referral point. To adequately capture the complexity of abusive and violent behaviour multiple measures of change are needed. These should not only measure criminal recidivism and behavioural and attitudinal change reported by the offender, but also the perspective of associated victim(s) and children.

In summary, there is a strong argument for developing more differentiated service responses determined by a detailed assessment of the dynamics and causes of the offence, as well as the severity and risk of reoffending. This is important in the effort to improve effectiveness; however, it also requires a concurrent change in program pathways and the relevant sequencing of multiple interventions where these are required. This is needed to ensure adequate numbers of referrals for specialist programs. One way to approach differentiated responses is through the classification of perpetrators into typologies (for example, as recommended by Bender and Roberts 2007), as well as considering how cognitive-behavioural treatment methods can be implemented within current program content.

Chapter 16

The Role of the Facilitator[1]

Andrew Day and Ed Carson

Domestic violence is now widely recognised as a major social problem around the western world. International surveys have suggested that around one third of all adult women will experience abuse perpetrated by an intimate male. A recent National Crime Victimization Survey in the United States found that 64 per cent of women who were raped, physically assaulted or stalked were victimised by a current or former partner (Tjaden and Thoennes 2000). Nearly half of all incidents involve physical injury, and approximately two thirds of all women who are murdered are killed by their husband or live-in partner (Davis and Mouzos 2007). Given that domestic violence is rarely an isolated event and that perpetrators are known to often repeatedly offend (Gondolf 2007), the logic underpinning calls to develop effective community responses to this problem is compelling.

One of the most interesting and important types of response has been to address the problem by working with the abuser (Buttell and Carney 2008). Programs for domestically violent men began to emerge in the later 1970s and 1980s (Dobash and Dobash 1992), and there are now literally hundreds of different types of program currently offered around the world. Programs range from those which are run by community based agencies where men attend on a voluntary basis to those designed specifically for men who have been found guilty of criminal offences related to domestic violence and who are legally mandated to attend. In Chapter 15 we noted that, as a consequence, programs vary considerably in terms of their stated purpose, disciplinary emphases and core understandings of the nature of domestic violence.

Our interest in writing this chapter is on those services and programs which are delivered in the context of a criminal justice response to domestic violence, rather than those that target voluntary clients. The aim is to explore the broader systemic issue of how the criminal justice

1 A version of this chapter is to be published by the *Psychology Journal* (with permission).

system can be used in a therapeutic manner to engage violent men in a behaviour change process, with particular reference to the way in which the practitioner might balance his or her responsibilities towards clients, the legal system, and the broader community. Those who deliver domestic violence programs typically hail from a wide range of professional backgrounds, and few have formal training in issues relating to the administration of justice and the consequent responsibilities that practitioners have in working in this specific therapeutic context. A key question for all therapeutic jurisprudence initiatives is the extent to which the use of the law in this way promotes therapeutic or anti-therapeutic outcomes (Wexler and Wexler 1991). Whilst such issues have received surprisingly little attention in both the academic and professional literature, it is suggested that they are likely to be important determinants of the likely success of any program for men who are legally coerced into treatment.

Program effectiveness

The primary goal of mandating clients to attend domestic violence programs is to prevent further offending. As a consequence, the issue of program effectiveness becomes critical to any discussion of how programs should be delivered. Although there is some debate within the field about the meaning and value of evaluation studies (see Gondolf 2001), meta-analytic reviews of program outcomes have tended to suggest that, on average, the effects of perpetrator programs on improving the safety of women are rather modest. As is noted in the previous chapter, a meta-analysis by Babcock, Green and Robie (2004) involving the results of a number of different program evaluations concluded that the effect sizes associated with different types of approach to domestic violence intervention were typically small (d=0.35 for Duluth programs; d=0.29 for cognitive behavioural programs), with the base rates of reoffending across studies reported to be 21 per cent based on police reports, and 35 per cent based on partner reports. However, when only those studies employing experimental designs were reviewed, these effect sizes reduced to d=.09 using victim reports as the outcome measure and d=0.12 based on police reports. This was interpreted by the authors to mean that "a woman is 5 per cent less likely to be reassaulted by a man who was arrested, sanctioned, and went to a batterers' program than by a man who was simply arrested and sanctioned" (Babcock et al 2004: 1032).

Another meta-analytic review by Feder and Wilson (2005: 239) investigating the effects of program attendance on mandated offenders produced even more disheartening results. They concluded that "the mean effect for victim reported outcomes was zero". Such findings have provoked a number of, at times heated, debates between researchers and practitioners about the value and appropriateness of different approaches to intervention (see Dutton and Corvo 2007; Gondolf 2007). In Chapter 15, for example, we suggested that further consideration should be given to the ways in which men's intervention groups are designed and delivered, and in particular to the articulation of a program logic linking specific interventions to particular intervention goals more closely. One difficulty that arises in relation to domestic violence programs is in articulating what the goals of the program should be, and the extent to which the practitioner responds to any inconsistencies between the goals of the individual client, the program, the criminal justice system, the broader community, and indeed his or her own personal and professional beliefs about how intervention should proceed.

Client perspectives

One of the major therapeutic tasks in domestic violence perpetrator programs is to reach a shared understanding with the client about the nature, extent and seriousness of their violence. Domestic violence differs from other types of violent offending in so far as offending typically occurs behind closed doors, where the only witnesses are victims. As a result the facts of the offence are often difficult to establish, and male perpetrators often dispute the evidence that is presented to the police or the courts in relation to the frequency and intensity of their violence, the reliability of the victim statements, and on a basic level the extent to which they consider themselves personally responsible. Indeed men typically arrive in programs believing that their behaviour was justified, that their violence was appropriate, and even that it would have been inappropriate for them to have acted in any other way (see Chapter 12). To borrow the phrase of Howells (1989), their behaviour is ego-syntonic. Given that angry and aggressive behaviour can lead to social perceptions of status, strength and competence (Tiedens 2001), any attempt to induce change is likely to elicit ambivalent reactions in the client and greater treatment resistance.

Howells and Day (2003) have applied Ford's (1992) motivational analysis of goals as a framework for understanding readiness for anger management. They suggest that for therapeutic goals to be realised, the client's personal goals need to be constituted by, supportive of, or consistent with, the therapeutic goal. Therapeutic change then involves the therapist examining with the client what goals the client is pursuing, how these goals are organised and how they are being regulated or misregulated (Karoly 1999). Karoly (1993: 279) further stresses the need to examine treatment targets in the context of broader client goals and the motivational salience of change. He suggests, also, that "therapeutic failures of various kinds (premature termination, resistance, relapse etc) can result from the therapist-assessor's failure to appreciate the structural relation between time-limited treatment goals and life goals in general".

Given that many clients may not, at least in the early stages of intervention, have personal goals that are consistent with program goals (that is, women's safety) or have goals that are incompatible with program goals (for example, to fulfil the obligations of the order; to change the partner's behaviour; to punish the partner etc), it is perhaps unsurprising that program facilitators commonly find difficulties in engaging clients in a change process and encounter hostility, resistance, and non-compliance. One issue that is undisputed in the domestic violence field is the very high attrition rates from programs, typically between 50 and 75 per cent (Buttell and Carney 2008). Gondolf (2008), for example, recently reported a completion rate of approximately 55 per cent for a 16 week group based program. Such statistics are of major concern given the evidence that those who start but who do not complete rehabilitation programs are left at higher risk of reoffending than those who do not enter programs at all (see DeMaris and Jackson 1987; McMurran and Theodosi 2006).

Victim perspectives

In many ways the focus on victim issues (that is, women's safety) in domestic violence programs is a defining feature of this type of work. Rather than the therapeutic contact occurring *because of the past harm* caused to a victim, program facilitators are obliged to monitor the *ongoing and future* risks of further harm, mainly because the context in which the original offence took place is often largely unchanged when a perpetrator enters a program.

The need to attend closely to the needs of victims is also likely to be an important determinant of therapeutic practice. A strong awareness of the harm caused by an individual client will influence the way in which the practitioner relates to him in a program, and sets the tone for the sessions that follow. In relation to sentencing, some have suggested that victim involvement can lead to vengeful and disproportionate punishments (Ashworth 2002) which is one reason why the conventional criminal justice system continues to place victim's rights on the periphery of justice proceedings (Ward and Langlands 2009). In a provocative analysis of the ethical issues underlying mandated offender rehabilitation with sex offenders, Glaser (2003) has argued that much of the way in which treatment is delivered should be understood in terms of treatment providers' desire to administer punishment to their clients on behalf of the community, motivated by their identification with child victims. The use of intense confrontation in some domestic violence programs (Murphy and Baxter 1997) might attract a similar analysis, though one which we would reject for reasons discussed later in this chapter. Furthermore it is clearly problematic to assume that all victims of domestic violence will respond in the same way. Indeed many victims are, if anything, overly forgiving, to the extent that on occasion they have appeared as defence witnesses when the matters comes to court (Fletcher 2008; Opitz 2008).

Practitioner perspectives

Little is known about the ways in which program providers view their clients and, in particular, about their emotional reactions to their work. Not only are there likely to be marked individual differences in the personal values that practitioners hold about their client, but also important differences in the values espoused in their professional training. Those from social work backgrounds, for instance, are likely to be trained in theories that explain crime from structural, geographical and gendered perspectives; perspectives which do not emphasise personal agency or individual responsibility. Those from psychology and counselling backgrounds are more likely to understand behaviour in the context of individual social and emotional learning histories (see McGuire 2002).

The extent to which practitioners can and should accept the validity of the phenomenology of male clients raises interesting issues and can be approached from the perspective of the therapeutic alliance. The therapeutic alliance has been shown to be a moderate but significant and consistent predictor of treatment outcome across a variety of therapeutic modalities and patient groups (for example, Bambling and King 2001), and has been put forward as a central mechanism to explain findings that different models of treatment deliver broadly equivalent outcomes. Theoretically, most definitions of a therapeutic alliance emphasise three related themes: (1) the collaborative nature of the relationship; (2) the affective bond between client and therapist; and (3) the client's and therapist's ability to agree on treatment goals and tasks.

Whilst general counselling techniques can be used to develop an affective bond (through the development of rapport and trust), and treatment goals and tasks can be set in the process of developing change plans, it is less clear whether the defining feature of the alliance, collaboration, should be a goal in this type of intervention. The process of confrontation and the underlying assumption that the client must be jolted into active behaviour change in order to overcome any claims that their behaviour was not serious or that their victims provoked or deserved the violence (Dutton 1986; Pence and Paymar 1983), is critical here. There is a choice that each practitioner makes between confronting, persuading, cajoling and motivating clients into some form of agreement with the basic goal of non-violence, and a different approach which begins with the client's frame of reference. The former is associated with a didactic, educational approach to group work, the latter with a more therapeutic approach.

The values that the practitioner holds can also directly influence the formation of strong therapeutic alliances with clients. Highly discrepant therapist-client values are likely to adversely affect treatment outcomes by impairing the development of a strong relational bond. Ward and Marshall (2007: 280) recently argued that the rehabilitation of offenders can be understood as an essentially evaluative process. For them, effective rehabilitation is based on enabling offenders to pursue ways of living that are constructed around core values, requiring that offenders "receive exposure to primary values, adaptive beliefs, constructive self- and other-regarding attitudes, and social recognition". Similarly Thigpen, Beauclair, Keiser, Guevara and Mestad (2007) identified some unique characteristics of the forensic counselling relationship that they believe serve to enhance effectiveness in working with offenders. For example, they suggest that the provider should act as a model and demonstrate anti-criminal expressions of behaviour, and that the effective practitioner must be consistent and unerring in communicating pro-social and high moral values.

Systemic perspectives

There are a number of systemic and organisational issues that will also influence any decisions about the goals of intervention. Systemic issues appear to have a great influence on treatment outcomes, even in integrated services (O'Leary, Chung, and Zannettino 2004). For example, referral to intervention programs often takes place after a significant time delay (sometimes up to a year or more) since the offence. Furthermore, the power to legally enforce an offender's program attendance can be inconsistent and in many cases non-attendance leads to few or lenient statutory consequences. This suggests that there is a need for participants to be aware that the criminal justice system seeks particular outcomes from program attendance and that the consequences for non-attendance and reoffending will be consistently applied.

Legally coerced treatment

In many ways, however, the defining feature of domestic violence programs is the legal mandate that provides the entry into the therapeutic situation. A number of important and specific therapeutic issues arise in circumstances when interventions are legally coerced (see Day, Tucker and Howells 2003), although relatively little is known about the effects of legally coerced treatment on treatment outcomes.

A recent review of compulsory treatment for substance using offenders by the ANDC (1997: 65) concluded that the current research evidence supporting the effectiveness of compulsory treatment is both "inadequate and inconclusive". This report cites Wild's (2006: 46) observation that the: "proliferation of social control tactics to facilitate addiction treatment is a worldwide social experiment being implemented without a compelling evidence base on its utility". In short, insufficient effectiveness research exists in order to lay any claim that legally coerced substance abuse interventions would fulfill the criteria required to be called "empirically supported" (Hollon and Chambless 1998). The same accusation might also be levelled at domestic violence programs, particularly in light of the Feder and Wilson (2005) meta-analysis (see above).

The use of the criminal justice system to force offenders to receive psychological treatment is also one of the most controversial aspects of service provision. Some service providers have expressed strong reservations about working with clients who are coerced into attending. Marlowe et al (2007: S5), for example, have suggested that the intrusion of a judge into the treatment process can be disruptive or harmful to the formation of a therapeutic alliance. They suggest that:

> [C]lients may be hesitant to confide important information to their counsellors for fear the information would be disclosed to the court and used against their legal interests. Moreover, being "treated like a criminal" by being brought into court on a regular basis might elicit counterproductive feelings of resistance or reactance. Under such circumstances, judicial monitoring could both waste scarce resources and elicit iatrogenic effects. On the other hand, high-risk offenders often fail to meet their obligations and may pose a continuing threat to public safety if they are not closely monitored and do not face immediate and consistent consequences for non-compliance in treatment.

There is theoretical literature in relation to working with coerced clients which is relevant to practice in this area. Whilst involuntary clients may range in their levels of motivation to engage with a mandated treatment, there will be some clients who are resistant, either actively or passively, to the intervention (see above). Chambers et al (2008) have suggested that when an individual's perceived freedom to engage in a specific action, belief or emotion is threatened, that individual enters a motivational state directed toward re-establishing their freedom. Re-establishing behavioural freedom manifests itself as psychological reactance in treatment, and might involve engaging in the prohibited behaviour, or even increasing it (Brehm 1966; Brehm and Brehm 1981). Reactance may also be expressed by engaging in aggression towards a prohibitor, in this case, the therapist (Johnson and Buboltz 2000).

Coerced treatment can be distinguished from pressured treatment, although both have objective and subjective dimensions. The available research evidence (see Day, Tucker and Howells 2003) suggests that coercing offenders into attending programs (or placing legal pressure on them to attend) is unlikely by itself to lead to poorer therapeutic outcomes. Rather, it is the individual's perception of coercion that will be more influential in determining how she or he approaches treatment. Even when clients do perceive they are being coerced, it is likely that pre-treatment anti-therapeutic attitudes can change over the course of a program, such that therapeutic gains (risk reduction) can occur. This suggests that the way in which the issue of coercion is approached by practitioners is likely to have a profound influence on the treatment process.

Practice implications

Barber (1991: 45) has discussed case work with the involuntary client from a social work perspective, making the following observations:

> [W]ork with involuntary clients must begin with the recognition that the interaction between the worker and client is based on *conflict* rather than co-operation, that social work with involuntary clients is a *political,* not a therapeutic, process involving the socially sanctioned use of power. The political nature of this activity becomes obvious when one calls to mind what it means to be an involuntary client in the first place.

He goes on to note that the "ultimate beneficiary of the work done will be those who in some way suffered from the client's aberrant behaviour in the first place" (1991: 45). Thus for Barber at least the role of the worker is to negotiate a settlement between the client and society at large, and it is important that the client is aware of this from the very outset of any intervention. Barber proposed a six step model of what he termed "negotiated casework" (see Table 16.1) below.

Table 16.1 Negotiated Casework (Barber 1991)

Steps	Description
1. Clear the air	Begin by directing attention to the order that led to the meetings. Read out a copy of the court order and elicit client perspectives.
2. Identify legitimate client interests	Attend to any objections to engagement in treatment and the goals of the client.
3. Identify non-negotiable aspects of intervention	Clarify which aspects cannot be compromised and the reporting requirements (for example, attendance).
4. Identify negotiable aspects of intervention	Define the problem and identify possibilities for change.
5. Negotiate the case plan	The aim here is to make decisions about the way forward, identifying goals and responsibilities.
6. Agree on criteria for progress	Clarify how judgments will be made about whether the case plan is working or not, and what happens if the client fails to comply with aspects of the case plan.

An advantage of this approach is that it clarifies the goals of the program and the responsibilities of the practitioner to other agencies, particularly in regard to reporting or evaluating clients for legal purposes. There are a range of ethical issues associated with offering treatment to an individual

Table 16.2. Differences between Therapeutic and Forensic Relationships (adapted from Greenberg and Shuman 1997)

	Healthcare provision	Evaluation for court
1. Whose client is the patient/litigant?	The mental health practitioner	The lawyer
2. The relational privilege that governs disclosure in each relationship	Therapist-patient privilege	Lawyer-client and lawyer work-product privilege
3. The cognitive set and evaluative attitude of each expert	Supportive, accepting, empathic	Neutral, objective, detached
4. The differing areas of competency of each expert	Therapy techniques for treatment of the impairment	Forensic evaluation techniques relevant to the legal claim
5. The nature of hypotheses tested by each expert	Diagnostic criteria for the purpose of therapy	Psycho-legal criteria for the purpose of legal adjudication
6. The scrutiny applied to the information used in the process and the role of historical truth	Mostly based on information from the person being treated with little scrutiny of that information by the therapist	Litigant information supplemented with that of collateral sources and scrutinised by the evaluator and the court
7. The amount and control of structure in each relationship	Therapist attempts to benefit the patient by working within the therapeutic relationship	Evaluator advocates for the results and implications of the evaluation for the benefit of the court
8. The nature and degree of adversarialness in each relationship	A helping relationship; rarely adversarial	An evaluative relationship; frequently adversarial
9. The goal of the professional in each relationship	Therapist attempts to benefit the patient by working within the therapeutic relationship	Evaluator advocates for the results and implications of the evaluator for the benefits of the court
10. The impact on each relationship of critical judgment by the expert	The basis of the relationship is the therapeutic alliance and critical judgment is likely to impair that alliance	The basis of the relationship is evaluative and critical judgment is unlikely to cause serious emotional harm

while also undertaking some form of evaluation or monitoring for legal purposes, although examples of practitioners undertaking both roles are still relatively common (see Freckelton 2006). These can be understood in terms of the conflict of roles between therapists and evaluators which are summarised in Table 16.2. It perhaps helps to explain some of the discomfort experienced by practitioners who seek to work therapeutically with domestically violent men, and yet are also asked to make disclosures to a third party, such as the court or community corrections officer.

The ANCD (2007: 26) report on compulsory treatment for substance users argued that:

> [F]or service providers, the monitoring and reporting required in some compulsory treatment programs, and thus the possibility that boundaries of confidentiality may need to be breached, raise two main concerns: they call into question the ethics of their practice; and they may compromise client trust and rapport, and thereby jeopardise the entire therapeutic relationship.

However, Thigpen at al (2007: 43) have also suggested that the provider must "approve (reinforce) the client's anti-criminal expressions and disapprove (punish) the client's pro-criminal expressions. Often, the latter requires going beyond disapproval to reporting violations of corrections policies and probation conditions". For domestic violence program providers, the issue of reporting is often unproblematic - it is commonly assumed that clients forfeit the right to confidentiality when issues of safety arise. However, the conflict of roles that results may not only undermine their ability to provide neutral and objective expert advice to the legal system, but also to develop the type of relationship with their clients that is ultimately likely to bring about behaviour change.

In conclusion then, this chapter has sought to discuss the ways in which different perspectives about the goals of intervention can surface in domestic violence perpetrator programs. These are key issues for practice, and whilst practitioners will take different positions on an appropriate standpoint in relation to these issues, what is apparent is that clarity about goals, and the way in which conflict is negotiated, is likely to influence the likely success of any program.

Chapter 17

Courage, Hope and Resilience: Aspirations for the Future

Andrew Day, Patrick O'Leary, Donna Chung and Donna Justo

It is widely acknowledged that domestic violence remains amongst the most common and the most under-reported of all crimes. Whilst the rate of females reporting incidents of physical assault by a male perpetrator has almost doubled over the last decade (from 19 per cent to 36 per cent: ABS 2006), it is estimated only 14 per cent of women report the most recent incident of domestic violence to police (see Mouzos and Makkai 2004).

There are a number of possible explanations for these statistics, but the material contained in this book suggests that, at least for some women, the reluctance to report offences relates in part to: a fear that they will not be taken seriously; have previously experienced an unhelpful police response; have a propensity to blame themselves; not viewing the situation as domestic violence or criminal behaviour (particularly when there is limited physical violence); that it will not lead to greater safety for them and their children; and/or that reporting will place them at greater risk of further and ongoing victimisation. In addition, and importantly for this book, women may not feel confident that either the legal process or any referral to a men's program will lead to significant changes in the attitudes, beliefs or behaviours of the male perpetrator.

Many of those who have been involved in writing this book would argue that these fears and barriers are realistic and reasonable. We would all agree that much more can, and should, be done to ensure that community responses to domestic violence are as effective as possible. Nevertheless, there are differences of opinion in relation to how services should be configured, how men's programs should be delivered, and how program effectiveness should be assessed. These are some of the issues which this book has aimed to explore, and are critical to the success and sustainability of domestic violence services. It will have been apparent from reading this book that significant challenges face those who are interested in working constructively with both men and women whose lives are affected by domestic violence.

The last 10 years have seen a significant investment in the development and delivery of a broad suite of offender rehabilitation programs across Australia, in both prison and community corrections settings, and support for rehabilitative ideals is now more clearly enshrined in public policy than perhaps at any time in the past. That is not to say that the value of offender rehabilitation has been universally recognised. As Ward, Day and Casey (2006: 73) put it:

> The balance between punishment and rehabilitation for public policy makers is a delicate one, and the rise of the victim's movement has added a new and different perspective to sentencing. The voice of victims is now much more widely heard than it had been before, and sentencing and release decisions are now often obliged to take these into account. There is conflict between the rehabilitative ethos and a countervailing political and legal pressure to introduce and/or maintain regressive measures for dealing with offenders.

This book suggests that nowhere is this balance more difficult to achieve than in the area of domestic violence. In many ways domestic violence programs are at the forefront of what have been termed therapeutic jurisprudence initiatives in Australia. The central notion here is using the law in ways which promote therapeutic outcomes, in this case reduction in the risk of violent behaviour being repeated. When men's intervention programs are considered, it would appear that the evidence supporting their effectiveness is far from conclusive. Nevertheless this book has shown a number of indicators of effectiveness that are not solely linked to men's change, as the pathway into men's program entry within an integrated response also enables the provision of support and services to women and children. Therefore, the positive outcomes for men's entry into a program may be that women and children get access to help and can live more safely even if his behaviour and attitudes ostensibly show little or no change. If women continue in the relationship then the women's contact aspect can offer women realistic advice on what change may be expected so that women do not gain false hope or a false sense of safety just because their partner has entered a program. It can therefore be misleading, but not unimportant, to measure men's progress in a group program as the only indicator of success or otherwise. Policy and service design needs to identify effectiveness measures relating to both men's attitude and behaviour change and women's and children's safety, as we can not always assume there is a correlation between these two elements. However, this requires that the delivery of a men's program sits within an integrated response.

At the men's program delivery level there is considerable, and growing, debate in relation to how program providers should position themselves in relation to the male participants, and the extent to which they should develop relationships with them that are educational, therapeutic or punitive. This is not a debate which should be regarded as either academic or ideological – it has important implications for how programs are delivered, the content, and the type of messages that are given to male perpetrators and female victims about their behaviour.

There would appear to be a need for further work to be conducted in the area of identifying the intervention needs of domestically violent men. For example, there is evidence to suggest that research on anger, alcohol and aggression does apply to some types of offender, leading a number of people to suggest that interventions for domestic violence may often need to be delivered in conjunction with services related to co-existing problems such as alcohol and drug rehabilitation (McMurran and Gilchrist 2007). Underpinning this work is the notion that individual differences are important to effective service provision – with the idea that not all offenders will benefit from the same type of program or intervention processes. The work of Gilchrist (2009), identifying the core beliefs or implicit theories of offenders about their offending, holds great promise here, but further work is required on the identification of offence pathways, and assessing both risk and dangerousness in ways that can inform the matching of offenders to appropriate levels of supervision and intervention. Another area of promise is in the area of treatment readiness (Ward et al 2004), and how to work most effectively with those offenders who appear to be neither interested nor engaged in any process of behaviour change. Finally there is a need to further develop methodologies for conducting evaluation research and develop psychometrically sound measures to assess change in program participants.

A commonly voiced concern with adopting an intervention focus on individual differences is that it may in some way allow offenders to avoid taking personal responsibility for their behaviour, by blaming other factors, such as childhood abuse, substance use, or provocation. Clearly the way in which issues of personal responsibility are approached and the balance struck between the personal histories of offenders and the particular context in which their offences occurred and the broader effects on women and children is likely to be critical to the effectiveness of any intervention. Such an approach clearly moves beyond a psycho-educational model of intervention, which has been commonly used in the past. This emerging area is a complex area which requires great skill, and in which program facilitators require support and supervision.

It is important, at this point, to acknowledge again that domestic violence services and programs have a very different history from those developed in other areas of criminal justice. They were born out of political activism placing women's rights to safety at the front and centre of any response. This focus on victim's rights and the associated notions of offender accountability in some ways distinguishes domestic violence programs from other types of offender rehabilitation programs and highlights the need for service integration. Women are typically not victimised once, but exposed to ongoing and repeated violence, from which they are often powerless to escape. Another key issue with this area of service delivery is that there has often been a history of intimate relationships between the perpetrator and victim, which conclude and recommence. This intimacy between perpetrator and victim shapes her help-seeking behaviour and decision-making about the relationship, and his response to criminal sanctions and mandated program attendance. The need for effective and timely responses from the police, child protection services, the criminal justice system and community corrections services is undisputed. The ongoing monitoring of risk by multiple agencies lies at the heart of successful service delivery. There is also an obvious need for the provision of education, advocacy and mental health services for those who have been victimised. The impact of living in fear over long periods of time should be evident to all, as is the need for support in reporting when crimes have been committed and following the legal process through to a conclusion. This is aside from the other direct effects of domestic violence on the physical health, wellbeing and financial security of women and their children.

Our hope in writing this book is that it will offer a resource to practitioners and researchers alike to help inform their work in this area. There are a number of common goals which unite the sector. The responses and support for them will always be influenced by community attitudes about what is unacceptable and what is a reasonable sanction to impose. The community now has a much greater awareness of domestic violence and its unacceptability. This reflects the work of second wave feminists' efforts to raise the issue publicly. This has seen changes evolve and develop in domestic violence responses, although many challenges remain to stopping domestic violence in the community. Domestic violence is a complex problem with ripple like effects and there remains considerable debate about how best to intervene. In essence, domestic violence continues to be a complex socio-political problem with considerable individualised effects. It is therefore important to ensure that the community responds in an appropriate way to perpetrators of domestic violence; that victims receive appropriate support and services; and that services are as successful as they can be in reducing the risk of known perpetrators committing further acts of violence against women and children.

Appendix: Data on Men's Change – Conflict Tactics Scale

Prior to entering the program, the majority of participants indicated that they had engaged in at least one behaviour indicative of relationship negotiation, such as showing respect for the feelings of their partner, or suggesting that they had been able to explain their perspective to their partner regarding a disagreement. In fact, the highest number of individual acts at Time 1 was for acts of a negotiation nature (an average of 68.89[1] individual acts).

Reports of physical assault (for instance, presence or absence) at program commencement were rather high (with a mean number of acts for the total sample of 13.00). While ten participants indicated no acts of physical assault, 27 participants (almost 60% of these from the 12-month group) did report that they had engaged in a minor act (for example, pushing/shoving, grabbing partner), and more than half of these men also indicated an act of greater severity (for example, slamming partner against wall), with these severity reports almost evenly distributed between time groups. Injuries to the participant as a result of a fight with their partner were reported, with having a sprain/bruise/cut and feeling physical pain the next day the most selected, but six participants indicating at least one injury of greater severity (three of the six-month participants indicated two different types of acts, and one of the 12-month participants indicated three types of acts), which usually involved going to see a doctor/needing to see a doctor (in two cases the fight involved passing out or sustaining a broken bone). Reports of the number of times such injuries had occurred, however, were rather low, supporting somewhat the lower reports of severe physical assault.

At program commencement, psychological aggression was endorsed somewhat more than that of physical aggression, with only three participants indicating no instances of psychological aggression. While most aggressive acts committed fell into the category of minor aggression (for example, insulting/swearing at partner), almost 60% of these participants had also committed more severe acts of psychological aggression (for example, threats of violence, destroying property), with those in the 12-

1 While 'individual acts' are referred to, this does not mean that each act was committed in isolation from others (for example, that two different types of psychological aggression did not occur together).

month group more likely to report at least one of these types of act. Behaviours indicative of psychological aggression were the highest reported negative behaviours by participants, with an average of 33.41 (total scale) single acts of different types of psychological aggression committed.

Sexual coercion was least endorsed, with three participants indicating at least one act of sexual coercion at Time 1 (two participants made their partner engage in intercourse without a condom—one participant did this once, one participant did this 25 times; one of these participants once also insisted on sex when their partner did not want to, without the use physical force; and one participant once used threats to make their partner engage in sex).

Comparison of prevalence and frequency reports (particularly frequency reports) between Time 1 and Time 2 are problematic due to the different time periods sampled for eight of the 11 post-program participants. Since reports of 12-month behaviours and six-month behaviours were similar, however, pre- and post-program scores are compared, although the conclusions remain cautious. In addition, analysis of individual cases is undertaken, since analysis at the group level where such variation between participant behaviours exists (in terms of reported prevalence and chronicity of acts) may be somewhat misleading.

At Time 2, analysis at the general level suggested some small to moderate changes. Negotiation linearly increased, mostly due to increases in emotional negotiation strategies. Injury to self also linearly decreased, and sexual coercion was at a similarly low level from Time 1 to Time 2 (for sexual coercion, one participant at post-test reported a severe sexually coercive act - two acts of using force to make their partner have oral or anal sex; this participant indicated no acts at Time 1). However, somewhat surprisingly, psychological aggression slightly increased (although there was wide variation between participants), and this was mostly due to an increase in severe psychological aggression. Similarly, physical assault also increased, with minor physically assaultive acts responsible for this increase.

It should be noted that two participants recorded scores of 0 for all scales at Time 2. It should also be noted that, in many cases, acts at Time 1 were rather low for these participants (see Tables A.1 and A.2), and so change is often small.

For negotiation, seven participants increased in their negotiation scores, two remained the same (one of these recorded the highest possible scores at both time periods), while two decreased (one decreased moderately, while the other participant was the program participant who recorded scores of 0 for all scales at Time 2). As mentioned, the increase seemed mostly due to a greater number of emotion negotiation tactics being employed by participants.

As mentioned, results for psychological aggression suggested little change overall, and any change being mostly due to an increase in severe psychological aggression, in comparison to a slight decrease in minor psychological aggression. However, analysis by individual case indicates that the overall increase was due to one participant who increased quite substantially in the use of both minor (48-75) and severe aggression (10-54), and one other participant who reported scores of 0 for all scales at Time 1 (an increase from 0-46 and 0-3 for minor and severe psychological aggression, respectively). When these two participants are excluded from analysis, it is notable that all other participants decreased (one participant remained at 0), with a mean change of 12 less acts of psychological aggression (three participants decreased to 0).

Results for physical assault were similarly influenced by these two participants (recording total scores of 8-80 and 0-25, with four and eight of these acts being of a severe nature, respectively), although other changes were rather modest. Of the other participants, there were four decreases (1-0, 7-0, 2-0, 18-13, although this participant increased slightly in minor physical assault and decreased in the use of more severe assault), while the other five reported scores of 0 at both Time 1 and Time 2. Thus, for those participants for whom a positive change was possible, three of four evidenced desired change.

For injury to self, again the two participants already discussed increased (10-27 and 0-2 minor injuries), four other participants decreased (from 2-0 and 8-4 minor injuries; 14 injuries to 0, six of which were major; and 39 to 0, 15 minor injuries and 24 more severe injuries, although this latter participant indicated no acts, including negotiation, at Time 2), and the remainder recorded 0 at both time periods.

Participant reports of partner behaviours

Participant reports of partner behaviours at Time 1 were also rather similar across time periods (12 or six months). Participant reports of their partner's negotiation behaviours were somewhat lower than their own, although tended to match in terms of prevalence.

However, the prevalence and frequency of reported instances of psychological and physical aggression by their partners were less related to their own. While reports were often related for minor acts (in terms of prevalence), frequency scores were still higher for partners for these minor acts. In addition, some participants reported that their partners had committed at least one act of severe psychological aggression (six participants) or severe physical attack (seven participants) when they had not, and also reported more of these acts by their partners (frequency). Reports of injury were also reported to be lower (frequency) for partners (although eight participants who reported minor injury had one partner sustaining an injury and the other not: six of these participants indicated such an injury to their partner and not themselves, with the other two reporting the opposite trend—all other participants who reported minor injuries reported that both partners had sustained injuries. For reports for severe injury prevalence, however, ten participants reported an imbalance, such that five received an injury and their partner did not, and five reported the opposite trend).

At Time 1, in both twelve- and six-month groups, reports of self and partner behaviours were, however, positively correlated: negotiation, $r(21)=.63$, $p < .01$ (twelve-month), $r(15)=.83$, $p < .001$ (six-month); psychological aggression, $r(21)=.87$, $p < .001$ (12-month), $r(16)=.88$, $p < .001$ (six-month); physical assault, $r(21)=.61$, $p < .01$ (12-month), $r(16)=.70$, $p < .01$ (six-month); sexual coercion, $r(16)=.54$, $p < .05$ (six-month); injury, $r(21)=.70$, $p < .001$ (12-month).

At program completion, however, participant reports for their partners matched theirs very closely. In fact, there were only minor discrepancies (a participant reporting engaging in sexually coercive behaviour, but his partner not doing so; one participant indicating injury to their partner but not himself; one participant indicating that their partner had acted physically aggressive, but not them; and two participants differing on self-other reports of psychological aggression, one in each direction).

While reports of negative partner behaviours were rather low at Time 2[2], examination of frequencies indicated participants reported that their partners had engaged in lesser negotiation, but had also engaged in lesser physical assault, and sexual coercion, and had obtained a greater number of injuries. Participants reported that their partners had also engaged in a higher level of psychological aggression. Injury reports are useful as they provide some idea of partner injury (although they were reported upon by the participant). Three participants indicated that they and their partner had sustained a minor injury (frequencies self-other: 4-4, 27-29, 2-4), with the latter two of these participants reporting a more severe injury for their partner (1 and 2 severe injuries). All other participants indicated a score of 0 for both self and partner.

At Time 2, there was one participant who reported only acts of increased negotiation by both self and partner.

Information was available for two participants at Time 3. One participant, who reported no acts other than negotiation (an increase) at Time 1 and Time 2 for self, reported 6 acts of minor psychological aggression at Time 3 (and decreased on negotiation). He also reported that his partner had committed six acts of minor psychological aggression at Time 2 (8 at Time 1), and 20 minor acts at Time 3. This participant also reported that she had committed two acts of major physical assault at Time 3 from 0 at Time 1 and 2 (and had decreased on negotiation). The other

2 As mentioned, two participants contribute to the often high results reflected in the means for self, and also do so for the means for partner behaviours. When examining the number of participants who reported their partners had engaged in an act for each scale without these participants included, 7 of 9 indicated an act of negotiation, 4 of 9 indicated an act of psychological aggression, and 2 of 9 indicated an act of physical assault (with the physical assault being self=0 and partner=4 for one participant, and 13=self and 10=partner for another participant).

participant reported zeros for all acts (including negotiation) by both self and partner at Time 3. This participant had reported increases in negotiation from Time 1 to Time 2 for self (decreases for partner), decreases in acts of psychological aggression for self (partner increased), and physical aggression decreased for both self and partner. Minor injuries had increased for the partner from Time 1 to Time 2 (from 2 to 25).

Table A.1. Participant reports of self and partner conflict tactics (prevalence and frequency) – Time 1

	Self						Partner					
	Total		Twelve Months		Six months		Total		Twelve Months		Six months	
	Prev.	Freq.	Prev.	Freq.	Prev.	Freq.	Prev.	Freq.	Prev.	Freq.	Prev.	Freq.
Negotiation – Total	33	68.89 (44.69)	21	74.38 (41.53)	12	61.20 (49.20)	33	55.67 (39.48)	21	60.95 (32.36)	12	48.57 (47.96)
Negotiation – Emotional	33	38.53 (26.10)	21	41.00 (23.26)	12	35.07 (30.14)	33	30.86 (22.15)	21	32.57 (18.16)	12	28.47 (27.30)
Negotiation – Cognitive	32	30.36 (22.19)	21	33.38 (20.96)	11	26.13 (23.89)	32	24.61 (20.75)	21	28.48 (18.59)	11	19.20 (23.00)
Psychological Aggression – Total	34	33.41 (33.16)	20	33.90 (27.78)	14	32.75 (40.12)	34	42.92 (41.03)	20	40.29 (35.15)	14	46.38 (48.69)
Psychological Aggression – Minor	33	26.32 (24.26)	20	27.57 (20.64)	13	24.69 (28.99)	34	31.35 (26.81)	20	30.57 (23.31)	14	32.38 (31.60)
Psychological Aggression – Severe	22	7.08 (10.59)	14	6.33 (9.19)	8	8.06 (12.43)	26	11.57 (19.19)	16	9.71 (15.21)	10	14.00 (23.75)
Physical Assault – Total	27	13.00 (19.13)	16	12.29 (17.28)	11	13.94 (21.87)	29	24.73 (40.26)	17	18.29 (36.56)	12	33.19 (44.41)
Physical Assault – Minor	27	10.11 (15.00)	16	9.48 (14.20)	11	10.94 (16.43)	28	16.43 (27.02)	17	13.05 (23.89)	11	20.88 (30.90)
Physical Assault – Severe	18	2.89 (5.87)	10	2.81 (4.45)	8	3.00 (7.50)	23	8.30 (16.58)	12	5.24 (13.07)	11	12.31 (20.03)
Sexual Coercion – Total	4	.84 (4.14)	2	.24 (.89)	2	1.63 (6.24)	2	1.62 (6.98)	0	.00 (.00)	2	3.75 (10.41)
Sexual Coercion – Minor	3	.82 (44.14)	1	.19 (.87)	2	1.63 (6.24)	2	1.57 (6.71)	0	.00 (.00)	2	3.63 (10.01)
Sexual Coercion – Severe	1	.03 (.16)	1	.05 (.22)	0	.00 (.00)	1	.05 (.33)	0	.00 (.00)	1	.13 (.50)
Injury – Total	19	4.03 (7.59)	11	4.19 (5.93)	8	3.81 (9.56)	23	2.76 (4.39)	13	3.10 (4.90)	10	2.31 (3.74)
Injury – Minor	19	3.00 (4.67)	11	3.57 (5.25)	8	2.25 (3.80)	22	2.57 (4.39)	12	2.81 (4.92)	10	2.25 (3.73)
Injury – Severe	6	1.03 (4.07)	4	.62 (1.56)	2	1.56 (5.99)	6	.19 (.46)	5	.29 (.56)	1	.06 (.25)

Note: N=37 for all total cells, with the exception of the Negotiation scores (N=36)

N=21 for all 12-month cells

N=16 for all 6-month cells, except the Negotiation scores (N=15)

Table A.2. Participant reports of self and partner conflict tactics (prevalence and frequency) – Time 2

	Self				Partner			
	Time 1		Time 2		Time 1		Time 2	
	Prev.	Freq.	Prev.	Freq.	Prev.	Freq.	Prev.	Freq.
Negotiation – Total	9	51.18 (51.36)	9	56.27 (42.60)	9	46.18 (40.05)	9	54.00 (44.49)
Negotiation – Emotional	9	26.27 (25.87)	9	35.27 (23.18)	9	24.09 (20.54)	10	33.00 (23.50)
Negotiation – Cognitive	9	24.91 (26.83)	9	21.00 (22.39)	9	19.55 (21.44)	9	19.09 (22.56)
Psychological Aggression – Total	9	18.91 (18.38)	6	20.00 (39.87)	10	31.36 (26.64)	6	20.09 (39.08)
Psychological Aggression – Minor	9	15.91 (14.65)	6	14.18 (25.27)	10	24.27 (20.73)	6	13.09 (21.36)
Psychological Aggression – Severe	6	3.00 (5.20)	4	5.82 (16.09)	8	7.09 (11.64)	4	7.00 (19.36)
Physical Assault – Total	5	3.27 (5.69)	3	10.73 (24.35)	7	12.00 (17.79)	4	9.55 (22.89)
Physical Assault – Minor	5	2.27 (3.35)	3	9.45 (22.81)	6	5.45 (9.44)	4	9.10 (22.28)
Physical Assault – Severe	2	1.00 (3.00)	3	1.27 (2.57)	4	6.55 (14.49)	3	.45 (.82)
Sexual Coercion – Total	1	.09 (.30)	1	.18 (.60)	0	.00 (.00)	0	.00 (.00)
Sexual Coercion – Minor	0	.00 (.00)	0	.00 (.00)	0	.00 (.00)	0	.00 (.00)
Sexual Coercion – Severe	1	.09 (.30)	1	.18 (.60)	0	.00 (.00)	0	.00 (.00)
Injury – Total	5	6.64 (11.83)	3	3.00 (8.06)	3	1.36 (3.04)	4	5.91 (10.92)
Injury – Minor	5	3.91 (5.38)	3	3.00 (8.06)	3	1.27 (3.00)	4	5.64 (10.72)
Injury – Severe	2	2.73 (7.28)	0	.00 (.00)	1	.09 (.30)	2	.27 (.65)

Note: N=11

Bibliography

Access Economics Pty Ltd (2004), *The Cost of Domestic Violence to the Australian Economy*. Sydney, Office of the Status of Women, Australian Government.

Ainsworth, M, Blehar, M, Waters, E and Wall, S (1978), *Patterns of Attachment*. Hillsdale, NJ: Erlbaum.

Alcoff, LM (2000), Habits of Hostility - On seeing race. *Philosophy Today* 44(S): 30–40.

American Bar Association (1996) Concept Paper on Specialised Courts Washington DC: www.abanet.rog/ceeli/concept/papers/specourts/spc1.html (accessed on 27 June 2003). Referred to in Changing Practices: The Specialised Domestic Violence Court Process Eley, S, *The Howard Journal*, ISSN 0265-5527, 44(2): 113-124, May 2005.

Australian Bureau of Statistics (2006), *Personal Safety Survey*. Canberra: Australian Bureau of Statistics.

ANCD (2007), *Compulsory drug treatment in Australia*. Canberra: Australian National Council on Drugs.

Anderson, KL and Umberstson, D (2001), Gendering violence: Masculinity and power in men's accounts of domestic violence. *Gender and Society*, 15: 358-380.

Andrews, DA and Bonta, J (2004), *The psychology of criminal conduct*. (3rd ed), Cincinnati OH: Anderson.

Ashworth, A (2002), *Sentencing and criminal justice*. London: Weidenfield and Nicolson.

Australian Bureau of Statistics (2006), *Personal Safety Survey*. Canberra: Australian Bureau of Statistics.

Babcock, JC, Green, CE and Robie, C (2004), Does batterers' treatment work? A meta-analytic review of domestic violence treatment. *Clinical Psychology Review, 23,* 1023-1053.

Babcock, J and Steiner, R (1999), The relationship between treatment, incarceration and recidivism of battering: A program evaluation of Seattle's coordinated community response to domestic violence. *Journal of Family Psychology* 13(1): 46-59.

Bagshaw D, Chung D, Couch M, Lilburn S and Wadham B (2000), *Reshaping responses to domestic violence: research into the needs of women, men and young people's who have experienced domestic violence* (Vols 1and2) Office for Status of Women, Department of the Prime Minister and Cabinet.

Bagshaw, D and Chung, D, (2000), Gender Politics and Research: male and female violence in intimate relationships. *Violence Against Women*, 8: 4-23.

Bambling, M and King, R (2001), Therapeutic alliance and clinical practice. *Psychotherapy in Australia*, 8(1): 38-47.

Barber, JG (1991), *Beyond Casework*. Basingstoke, UK: MacMillan.

Barratt, ES and Slaughter, L (1998), Defining, measuring and predicting impulsive aggression: A heuristic model. *Behavioral Sciences and the Law*, 16: 285-302.

Beesley, F and McGuire, J (2009), Gender-role identity and hyper-masculinity in violent offending. *Psychology, Crime and Law*, 15: 251-268.

Bender, K and Roberts, AR (2007), Battered women versus male batterer typologies: Same of different based on evidence based studies? *Aggression and Violent Behavior*, 12: 519-530.

Benhabib, S, Butler, J, Cornell, D and Fraser, N (eds) (1995), *Feminist Contentions: A Philosophical Exchange*. New York, Routledge.

Berman, G and Feinblatt, J (2001) Problem Solving Courts: A Brief Primer. *Law and Policy* 23(2): 125-140

Bird, J, (2002), *The Heart's Narrative*. Auckland: Edge Press.

Birgden, A (2002), Therapeutic jurisprudence and "good lives": A rehabilitation framework for corrections. *Australian Psychologist*, 37: 180-186.

Block, CR (2003), How Can Practitioners Help an Abused Woman Lower Her Risk of Death? *NIJ Journal*, 250: 4-7.

Bordin, ES (1994), Theory and research on the therapeutic working alliance: New directions, in AO Horvath and LS Greenberg (eds), *The working alliance: Theory, research and practice*. New York: Wiley.

Bourdieu, P, (2001), *Masculine Domination*, California: Stanford University Press.

Bowen, E, Gilchrist, E and Beech, AR (2008), Change in treatment has no relationship with subsequent re-offending in UK domestic violence sample: A preliminary study. *Journal of Offender Therapy and Comparative Criminology*, 52: 598-614.

Bowlby, J (1969), *Attachment and Loss*. New York: Basic Books.

Bowlby, J (1979), *The Making and Breaking of Affectional Bonds*. London: Tavistock.

Bowlby, J (1988), *A secure base: Parent-child attachment and healthy human development*. New York: Basic Books.

Bowlen, R (2005) Attachment and Family Violence: Complexities in knowing. *Child Abuse and Neglect*, 29: 845–852.

Brehm, J W (1966), *A theory of psychological reactance*. New York: Academic Press.

Brehm, SS and Brehm JW (1981), *Psychological reactance: A theory of freedom and control*. New York: Academic Press.

Briggs, F (1995), *From victim to offender: How child sexual abuse victims become offenders*. Sydney: Allen and Unwin.

Brown, PD and O'Leary, KD (2000), Therapeutic alliance: Predicting continuance and success in group treatment for spouse abuse. *Journal of Consulting and Clinical Psychology*, 68: 340-345.

Brown, PD, O'Leary, KD and Feldbau, S (1997), Dropout in a treatment program for self-referring wife abusing men. *Journal of Family Violence, 12*, 365-387.

Browne, C and Winkelman, C (2003), *The Legacy of Childhood Trauma: The Effect of Adult Attachment and Cognitive Distortion on Psychological Adjustment*. Unpublished paper – International Conference on Trauma, Attachment and Dissociation, Melbourne.

Buchbinder, D, (1998), *Performance Anxieties: Reproducing Masculinity*. Sydney: Allen and Unwin.

Burke, C (1999), Re-dressing the balance: child protection intervention in the context of domestic violence, in J Breckenridge and L Laing (eds) *Challenging the Silence: Innovative responses to sexual and domestic violence*. Sydney: Allen and Unwin.

Bushman, BJ and Anderson, CA (2001), Is it time to pull the plug on the hostile versus hostile versus instrumental aggression dichotomy? *Psychological Review*, 108: 273-279.

Butler, J, (1990), *Gender Trouble: Gender Trouble: Feminism and the Subversion of Identity*. London: Routledge.

Butler, J, (1995), *Bodies that Matter: On the discursive limits of sex*. London: Routledge.

Buttell, FP and Carney, MM (2008), A large sample investigation of batterer intervention program attrition: Evaluating the impact of state program standards. *Research on Social Work Practice*. 18: 177-188.

Buzawa, E and Austin, T and Buzawa, C (1995), Responding to Crimes of Violence against Women: Gender Differences Versus Organizational Imperatives, *Crime and Delinquency*. 41: 443-466.

Buzawa, E and Austin, T (1993), Determining Police Response to Domestic Violence Victims: The Role of Victim Preference, *American Behavioural Scientist*, 36, 610-624.

Buzawa, E and Buzawa, C (1993), The Impact of Arrest on Domestic Violence, *American Behavioural Scientist*, 36: 558-574.

Buzawa E and Buzawa C (2002) *Domestic violence: the criminal justice response* (3rd ed) Thousand Oaks CA: Sage.

Cady, KM (1999), Tactics to Uncover Evidence of Defendant's Prior Bad Acts. *Homefront*, 4: 1-3.

Campbell, J, Webster, D, Koziol-McLain, J, Block, CR, Campbell, D, Curry, M, Gary, F, McFarlane, J, Sachs, C, Sharps, P, Ulrich, Y, Wilt, S (2003), Assessing Risk Factors for Intimate Partner Homicide, *NIJ Journal*, 250: 15-19.

Carney, T (2000) 'New configurations of justice and services for the vulnerable: panacea or panegyric', *Australia and New Zealand Journal of Criminology*, 33(3): 318-40.

Casey, S, Day, A and Howells, K (2005), The application of the transtheoretical model to offender populations: Some critical issues. *Legal and Criminological Psychology*. 10: 1-15.

Chambers, JC, Eccleston, L, Day, A, Ward, T and Howells, K (in press), Treatment readiness in violent offenders: The influence of cognitive factors on engagement in violence programs. *Aggression and Violent Behavior*, 13:276-284.

Chambless, DL and Hollon, SD (1998), Defining empirically supported therapies. *Journal of Consulting and Clinical Psychology*, 66: 7-18.

Chronister, K (2007), Contextualizing women domestic violence survivors' economic and emotional dependencies. *American Psychologist*, 62: 706-708.

Chung D, Kennedy R, O'Brien B, Wendt, S (2001) *Home Safe Home: A national study of the links between domestic and family violence and women's homelessness.* Canberra: Partnerships Against Domestic Violence, Department of the Prime Minister and Cabinet.

Chung D, O'Leary P and Zannettino, L (2003), *National review of integrated programs for perpetrators of domestic violence.* Office for Status of Women, Department of the Prime Minister and Cabinet, Canberra.

Chung, D and Zannettino, L (2006), Feminists researching domestic violence perpetrator programs: Improving women's and children's safety or misplaced effort? *Women Against Violence,* 18: 37-45.

Clark, S, Burt, MR, Schulte, MM and Maguire, K (1996) *Coordinated Community Responses to Domestic Violence in Six Communities, Beyond the Justice System* (Report to the Urban Institute for the Office of the Assistant Secretary of Planning and Evaluation) (available online at www.problemsolvingcourts.com/resolutions.html (accessed on 18 November 2003).

Coker, D (2004), Race, Poverty and the Crime-Centered Approach to Domestic Violence, *Violence Against Women,* 10: 1331-1353.

Commonwealth of Australia, Partnerships Against Domestic Violence (2003) *Against the Odds; How women survive domestic violence* (3rd ed). Canberra: Office of Status of Women.

Connell, RW (1995), *Masculinities,* Berkeley: University of California Press.

Connell, RW (1996), Politics of Changing Men, *Australian Humanities Review,* December.

Connell, RW (2000), *The Men and The Boys.* Sydney: Allen and Unwin.

Connell, RW (2005), *Masculinities* 2nd ed. Sydney: Allen and Unwin.

Cooley-Quille, M and Lorion, R (1999), Adolescents' exposure to community violence: Sleep and psychophysiological functioning. *Journal of Community Psychology,* 27: 367-375.

Corey, M and Corey, G (1997), *Groups: Process and Practice* (5th ed). Pacific Grove, CA: Brooks/Cole.

Cox, B (2002), *Domestic Violence: Understanding Victim Behaviour.* NLETA Online <www.aco.state.nc.us/www/ids/Brief%20Bank/.../In%80re%20BP/doc>

Cramer, E (1999), Variables That Predict Verdicts in Domestic Violence Cases. *Journal of Interpersonal Violence,* 14: 1137-1150.

Crime and Misconduct Commission - Queensland, 2005, *Policing Domestic Violence in Queensland: Meeting the Challenges,* Brisbane, <www.cmc.qld.gov.au/data/portal/00000005/content/73653001131400781353.pdf> (accessed 25 August 2006).

Davies, M and Mouzos, J (2007), *Homicide in Australia: 2005-06 national homicide monitoring program annual report.* Canberra: Australian Institute of Criminology.

Davis, LV (1984), Beliefs of service providers about abused women and abusing men. *Social Work,* 29: 243-250.

Day, A (2003), Reducing the risk of re-offending among Australian indigenous offenders: What works for whom? *Journal of Offender Rehabilitation,* 37(2): 1-16.

Day, A, Bryan, J, Davey, L and Casey, S (2006), Processes of change in offender rehabilitation. *Psychology, Crime and Law,* 12 (5): 473-489.

Day, A, Chung, D, O'Leary, P and Carson, E (2009), Programs for men who perpetrate domestic violence: An examination of the issues underlying the effectiveness of intervention programs. *Journal of Family Violence,* 24(3): 203-212.

Day, A and Howells, K (2008), *Theory manual for the Violent Offender Treatment Program.* Dept of Correctional Services, WA.

Day, A, Howells, K, Casey, S, Ward, T, Chambers, JC and Birgden, A (2009), Assessing treatment readiness in violent offenders. *Journal of Interpersonal Violence,* 24: 4.

Day, A, Howells, K, Mohr, P, Schall, E and Gerace, A (2008), The development of CBT programmes for anger: The role of interventions to promote perspective-taking skills. *Behavioural and Cognitive Psychotherapy,* 36: 299-312.

Day, A, Tucker, K and Howells, K (2004), Coercing offenders into treatment, invited paper for special issue of *Psychology, Crime and Law,* 10: 259-269.

DeMaris, A and Jackson, JK (1987), Batterers' reports of recidivism after counseling. *Social Casework,* 68: 458-465.

Dempsey, B (2009), *Implicit Theories in Domestic Violence.* Unpublished Master of Psychology (Forensic) thesis. Adelaide: University of South Australia.

Denzin, N.K (1984), Toward a phenomenology of domestic, family violence. *American Journal of Sociology* 90(3): 483-513.

DiGiuseppe, R and Linscott, J (1993), Philosophical differences among cognitive behavioural therapists: Rationalism, constructivism, or both? *Journal of Cognitive Psychotherapy: An International Quarterly,* 7: 117-130.

Dobash, RP and Dobash, RE (2005), Abuser Programmes and Violence Against Women, in W Smeenk and M Malsch (eds), *Family Violence and Police Reaction: Learning from research, policy and practice in European countries.* London: Ashgate.

Dobash, RE and Dobash, RP Cavanagh, K and Lewis, R (2000), *Changing Violent Men.* California: Sage Publications Ltd

Dobash, RP and Dobash, RE (1992), *Women, violence and social change.* London: Routledge.

Dobash, RP and Dobash, RE (2000), Criminal justice programs for men who assault their partners, in CR Hollin (ed), *Handbook of Offender Assessment and Treatment.* New York: John Wiley and Sons.

Domestic Violence Protocol for Law Enforcement 2002, Police Chief's Association of Santa Clara County, February 2002.

Douglas, H and Godden, L (2003), Intimate Partner Violence: Transforming Harm into a Crime, *Murdoch University Electronic Journal of Law,* vol 10, no 2 <www.austlii.edu.au/au/journals/MurUEJL/2003/17.html> (accessed 26 October 2005).

Dragiewicz, M.A, (2005), *The Batterers Voice: Equal Protection,* Gender and Domestic Violence Discourse, PhD Dissertation, George Mason University.

Dutton DG (2000), Witnessing Parental Violence as a Traumatic Experience Shaping the Abusive Personality, in P Jaffe (ed), *Children Exposed to Domestic Violence: Current issues in Research, Intervention, Prevention and Policy.* New York: Routledge.

Dutton, DG (1986), The outcome of court-mandated treatment for wife assault: A quasi-experimental evaluation. *Violence and Victims,* 1: 163-175.

Dutton, DG (2007), The complexities of domestic violence. *American Psychologist,* 62: 708-710.

Dutton, DG and Corvo, K (2007), The Duluth model: A data impervious paradigm and a failed strategy. *Aggression and Violent Behavior,* 12: 658-667.

Dutton, D and Corvo, K (2006), Transforming a flawed policy: A call to revive psychology and science in domestic violence research and practice. *Aggression and Violent Behaviour,* 11: 457–483.

Dutton, DG and Corvo, K (2007), The Duluth model: A data impervious paradigm and a failed strategy. *Aggression and Violent Behavior,* 12: 658-667.

Dworkin, A, (1983), *Right Wing Women.* London: Women's Press.

Eckhardt, CI, Babcock, J and Homack, S (2004), Partner assaultive men and the stages and processes of change. *Journal of Family Violence,* 19: 81-93.

Eden, KE, Lalos, A, Högerberg, U and Dahlegren, L (2008) Violent Men: Ordinary and Deviant, *Journal of Interpersonal Violence,* 23(2): 225-244.

Eley, S, Changing Practices: The Specialised Domestic Violence Court Process, *The Howard Journal,* 44(2): 113-124, May 2005.

Ellison, L (2003), Responding to victim withdrawal in domestic violence prosecutions, *Criminal Law Review* 3: 760-772

Ellison, L (2002), Prosecuting Domestic Violence without Victim Participation, *Modern Law Review,* 65: 834-858.

Ewing, CP and Aubrey, M (1987), Battered women and public opinion: Some realities about the myths. *Journal of Family Violence,* 12: 70-82.

Feazell, CS, Mayers, RS and Deschner, J (1984), Services for men who batter: Implications for programs and policies. *Family Relations,* 33: 217-223.

Feder, L and Wilson, DB (2005), A meta-analytic view of court mandated batterer intervention programs: Can courts affect abuser's behavior? *Journal of Experimental Criminology,* 1: 239-262.

Fletcher, A (2008), *Facilitators working with male perpetrators of domestic violence.* School of Social Work and Social Policy Seminar Series 15 May 2008: University of South Australia.

Fonagy, P (1999) Male perpetrators of violence against women: An attachment theory perspective. *Journal of Applied Psychoanalytic Studies,* 1: 7-27.

Ford, ME (1992), *Motivating humans: Goals, emotions and personal agency beliefs.* Newbury Park, CA: Sage.

Form for Evaluating Police Response to Domestic Violence, Women's Justice Centre, California, undated.

Foucault, M (1971), Orders of Discourse, Inaugural lecture at the College de France, *Social Science Information,* 10(2): 7-30

Foucault, M (1972), *The Archaeology of Knowledge.* London: Tavistock.

Foucault, M (1991), Politics and the Study of Discourse, in G Burchell, C, Gordon, and P Miller (eds), *The Foucault Effect: Studies of Governmentality* with two lectures by and an interview with Michel Foucault. Chicago: University of Chicago Press.

Freckelton, I (2006) Ethics and the legal context, in S Morrissey and P Reddy (eds), *Ethics and professional practice for psychologists.* Melbourne: Thomson.

Freiberg, A (2001) Problem-oriented courts: innovative solutions to intractable problems? *Journal of Judicial Administration* 11(1): 7-27.

Gilchrist, E (2009), Implicit Thinking about Implicit Theories in Intimate Partner violence. *Psychology, Crime and Law,* 15: 131-145.

Glaser, B (2003), Therapeutic jurisprudence: An ethical paradigm for therapists in sex offender treatment programs, *Western Criminology Review,* 4: 1–16.

Goldner, V (1999), Morality and multiplicity: Perspectives on the treatment of violence in intimate life, *Journal of Marital and Family Therapy* 25(3): 325-336.

Gondolf, E (1997), Batterer Programs: What we know and need to know. *Journal of Interpersonal Violence,* 12: 83-98.

Gondolf, E (2002), *Batterer Intervention Systems: Issues, Outcomes and Recommendations.* Thousand Oaks, CA: Sage.

Gondolf, EW (1988), Who are those guys? Towards a behavioral typology of batterers, *Violence and Victims,* 3: 187-203.

Gondolf, EW (2000), How batterer program participants avoid reassault. *Violence Against Women,* 6: 1204 - 1222.

Gondolf, EW (2001), *The Way to Change Series for Men Who Have Abused Their Women Partners. Workbook 1, The Nature of Abuse.* Washington DC: Learning Publications.

Gondolf, EW (2002), *Batterer Intervention Systems: Issues, Outcomes and recommendations.Recommendations.* Thousand Oaks, CA: Sage Publications.

Gondolf, EW (2006), *The System Matters.* Two day Workshop, Brisbane, 13-14 November.

Gondolf, EW (2007), Theoretical and research support for the Duluth model: A reply to Dutton and Corvo. *Aggression and Violent Behavior,* 12: 644-657.

Gondolf, EW (2008), Program completion in a specialized batterer counseling for African-American men. *Journal of Interpersonal Violence,* 23: 94-116.

Gondolf, EW, Chang, YF and Laporte, R (1999), Capture-recapture analysis of batterer reassaults: An epidemiological innovation for batterer program evaluation. *Violence and Victims,* 14: 191-202.

Gondolf EW and Heckert A (2003) Determinants of women's perceptions of risk in battering relationships. *Violence and Victims,* 18(4): 371-386.

Gondolf, E.W and White, R.J (2000), Consumer recommendations for batterer programs. *Violence Against Women,* 6: 198-217.

Gondolf, EW, Chang, YF and Laporte, R (1999), Capture-recapture analysis of batterer reassaults: An epidemiological innovation for batterer program evaluation. *Violence and Victims,* 14: 191-202.

Goodman, L, Dutton, M, Bennett, L (2000), Predicting Repeat Abuse Among Arrested Batterers: Use of the Danger Assessment Scale in the Criminal Justice System. *Journal of Interpersonal Violence*, 15: 63-74.

Government of Tasmania 2004, *Safe at Home,* no 1, <www.women.tas.gov.au/news/safeathome.html> (accessed 8 September 2006).

Gregory, J (2008), Wife-killer 'Provoked' by Affair, *The Courier Mail*, Brisbane, 15 April.

Gwinn, C (2004), Toward Effective Intervention: Trends in the Criminal Prosecution of Domestic Violence. San Diego City Attorney's Domestic Violence Unit, <www.sandiegodvunit.org/article1.htm> (accessed 20 February 2004).

Hague, G and Malos, E (1998), Inter-Agency Approaches to Domestic Violence and the Role of Social Services. *British Journal of Social Work*, 28: 369-386.

Hall, R, (1996), Partnership Accountability, in McLean, C, Carey, M and White. C, (eds) *Men's Ways of Being: New Directions in Theory and Practice*, Westview Press, Oxford

Hall, R, (2001), Pitfalls and challenges in work with men who use violence against their partners, in Pease, B and Camilleri, P (eds) *Working With Men in the Human Services*. Crows Nest, NSW: Allen and Unwin.

Hart, BJ (1989), Domestic Violence: A Model Protocol for Police Response. MINCAVA, <www.mincava.umn.edu/documents/hart/modelpo.shtml> (accessed 24 February 2004).

Hazen, C and Shaver, P (1987), Romantic love conceptualized as an attachment process. *Journal of Personality and Social Psychology*, 52: 511-524.

Hearn, J and Whitehead, A, (2006), Collateral Damage; Men's Domestic Violence to women seen through men's relations with men, *The Journal of Community and Criminal Justice*. 53(1): 38-56.

Hearn, J (2000), *Implications for the Critical Studies of Men*, <www.rolstad.no/mannsfroskning/mannsforsking/1-98/hearn.htm, (accessed 04/03/2008).

Hearn, J (2001), Men, Social Work and Men's Violence to Women, in Christie, A (ed) *Men and Social Work – theories and practices*. Palgrave, New York

Henry, S (2003), *Inside Pandora's Box: Healing the Connection Between Victimization and Perpetration*. Unpublished paper - International Conference on Trauma, Attachment and Dissociation, Melbourne, Australia.

Holder, R, (2001), Domestic and Family Violence: Criminal Justice Interventions, *Australian Domestic and Family Violence Clearinghouse Issues Paper 3*, Australian Domestic and Family Violence Clearing House, UNSW, Sydney.

Holder, R and Mayo, N (2003), What Do Women Want? Prosecuting Family Violence in the ACT, *Current Issues in Criminal Justice*, 15: 5-25.

Hollin, CR (1995), The meaning and implications of program integrity, in McGuire, J (ed), *What Works: Effective Methods to Reduce Reoffending*, Wiley, Chichester

Holtzworth-Munroe, A and Stuart, GL (1994), Typologies of male batterers: Three subtypes and the differences among them. *Psychological Bulletin*, 116(3): 476-497.

Horvath, AO and Symonds, BD (1991), Relation between working alliance and outcome in psychotherapy: A meta-analysis. *Journal of Counseling Psychology*, 38: 139-149.

Howells, K (2008), The treatment of anger in offenders, in A Day, M Nakata, and K Howells (eds), *Anger in Indigenous Men*. Federation Press: Sydney

Howells, K and Day, A (2003), Readiness for Anger Management: Clinical and Theoretical Issues. *Clinical Psychology Review*, 23: 319-337.

Howells, K and Day, A (2002), Grasping the nettle: Treating and rehabilitating the violent offender. *Australian Journal of Psychology*, 37(3): 222-228.

Howells, K and Day, A (2006), Affective determinants of treatment engagement in violent offenders. *International Journal of Offender Rehabilitation and Comparative Criminology*, 50: 174-186.

Howells, K, Daffern, M and Day, A (2005), Aggression and violence, in K Soothill, M Dolan and P Rogers (eds), *The Handbook of Forensic Mental Health*. Cullompton, Devon: Willan.

Howells, K, Heseltine, K, Sarre, R, Davey, L and Day, A (2004), Correctional Offender Treatment Programs: The National Picture in Australia. Report for the Criminology Research Council. <www.aic.gov.au/crc/reports/200203-04.html>

Humphreys, C (2007), *Issues Paper 13: Domestic Violence and Child Protection: Challenging directions for practice*. Canberra: Australian Domestic and Family Violence Clearinghouse.

Humphreys, C, Thiara, R, Regan, L, Lovett, J, Kennedy, L, Gibson, A (2005), *Prevention not Prediction? A Preliminary Evaluation of the Metropolitan Police Domestic Violence Risk Assessment Model (SPECSS+): Final Report*, [Warwick?].

Hyman, E, Judge Superior Court California, Presentation to AIJA Family Violence Conference in Adelaide in February 2006.

Investigation and Prosecution of Strangulation Cases: A Model Protocol for Maryland Prosecutors (2002), *Maryland Network Against Domestic Violence*.

Irwin, M, Judge and Chief Magistrate (2005), *Response to Domestic and Family Violence - New Directions* Address delivered to Domestic Violence Court Assistance Network Conference at Cairns, 11 November.

Irwin, M, Judge and Chief Magistrate (2007), *What would a Specialised Domestic Violence Court mean for the Gold Coast*. Address delivered to the Domestic Violence Forum, Southport, 9 May.

Jacobson, NS, Gottman, JM, Waltz, J, Rushe, R, Babcock, J and Hotzworth-Munroe, A (1994), Affect, verbal content and psychophysiology in arguments of couples with a violent husband. *Journal of Consulting and Clinical Psychology*, 62(5): 982-988.

Jenkins, A, (1990), *Invitations to Responsibility; The therapeutic engagement of men who are violent and abusive*, Adelaide: Dulwich Centre Publications.

Johnson, MP (1995), Patriarchal terrorism and common couple violence: Two forms of violence against women. *Journal of Marriage and the Family*, 57: 283-294.

Johnson, P and Buboltz, WC Jr (2000), Differentiation of self and psychological reactance. *Contemporary Family Therapy: An International Journal* 22: 91-102.

Kaplan, H and Sadock, B (eds) (1993), *Comprehensive Group Psychotherapy* (3rd ed). Baltimore: Williams and Wilkins.

Karoly, P (1993), Goal systems: An organizing framework for clinical assessment and treatment planning. *Psychological Assessment*. 5: 273-280.

Karoly, P (1999), A goal systems-self-regulatory perspective on personality, psychopathology and change. *Review of General Psychology,* 3: 264-291.

Kaufman, M, (1987), *Beyond Patriarchy: Essays by Men on Pleasure, Power and Change,* Oxford University Press: Toronto.

Laing, L, (2000), Progress, Trends and Challenges in Australian responses to domestic violence, *Australian Domestic and Family Violence Clearinghouse Issues Paper 1,* Australian Domestic and Family Violence Clearinghouse, UNSW, Sydney.

Laing, L (2002), Responding to men who perpetrate domestic violence; controversies, interventions and challenges. *Australia Domestic and Family Violence Clearing House. Issues Paper No 7.*

Laing, L (2004), Risk Assessment in Domestic Violence. *Australian Domestic and Family Violence Clearinghouse,* Topic Paper, 1-17.

Laing, L and Bobic, N (2002), *Economic Costs of Domestic Violence: Literature Review.* Sydney, Australian Domestic and Family Violence Clearinghouse.

Levesque, DA, Gelles, RJ and Velicer, WF (2000), Development and validation of a stages of change measure for men in batterer treatment. *Cognitive Therapy and Research,* 24: 175-199.

Levesque, DA, Velicer, WF, Castle, PH and Green, RN (2008), Resistance among domestic violence offenders. *Violence Against Women,* 14: 158-184.

Levesque, D and Gelles, R (1998), *Does treatment reduce recidivism in men who batter? A meta-analytic evaluation of treatment outcome research.* Conference presentation. Durham, New Hampshire.

Levesque, DA, Velicer, WF, Castle, PH and Green, RN (2008), Resistance among domestic violence offenders. *Violence Against Women,* 14: 158-184.

Lines, B (2003), System Change in Bite-sized Chunks: Domestic Violence Revisited in the ACT, *Platypus Magazine,* 78: 32-37.

Littel, K, Malefyt, M, Walker, A, Buel, S, Tucker, D and Kuriansky, J (ed) (1998), Assessing Justice System Response to Violence Against Women: A Tool For Law Enforcement, Prosecution and the Courts to Use in Developing Effective Responses. *Violence Against Women Online Resources,* <www.vaw.umn.edu/documents/promise/pplaw/pplaw.html> (accessed 26 October, 2006).

Logar, R (2005), *The Austrian Model of Intervention in Domestic Violence Cases,* United Nations Division for the Advancement of Women. <www.un.org/womenwatch/daw/egm/vaw-gp-2005/docs/experts/logar.dv.pdf>.

Makkai, T (2006), Director, Australian Institute of Criminology Presentation to AIJA Family Violence Conference in Adelaide in February 2006

Marlowe, DB, Festinger, DS, Dugosh, KL, Lee, PA and Nenasutti, KM (2007), *Drug and Alcohol Dependence.* 88S: S4-S13.

Maryland Network Against Domestic Violence (2002), Pro-Prosecution Initiative Evaluation. <www.jcjs.org/Products/Domestic%20Violence/Maryland/Pro-Prosecution%20Initiative%20Evaluation.pdf>.

Mazur, R and Aldrich, L (2003), What Makes a Domestic Violence Court Work? Lessons from New York, *The Judge's Journal,* Spring: 5-9.

McEllistrem, JE (2004), Affective and predatory violence: A bimodal classification system of human aggression and violence. *Aggression and Violent Behavior,* 10: 1-30.

McGuire, J (2000), Explanations of offence behaviour, in McGuire, J, Mason, T and O'Kane, A (eds) *Behaviour, Crime and Legal Processes* Chichester: Wiley.

McGuire, J (2002), Explanations of criminal behaviour, in J McGuire, T Mason, and A O'Kane (eds), *Behaviour, crime and legal processes: A guidebook for practitioners.* Chichester: Wiley.

McGuire, J (2002), *Offender rehabilitation and treatment: Effective programmes and policies to reduce re-offending.* Chichester: John Wiley and Sons.

McGuire, J (ed) (1995), *What Works: Reducing Re-offending, Guidelines from Research and Practice.* Wiley: Chichester. UK.

McGuire, L (2004), Criminal Prosecution of Domestic Violence. *Violence Against Women Online Resources,* <www.vaw.umn.edu> (accessed 20 February 2004).

McKendy, J (1992), Ideological Practices and the Management of Emotions, *Critical Sociology,* 19(2): 47-73.

McKendy, JP (2006), I'm very careful about that': narrative and agency of men in prison, *Discourse and Society,* 17: 4.

McLaren, M, (1997), Foucault and the Subject of feminism, in *Social Theory and Practice.* 23(1): 109-127

Mclean, C, (1996), The Politics of Men's Pain, in McLean, C, Carey, M and White, C, (eds) *Men's Way of Being: New Directions in Theory and Psychology,* Westview Press, UK

McMurran, M and Gilchrist, E (2007), Anger control and alcohol use: Appropriate interventions for perpetrators of domestic violence? *Psychology, Crime and Law,* 10: 1-10.

McMurran, M and Theodosi, E (2007), Is treatment non-completion associated with increased reconviction over no treatment? *Psychology, Crime and Law,* 13: 333-343.

McNay, L, (1992), *Foucault and Feminism.* Boston: Northern University Press.

Milkman, H and Wanberg, K (2007), *Cognitive-behavioral treatment: A Review and Discussion for Professionals for Corrections Professionals.* US Department of Justice National Institute of Corrections.

Miller, S, Gregory, C and Iovanni, L (2005), One size fits all? A gender-neutral approach to a gender-specific problem: contrasting batterer treatment programs for male and female offenders, *Criminal Justice Policy Review.* 16(3): 336-359.

Mills, LG, (2004), Insult to Injury: Rethinking our Responses to Intimate Abuse, *British Journal of Criminology,* 44(6): 983-985.

Minnesota Program Development Inc, (2008), The Duluth model. <www.duluth-model.org> (accessed 11 February 2008).

Misso, D (2004), *Interview Techniques for Domestic Violence.* One day workshop, Brisbane, Queensland, 12 November.

Mouzos, J and Makkai, T (2004), Women's Experiences of Male Violence: Findings from the Australian component of the International Violence Against Women Survey. *Australian Institute of Criminology, Research and Public Policy Series, 56.*

Mullender, A and Hague, G (2005), Giving a Voice to Women Survivors of Domestic Violence through Recognition as a Service User Group. *British Journal of Social Work*, 35(8): 321-41

Mulroney, J (2003), Trends in Interagency work. Australian Domestic and Family Violence Clearinghouse, Topic Paper, 1-17.

Murphy, CM and Baxter, VA (1997), Motivating batterers to change in the treatment context. *Journal of Interpersonal Violence*, 12: 607-620.

Novaco, RW, Ramm, M and Black, L (2001), Anger treatment with offenders, in Hollin, CR (ed) *Handbook of Offender Assessment and Treatment*. Chichester: John Wiley and Sons.

O'Leary, KD, Malone, J and Tyree, A (1994), Physical aggression in early marriage: Pre-relationship and relationship effects. *Journal of Consulting and Clinical Psychology*, 62: 594-602.

O'Leary, P, Chung, D and Zannettino, L (2004), *A Comparative Assessment of Good Practice in Programs for Men who use Violence Against Female Partners*. Canberra: Office of the Status of Women, the Department of the Prime Minister and Cabinet.

O'Leary, P, Richards, J, Chung, D and Zannettino, L (2005), *Project S.A.F.E.R.: Evaluation of Southport Pilot Program*, Research and Education Unit on Gendered Violence and Gold Coast Domestic Violence Integrated Response.

Office of Status of Women (1998), *Against the Odds; how women survive domestic violence*, Canberra: Government Press.

Opitz, C (2008), *Female victims of domestic violence*. School of Social Work and Social Policy Seminar Series 15 May, University of South Australia.

Pagelow, M (1990) The affects of domestic violence on children and their Consequences for Custody and Visitation Arrangements. *Mediation Quarterly* 7: 4.

Partnerships Against Domestic Violence (2004), The costs of domestic violence to the Australian economy. <www.ofw.facsia.gov.au/downloads/pdfs/cost_of_dv_to_australian_economy_I.pdf> (accessed 11 February 2008).

Payne, J (2006) Specialty courts: current issues and future prospects *Trends and Issues in Crime and Criminal Justice* AIC No 317, June.

Pease, B and Fook, J, (1999), *Transforming Social Work Practice: Post-modern Critical Perspectives*. Sydney: Allen and Unwin.

Pease, B, (1997), *Men and Sexual politics: towards a pro-feminist practice*. Adelaide: Dulwich Centre Publications.

Pease, B, (2001), Theoretical Issues and Political Dilemmas in Working With Men, in Pease, B and Camilleri, P (eds) *Working With Men in the Human Services*. Sydney: Allen and Unwin.

Pease, B, (2002), Rethinking Empowerment; A Post-modern Appraisal for Emancipatory Practice, *British Journal of Social Work*, 32: 135-147.

Pease, B and Fisher, S, (2001), Preventing Men's Violence: a response to the Victorian whole of government discussion paper on men's behaviour change programmes, *Women Against Violence*, 10: 49-53.

Pence, E and McDonnell, C (2000) Developing Policies and protocol in Duluth, Minnesota, in Hammer, J and Itzin, C (eds) *Home Truths about Domestic Violence: Feminist influences on policy and practice, a reader.* Routledge: London.

Pence, E and Paymar, M (2003), *Creating a process of change for men who batter. An Education Curriculum,* (revised ed). Duluth: Minnesota Program Development.

Pence, E and Paymar, M (1993), *Education groups for men who batter.* New York: Springer.

Pence, E and Paymar, M (1993), *Education Groups for Men who batter: The Duluth Model.* Duluth: Minnesota Program Development Inc.

People, J (2005), Trends and Patterns in Domestic Violence Assaults. *Crime and Justice Bulletin: Contemporary Issues in Crime and Justice,* 89 <www.search.informit.com.au> (accessed 24 January 2007)

Pepitone, A and Reichling, G (1955), Group Cohesiveness and the Expression of Hostility. *Journal of Human Relations,* 8: 327-337.

Perlesz, A, Young, J, Paterson, R and Bridge, S (1994), The Reflecting team as a reflection of second order therapeutic ideals. *ANZ Journal of Family Therapy,* 15: 117-127.

Perry, B (1997), Incubated in Terror: Neurodevelopmental Factors in the "Cycle of Violence", in Osofsky, J (ed) *Children, Youth and Violence: The search for solutions.* New York: Guildford Press.

Polaschek, DLL and Collie, RM (2004), Rehabilitating serious violent adult offenders: an empirical and theoretical stocktake. *Psychology, Crime and Law,* 10(3): 321-334.

Pollitz-Worden, A (2000), The Changing Boundaries of the Criminal Justice System: Redefining the Problem and the Response in Domestic Violence. *Criminal Justice,* 2: 215-266.

Pozatek, E, (1994), The Problem of Certainty: Clinical Social Work in the Post-modern Era, *Social Work,* 39: 4

Prochaska, JO and DiClemente, CC.(1992), *Stages of change in the Modification of Problem Behaviours.* Newbury Park: Sage.

Queensland Corrective Services (2006), *The Principles of What Works.* <www.correctiveservices.qld.gov.au/Resources/Procedures/Offender_Management/documents/ofmappwhatworks.doc>.

Renwick, SJ, Black, L, Ramm, M and Novaco, RW (1997), Anger treatment with forensic hospital patients. *Legal and Criminological Psychology.* 2: 103-116.

Roberts, AR and Roberts, B (2005), *Ending intimate abuse: Practical guidance and survival strategies.* New York: Oxford University Press.

Robertson, N (1999), *Stopping violence programs: Enhancing the safety of battered women or producing better-educated batterers,* New Zealand Journal of Psychology, 28(2): 68-78.

Robinson, AL (2004), *Domestic Violence MARACs (Multi-Agency Risk Assessment Conferences) for Very High-Risk Victims in Cardiff, Wales: A process and Outcome Evaluation,* <www.cardiff.ac.uk/schoolsanddivisions/academicschools/socsi/staff/acad/robinson.html> (accessed 12 October 2006).

Robinson, A and Chandek, M (2000), The Domestic Violence Arrest Decision: Examining Demographic, Attitudinal and Situational Variables, *Crime and Delinquency*, 46: 18-37.

Rogers, CR (1970) *On Encounter Groups*. NY: Harper and Row.

Rose, N, (1999), *Powers of Freedom: Reframing Political Thought*, Cambridge University Press, Cambridge.

Roy, K, (2005), Overcoming Nihilism: From Communication To Deleuzian Expression, *Educational Philosophy And Theory*. 36(3): 297-312

Russell, MN (2002), Changing beliefs of spouse abusers, in McGuire, J (ed), *Offender Rehabilitation and Treatment: Effective Programmes and Policies to Reduce Re-offending*. New York: John Wiley and Sons.

Salter, A (1995), *Transforming Trauma: A guide to understanding and treating adult survivors of child sexual abuse*. Thousand Oaks, CA: Sage Publications

Saunders, DG, Lynch, AB, Grayson, M and Linz, D (1987), The Inventory of Beliefs about Wife Beating: The construction and initial validation of a measure of beliefs and attitudes. *Violence and Victims*, 2: 39-57.

Saunders, DG (1984), Child custody decisions in families experiencing woman abuse. *Social Work*, 39: 51-59.

Sawicki, L (1991), *Disciplining Foucault: Feminism, Power and the Body*, Routledge: New York.

Schwandt, TA (1994), Constructivist, Interpretivist Approaches to Human Inquiry, in *Handbook of Qualitative Research*, Denzin, NK and Lincoln, YS (eds) Thousand Oaks, CA: Sage.

Scott, K and Wolfe, D (2000), Change among batterers: Examining men's success stories. *Journal of Interpersonal Violence*, 15: 827-842.

Selzer, ML (1971), The Michigan Alcoholism Screening Test: The quest for a new diagnostic instrument. *American Journal of Psychiatry*, 127: 1653-1658.

Serin, RC and Preston, DL (2001a) Programming for violent offenders. *Forum on Corrections Research*, 5: 3-5.

Serin, RC and Preston, DL (2001b) Managing and treating violent offenders, in Ashford, JB Sales, BD and Reid, W (eds.) *Treating Adult and Juvenile Offenders with Special Needs*. Washington DC: American Psychological Association.

Shepard, MF and Campbell, JA (1992), The Abusive Behavior Inventory: A measure of psychological and physical abuse. *Journal of Interpersonal Violence*, 7: 291-305.

Shepard, M (2005), Twenty Years of Progress in Addressing Domestic Violence: An Agenda for the Next 10. *Journal of Interpersonal Violence*, 20(4): 436-441.

Shlonsky, A and Friend, C (2007), Child maltreatment and domestic violence editorial: Current state of knowledge and emerging strategies for policy and practice. *Brief Treatment and Crisis Intervention*, 7: 249-252.

Sinfield, A (1992), *Faultlines: Cultural Materialism and the Politics of Dissident Reading*, Berkeley: University of California Press.

Smith, G (1996), Dichotomies in the Making of Men, in C McLean, M Carey and C White (eds), *Men's Way of Being: New Directions in Theory and Psychology*, Boulder, Colorado: Westview Press.

Sonkin, D and Dutton, D (2003), Treatment of assaultative men from an attachment perspective, in D Sonkin and D Dutton (eds), *Intimate Violence: Contemporary Treatment Innovations.* New York: Haworth Publishing.

Spence, DL (2003), Everett, Washington, Arrest Policies Project: A Process Evaluation, *Institute for Law and Justice*, Alexandria Virginia. <www.ncjrs.gov/pdffiles1/nij/grants/201870.pdf> (accessed 26 October 2006)

St Pierre, EA and Pillow, WS, (2000), *Working the Ruins: Feminist Poststructural Theory and Methods in Education.* Routledge: London

Stanko, EA (1985), *Intimate Intrusions: Women's Experiences of Male Violence.* London: Unwin Hyman.

Stark, E (2007) *Coercive Control: How Men Entrap Women in Personal Life.* New York: Oxford University Press.

Stark, E (2005), Reconsidering State Intervention in Domestic Violence Cases, *Social Policy and Society*, 5(1): 149-159

Stozny, S (1995), *Treating Attachment Abuse.* New York: Springer Publishing Co Inc.

Stozny, S (2008), *Compassion power.* <www.compassionpower.com/index.php> (accessed 26 May 2008).

Straus, M, Hamby, SL, Boney-McCoy, S and Sugarman, DB (1996), The Revised Conflict Tactics Scales (CTS2), *Journal of Family Issues,* 17: 283-316.

Strauss, A and Corbin, J (1990), *Basics of Qualitative Research.* London: Sage.

Suderman, M and Jaffe, P (1999) *A Handbook for Health and Social Service Providers and Educators on Children Exposed to Women Abuse/Family Violence,* Health Canada.

Sullivan, B (2006), *Compassionate, Collaborative, Confrontation.* Two day Workshop, Gold Coast, Queensland, 30-31 March.

Sutton, S (2005), *Putting the Baby Back in the Bath: Reintegrating psychology into domestic violence.* Unpublished paper.

Tamasese, K, Waldegrave C, Tuhaka, J and Campbell, (1998), Furthering conversation about partnerships of accountability: Talking about issues of leadership, ethics and care. *Dulwich Centre Journal.* 4: 51-62.

Thomas, SP (2003), Men's anger: A phenomoneological exploration of its meaning in a middle-class sample of American men. *Psychology of Men and Masculinity,* 4: 163-175.

Tiedens, LZ (2001), Anger and advancement versus sadness and subjugation: The effect of negative emotion on social status conferral. *Journal of Personality and Social Psychology,* 80: 86-94.

Tjaden, P and Thoennes, N (2000), *Extent, nature and consequences of intimate partner violence: findings from the National Violence Against women Survey* (Publication no. NCJ 181867), Washington DC: US Dept of Justice.

Ursel, J, Director, Winnipeg Family Violence Court, Presentation to AIJA Family Violence Conference in Adelaide in February 2006

Utah Government (1995), *Domestic Violence, Incidence and Prevalence Study.* Salt Lake City: Utah.

Van der Kolk, B (1987), *Psychological Trauma.* Washington DC: American Psychiatric Press.

Velicer, WF, Prochaska, JO, Fava, JL, Norman, GJ and Redding, CA (1998), Smoking cessation and stress management: Applications of the transtheoretical model of behavior change. *Homeostasis,* 38: 216-233.

Verco, J (2002), Women's outrage and the pressure to forgive: Working with survivors of child sexual abuse, *The International Journal of Narrative Therapy and Community.* Adelaide: Dulwich Centre Publications.

Victorian Law Reform Commission (2005), Family Violence and the Law: Putting 'Private' Violence on the Public Agenda, (J Peirce, Commissioner), in *Families Matter: 9th Australian Institute of Family Studies Conference,* Melbourne <www.aifs.gov.au/institute/afrc9/pierce.pdf> (accessed 25 August 2006).

Waldegrave, C, (1990), Just Therapy, *Dulwich Centre Newsletter,* 1: 5-46.

Ward, T and Langlands, RL (2009), Repairing the rupture: Restorative justice and the rehabilitation of offenders. *Aggression and Violent Behavior,* 14: 205-214.

Ward, T and Marshall, WL (2007), Narrative identity and offender rehabilitation. *International Journal of Offender Therapy and Comparative Criminology,* 51: 279-297.

Ward, T, Day, A and Casey, S (2006), Offender rehabilitation down under. *Journal of Offender Rehabilitation,* 43(3): 73-83.

Ward, T, Day, A, Howells, K and Birgden, A (2004), The multifactor offender readiness model. *Aggression and Violent Behavior,* 9: 645-673.

Wartenburg, TE (1990), *The Forms of Power: From Domination to Transformation,* Philadelphia: Temple University Press.

Watts, AG (2001), Career guidance and social exclusion: A cautionary tale. *British Journal of Guidance and Counselling,* 29: 156-176.

Weisz, A, Tolman, R and Saunders, D (2000), Assessing the Risk of Severe Domestic Violence: The Importance of Survivor's Predictions. *Journal of Interpersonal Violence,* 15: 75-90.

Wells, A (2003), Innovative Approaches to Stopping Family Violence, in K McMaster and A Wells (eds), *Innovative Approaches to Stopping Family Violence.* Wellington, NZ: Steel Roberts and Associates.

Western Australia Ombudsman (2003), *An Investigation into the Police Response to Assault in the Family Home,* Ombudsman Western Australia, <www.ombudsman.wa.gov.au/pdf/reports/Police_Response_to_Assault_in_the_Family_Home.pdf> (accessed 8 September 2006).

Westwood, S, (2002), *Power and the Social.* New York: Routledge.

Whitaker, DS (1987), *Using Groups to Help People,* Hove, UK: Routledge and Kegan.

White, M (1995) *Re-Authoring Lives: Interviews and Essays.* Adelaide: Dulwich Centre Publications.

White, M (1989), *Selected Papers.* Adelaide: Dulwich Centre Publications.

White, M (1991), Deconstruction And Therapy. Dulwich Centre Newsletter, *New Zealand Counselling And Guidance Journal,* 3: 21-40.

White, M (1995), *Re-Authoring Lives: Interviews And Essays.* Adelaide: Dulwich Centre.

White, M (1997), *Narrative Of Therapists' Lives.* Adelaide: Dulwich Centre.

White, M (2000), *Reflections On Narrative Practice: Essays And Interviews*. Adelaide: Dulwich Centre.

White, M and Epston, D (1989), *Literate Means To Therapeutic Ends*. Adelaide: Dulwich Centre.

White, M and Epston, D (1990), *Narrative Means To Therapeutic Ends*. New York: WW Norton.

Wild, TC, Newton-Taylor, B and Alletto, R (1998) Perceived coercion among clients entering substance abuse treatment: structural and psychological determinants. *Addictive Behaviors*, 23: 81-95.

Winick, B (2008), A therapeutic jurisprudence approach to dealing with coercion in the mental health system. *Psychiatry, Psychology and Law*, 15: 25-39.

Women's Services Network (2000), *Domestic Violence in Regional Australia; a literature review: A report for the Commonwealth Department of Transport and Regional services under the partnerships Against Domestic Violence Programme*. Canberra: Commonwealth of Australia.

Wormwith, JS, Althouse, R, Simpson, M, Reitzel, LR, Fagan, TJ and Morgan, RD (2007), The rehabilitation and reintegration of offenders: The current landscape and some future directions for correctional psychology. *Criminal Justice and Behavior*, 34: 879-892.

Yalom, ID and Leszcz, M (2005), *The Theory and Practice of Group Psychotherapy* (5th ed), NY: Basic Books.

Young, J, Perlesz A and Paterson, R (1989), The Reflecting Team Process in Training. *ANZ Journal of Family Therapy*, 10: 69-74.

Zweig, JM and Burt, MR (2003), Effects of Interactions Among Community Agencies on Legal System Responses to Domestic Violence and Sexual Assault in STOP Funded Communities. *Criminal Justice Policy Review*, 14: 249-272.

Index